THE BEST OF
family handyman

THE BEST OF
family
handyman.

by The Editors of *Family Handyman* magazine

A *FAMILY HANDYMAN* BOOK

ISBN 978-1-62145-924-8 (dated), 978-1-62145-925-5 (undated)

Component number 118300114H (dated), 118300116H (undated)

We are committed to both the quality of our products and the service we provide to our customers. We value your comments, so please feel free to contact us at TMBBookTeam@TrustedMediaBrands.com.

For more *Family Handyman* products and information, visit our website: *www.familyhandyman.com*

Printed in China
10 9 8 7 6 5 4 3 2 1

Text, photography and illustrations for *The Best of Family Handyman 2023* are based on articles previously published in *Family Handyman* magazine (*familyhandyman.com*).

WARNING
All do-it-yourself activities involve a degree of risk. Skills, materials, tools and site conditions vary widely. Although the editors have made every effort to ensure accuracy, the reader remains responsible for the selection and use of tools, materials and methods. Always obey local codes and laws, follow manufacturer's operating instructions, and observe safety precautions.

Photo Credits
p. 7, 201, Bulgac/Getty Images; p. 9, 37, courtesy of Cambria; p. 31, bottom: Archways and Ceilings (6); p. 32, sommersby/Getty Images; p. 34, left: Elenathewise/Getty Images; p. 35, Corian® (6); p. 36, top: stockstudioX/Getty Images; p. 36, bottom: vallefrias/Getty Images; p. 37, bottom: courtesy of Cambria; p. 38, top: chandlerphoto/Getty Images; p. 38, bottom: Mint Images/Getty Images; p. 39, top: seanoriordan/Getty Images; p. 39, bottom left: Stone Source USA (2); p. 39, bottom far right: Xinzheng/Getty Images; p. 52, background: Witthaya Prasongsin/Getty Images; p. 54, left: Natikka/Getty Images; p. 54, right: contrastaddict/Getty Images; p. 56, top left: Arman Zhenikeyev/Getty Images; p. 56, bottom left: Michael Vi/Getty Images; p. 56, right: GaryAlvis/Getty Images; p. 58, background: Xinzheng/Getty Images; p. 60, Matterport (2); p. 66, Westend61/Getty Images; p. 71, PowerShades (3); p. 75, bottom: Kohler Co.; p. 118, Knaupe/Getty Images; p. 129, 149, 151, night sky: Brandon Sherwood/Getty Images; p. 130, fiber cement: Kiattisak Thongtawee/Shutterstock; p. 130, wood: bruceman/Getty Images; p. 130, stucco: primeimages/Getty Images; p. 130, steel: Romanets/Shutterstock; p. 130, engineered wood: 501room/Shutterstock; p. 130, brick: Arne Klemp/Getty Images; p. 130, vinyl: Nenov/Getty Images; p. 137, top and right: Dragonfly Energy/Battle Born Batteries; p. 142, anela/Getty Images; p. 143, Tom Lau/Getty Images; p. 154, backyard: gmc3101/Getty Images; p. 154, patio: Afonkin_Yuriy/Getty Images; p. 155, figure: Jay Cork; p. 158, Jay Cork; p. 160-162, 164, 166 (left and bottom right), 167, 168, Brad Staley; p. 165, top: Mike Berner; p. 171, 206, constantgardener/Getty Images; p. 173, courtesy of Home Depot (2); p. 202, top: ewg3D/Getty Images; p. 203, bottom left: Hart Tools; p. 207, clockwise from top: Prairie Nursery, Ravi Krish/Getty Images, Laszlo Podor/Getty Images, maciu17/Getty Images; p. 208, top left: KenWiedemann/Getty Images; p. 208, top right: MartinPrescott/Getty Images; p. 208, bottom: Photos by R A Kearton/Getty Images; p. 209, top: constantgardener/Getty Images; p. 209, bottom left: Comstock/Getty Images; p. 209, bottom right: RiverNorthPhotography/Getty Images; p. 263, top: BLACK+DECKER (2); p. 263, bottom: Techtronic Industries; p. 264, bottom: Techtronic Industries (2); all cartoon illustrations throughout book: Steve Björkman

SAFETY FIRST—ALWAYS!

Tackling home improvement projects and repairs can be endlessly rewarding. But as most of us know, with the rewards come risks. DIYers use chain saws, climb ladders and tear into walls that can contain big and hazardous surprises.

The good news is that armed with the right knowledge, tools and procedures, homeowners can minimize risk. As you go about your projects and repairs, stay alert for these hazards:

Aluminum wiring

Aluminum wiring, installed in about 7 million homes between 1965 and 1973, requires special techniques and materials to make safe connections. This wiring is dull gray, not the dull orange characteristic of copper. Hire a licensed electrician certified to work with it. For more information, go to *cpsc.gov* and search for "aluminum wiring."

Spontaneous combustion

Rags saturated with oil-based paints and stains or oil finishes like Danish oil and linseed oil can spontaneously combust if left bunched up. Always dry them outdoors, spread out loosely. When the oil has thoroughly dried, you can safely throw them in the trash.

Vision and hearing protection

Safety glasses or goggles should be worn whenever you're working on DIY projects that involve chemicals, dust and anything that could shatter or chip off and hit your eye. Sounds louder than 80 decibels (dB) are considered potentially dangerous. Sound levels from a lawn mower can be 90 dB, and shop tools and chain saws can be 90 to 100 dB.

Lead paint

If your home was built before 1979, it may contain lead paint, which is a serious health hazard, especially for children 6 and under. Take precautions when you scrape or remove it. Contact your public health department for detailed safety information or call (800) 424-LEAD (5323) to receive an information pamphlet. Or visit *epa.gov/lead*.

Buried utilities

A few days before you dig in your yard, have your underground water, gas and electrical lines marked. Just call 811 or go to *call811.com*.

Smoke and carbon monoxide (CO) alarms

The risk of dying in reported home structure fires is cut in half in homes with working smoke alarms. Test your smoke alarms every month, replace batteries as necessary and replace units that are more than 10 years old. As you make your home more energy-efficient and airtight, existing ducts and chimneys can't always successfully vent combustion gases, including potentially deadly carbon monoxide (CO). Install a UL-listed CO detector, and test your CO and smoke alarms at the same time.

Five-gallon buckets and window covering cords

Anywhere from 10 to 40 children a year drown in 5-gallon buckets, according to the U.S. Consumer Products Safety Commission. Always store them upside down and store ones containing liquid with the covers securely snapped.

According to Parents for Window Blind Safety, hundreds of children in the United States are injured every year after becoming entangled in looped window treatment cords. For more information, visit *pfwbs.org* or *cpsc.gov*.

Working up high

If you have to get up on your roof to do a repair or installation, always install roof brackets and wear a roof harness.

Asbestos

Texture sprayed on ceilings before 1978, adhesives and tiles for vinyl and asphalt floors before 1980, and vermiculite insulation (with gray granules) all may contain asbestos. Other building materials made between 1940 and 1980 could also contain asbestos. If you suspect that materials you're removing or working around contain asbestos, contact your health department or visit *epa.gov/asbestos* for information.

CONTENTS

1. Interior Projects, Repairs & Remodeling

2. HVAC, Plumbing & High-Tech

3. Woodworking & Workshop Projects & Tips

4. Exterior Repairs & Improvements

5. Outdoor Structures, Landscaping & Gardening

6. Using DIY Tools & Materials

1 INTERIOR PROJECTS, REPAIRS & REMODELING

HIDEAWAY WORK-SPACE

NEED A ZONE TO CALL YOUR OWN?
LOOK INSIDE THE CLOSET!

BY BILL BERGMANN

Working from home has become a reality for many, and not every home has a spare bedroom that can become an office. Even if you don't work from home, you might long for a dedicated space for your craft or hobby, or a place for kids to do their homework.

Converting a closet allows you to gain space without taking over a room or remodeling. I will show you how to transform your closet into a multipurpose work space using hollow-core doors and basic tools. You can find doors at a reuse center, as I did, or buy them new at a home center.

When you are done, just fold up the desktop and call it a day!

WHAT IT TAKES

TIME	COST	SKILL LEVEL
2 days	$600	Intermediate

TOOLS
Drill/driver, basic hand tools, stud finder, circular saw, hacksaw, jab drywall saw, pull saw, 4-ft. level and/or torpedo level, electrical wire stripper/cutter, 3-in. hole saw, oscillating multi-tool

MATERIALS LIST

ITEM	QTY.
Hollow-core doors: 6' 8" x 2'	3
8' 2x6s (to cut for hollow-core filler)	2
Primed 1x2: 8' length	2
Primed 1x2: 12' length	1
3/4" x 3/4" piano hinge: 30"	2
1" 18-gauge nails	
2" 18-gauge nails	
2-1/2" trim screws	
Folding leg bracket hinges	2
Electrical supplies (outlets with USB ports, NM-B cable, remodel boxes, light fixture)	
Computer cord ports/grommets	
Power strip	
Construction adhesive, wood glue	

EDGE GUIDE

HOLLOW DOOR CAVITY

FILLER STRIP

STUD LOCATIONS

WALL CLEAT

1 MAKE FILLER STRIPS

After you cut the door slabs to fit your closet space, you need to make the filler pieces that fit inside to reinforce each hollow core. Measure the inner door cavity. Mine measured 1-1/8 in.; that's typical, but it can vary. You can cut filler pieces to that size from a 2x6. I have wood-topped sawhorses, so I fastened down the 2x6 with 2-in. screws. Clamps would work just as well.

With the blade depth set to 1-5/8 in., make a short test cut to be sure the edge guide is set to the right width and the zero stop on the saw's bevel gauge is cutting at 90 degrees. Keeping the wider part of the saw's baseplate on the 2x6, I was able to get two passes with a solid footing of my saw's baseplate on the board, which ensured accurate cuts. Despite some waste, this is a safe technique if you don't have a table saw.

2 INSTALL FILLER STRIPS

Most new hollow-core doors have a cardboard web inside to support the outer panels. With a sharp chisel and a pull saw, you can quickly cut and push that web out of the way. If you're repurposing older doors, you may encounter a thin wood filler that takes more time to clear. Install your new solid filler pieces with glue and 1-in. nails. Be sure to add filler pieces on the fold-down top and leg to give solid purchase for the leg bracket screws. Then sand the filler pieces smooth and flush with the outer panels.

3 INSTALL WALL CLEATS

A comfortable desk height is about 30 in. I wanted enough height between the desk and the first shelf for my computer monitor,

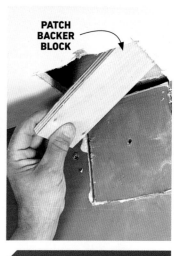

DRYWALL CUTOUTS

PATCH BACKER BLOCK

4

PRO TIP
Patch the holes using your 5-in. drywall cutouts. Install an 8 x 3 x 1/2-in. plywood backer, then screw the drywall cutouts back into place.

as well as enough room above the upper shelf to fit the boxes I previously had in the closet. With all this in mind, I marked the height for the desk and shelves inside the closet.

With a torpedo level taped to a straight piece of 1x2, I made level lines on the back closet wall for the cleats. Locate the wall studs and mark them with painter's tape. Nail the back wall cleats to the studs. In case I ever need to remove the desk, I skipped the glue here. A few small holes are easier to repair than long swaths of paint and drywall. I then used the torpedo level to install the side wall cleats. If you don't find studs to which you can fasten the side cleats, use hollow-wall anchors.

RUN THE WIRING
To add an outlet below the desktop, I pulled a wire from the closet ceiling fixture. The first step with any wiring project is to locate and turn off the breaker feeding the circuit you're working on. To get a wire up a wall and into a ceiling cavity, you'll need to drill through some framing members. To access them, cut two 5-in. square holes, one in the ceiling and the other in the wall directly behind the light fixture box. Save the drywall squares for reuse. Then drill a hole through the top plate of the wall framing.

EXPECT THE UNEXPECTED
What you find inside a wall often isn't "typical." I encountered a 2x6 drywall backer nailed over drywall that ran over the top plate, probably from a previous remodel. This kept me from simply pushing the wire through the top plate into the ceiling cavity. To make this 90-degree turn, I cut a notch in the 2x6 framing with a multitool to pull the wire through.

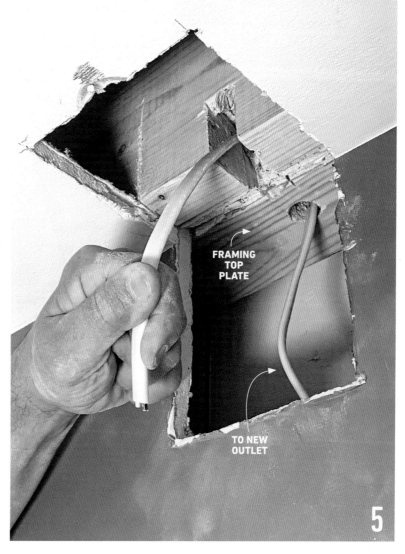

FRAMING TOP PLATE

TO NEW OUTLET

5

Before I cut that notch, I double-checked to be sure this 2x6 framing wasn't a structural piece, such as the bottom chord of a truss or a floor joist. I then fished the wire up through the wall from the outlet cutout below the desktop, through the top plate and into the ceiling to make my connections in the closet light fixture box. To complete this step, I installed the remodel box and outlet, patched the wall and ceiling, and installed a 6-in. flush-mount LED ceiling fixture to replace the old bulb socket in the closet.

FINISH AND PAINT

For the best results, paint or finish your desktop and shelves before installation. I used a water-based polyurethane finish for my desktop and shelves, and I coated the shelf cleats with latex enamel paint. Prime and repaint the wall and ceiling patches.

INSTALL THE DESKTOP AND SHELVES

You may need to install your desktop first if the upper shelves will prevent you from getting the desktop into place. Because I may want to restore this closet to its original configuration someday, I didn't use adhesive. A couple 2-1/2-in.

LEG BRACKET

PIANO HINGE

Speedhorse

8

trim screws at each alcove end and one in the center are all I needed to secure everything in place.

8 ASSEMBLE THE FOLDOUT
Cut the piano hinge to length and attach one of its leaves to the folding desktop. Using a combination square, mark the placement for the folding leg brackets on the back of the leg and underside of the folding desk. Predrill holes; install brackets with supplied screws.

9 ATTACH THE FOLDOUT
Using clamps to hold the folding desktop in position, attach the other leaf of the piano hinge to the desktop.

10 ADD CORD AND OUTLET GROMMETS
Mark the placement for the desktop outlets—whatever is convenient for your desktop. I put a cord grommet in the center of the desk and one outlet grommet in each of the back corners. Use a 3-in. hole saw to cut the holes through the desktop. Underneath the desk I attached a surge protector power strip with additional USB ports. Using zip ties, I secured all the cords under the desk.

PIANO HINGE

9

10

HOLE SAW

CORD GROMMET

OUTLET GROMMET

BEAUTIFUL
BEAMS

NO ONE NEEDS TO KNOW THEY'RE FAUX

BY MIKE BERNER

Magicians never reveal their secrets, but I'm a carpenter, so I'll tell you one of mine. You know those beautiful ceiling beams you see in rustic, industrial and farmhouse interiors? Most of them aren't real!

This is good news—it means you can get the look even if you don't have exposed beams. Add depth and character to any room by building your own beams. You can stain them, paint them white or choose a weathered, decades-old look. I'll show you how to make beams for any home.

MEET THE BUILDER

MIKE BERNER IS A CARPENTER AND WOODWORKER WHO LOVES UNCOVERING THE MAGIC BEHIND THE CRAFT.

WHAT IT TAKES

TIME	COST	SKILL LEVEL
A weekend	$600	Intermediate

TOOLS
Table saw or track saw, drill/driver, finish nailer, featherboard, basic woodworking tools, belt sander, ladder

MATERIALS
2x6 boards, red oak 1x6s and 1x8s, 3-in. construction screws, glue, reinforced packing tape, trim screws, stain and finishing supplies

Cabinetry and table courtesy of FindFurnish.com

AUTHENTIC, SEAMLESS BEAMS

For this project, I'm going for a real-beams look. Using a method called miter folding, I'll transform a pair of 1x6s and a 1x8 board into a hollow beam. The miter seams will be invisible, and each beam will look like an actual solid piece. You'll need a table saw or a track saw to pull this off, but your beams will look as if they are actually holding up the ceiling.

2x6 CLEAT

WEDGE BOARDS

1

NOTE THE SIZE OF THE GAP

2

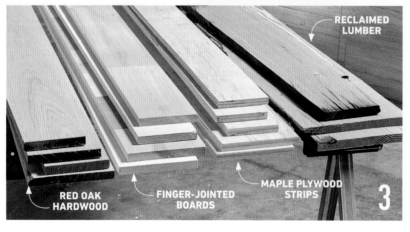

RECLAIMED LUMBER

MAPLE PLYWOOD STRIPS

FINGER-JOINTED BOARDS

RED OAK HARDWOOD

3

1 FASTEN CEILING CLEATS

First, locate and mark the position and direction of each ceiling joist around the edges of the ceiling. Then, avoiding ceiling fixtures, mark where the beams will be positioned. Keep their spacing even and ensure each beam will be attached to a joist. The beams can be installed across or along the ceiling joists. Next, attach 2x6 cleats to the ceiling joists where you will place the beams. I used a pair of 2x6 boards to wedge the cleats into position while I fastened them to the ceiling joists.

2 CHECK FOR FLATNESS

While you're installing the cleats, check to see how flat the ceiling is. Hold a straightedge along the 2x6 cleat. Take note of any gaps more than 1/8 in. between the level and the ceiling. This will come in handy when you scribe and trim the beams to get a perfect fit.

3 CHOOSE THE RIGHT BOARDS

Begin the actual beam-building process by choosing the material that suits your style.

■ **HARDWOOD:** Choose the straightest boards possible at a length that will span the entire room. Bowed boards will be trouble when you're cutting and assembling. Sight down the edges and put only straight ones in your cart.

■ **FINGER-JOINTED BOARDS:** Built to be straight, these are a great option if you'll be painting your beams.

■ **VENEERED PLYWOOD:** Perfectly straight factory edges ensure crisp corners, and strips are easy to cut and assemble. But lengths are limited.

■ **RECLAIMED LUMBER:** Go this route to nail the rustic look, but expect extra work to get a straight edge. You'll need to send one edge of reclaimed boards through a jointer, use a table saw with a jig or use a track saw.

4 CUT THE LONG MITERS

This is the trickiest part of building seamless faux beams. Set up a table saw to make a 45-degree bevel and adjust the fence so the narrow face between the bevel cuts is at least 5-1/2 in. wide. Cut a bevel on both long edges of the 1x8 boards. Use a featherboard to keep the material against the fence and press the board to the table as you feed it through the saw. Then cut the same bevel on one edge of the 1x6 boards.

5 BACK-BEVEL THE TOP EDGES

The 1x6 boards will turn into the sides of the beams, and the top edge will meet the ceiling. Cutting a slight bevel on the top edge, opposite the 45-degree bevel, will help you if your ceiling is not flat. If you found a 1/8-in. or smaller gap when you checked how flat the ceiling was (in Step 2), cut a 5-degree bevel. If your ceiling has 1/4-in. or larger gaps, cut a 15-degree bevel. Cutting a steeper bevel than necessary might cause the wood to split where the screws are installed.

6 TAPE THE SEAMS

Arrange the three boards on sawhorses with the bevel cuts down and the points of the miters touching. Using reinforced packing tape, join the boards across the seams, then down the lengths of the seams. I sandwiched the ends of the boards with scrap offcuts and clamps to secure them; this helped keep everything together when the boards were flipped for the next step.

Our blade guard is removed for demonstration only. Keep all safety devices in place.

45° BEVELS

5-1/2"

FEATHERBOARD

4

PRO TIP
The back bevel makes it easier to sand a piece of wood, like base trim or cabinet panels, to meet a scribed line. Instead of sanding the entire thickness of the board, you'll just sand the point of the bevel.

OUTER SIDE OF BEAM

POINT OF BACK BEVEL

5° TO 15° BACK BEVEL

5

REINFORCED PACKING TAPE

BEVELS FACING DOWN

6

7 GLUE AND FOLD

Flip the boards over, then spread glue on the beveled edges. Titebond III glue is great when I need extended working time, and it's easy to spread with a brush. I folded the edges of the beams up and used more packing tape to hold the tops in place while the glue dried. Don't be afraid to use a few 18-gauge brad nails to pin the miter together at the ends.

8 BURNISH THE CORNERS

With the tape still on and the glue still drying, run a screwdriver shaft along each corner. This presses the corner of the miter completely closed while the glue is still wet to make a tight, invisible miter that will last. Be careful not to rip the tape as you burnish the corners.

9 SCRIBE IN PLACE

Once the glue is dry and the beam is sanded and stained, fit each beam into place. Hold the beam tight to the ceiling. With your pencil flat on the ceiling, run the tip along the entire length of the beam.

SAND THE BEVELED POINT TO THE LINE

10

11

10 **SAND TO THE SCRIBE**
With the beams back on sawhorses, use a belt sander to sand the top edges to the scribed line. The back-beveled tops make this a quick and easy job. Instead of sanding down the entire 3/4-in. thickness, you need to remove only the point of the outside face.

11 **INSTALL THE BEAMS**
Drill pilot holes along the tops of the beams every 16 in. Then lift the beams back into place and fasten them to the cleats with trim screws. Fill the small screw holes with wood putty and touch them up with stain. The beams will look as if they've been holding up the ceiling since day one.

BEAM STYLES FOR ANY HOME

HARDWOOD + STAIN
This is the clean, modern real-beam look I used for this project. I used red oak lumber with Simply White 275 Minwax stain.

BOX BEAMS
You can build this beam style without a table saw by using 1x6 boards right from the store—no long bevel cuts needed.

■ **PAINTED:** Use finger-jointed preprimed boards, which come perfectly straight. Just nail them together, and then caulk, paint and install them.

■ **HARDWOOD:** Use straight-grained hardwood like mahogany, and the seams almost disappear. Nail the boards flush, apply finish and install.

VENEERED PLYWOOD
The advantage of veneered plywood is that the sheets come straight as an arrow, making them easy to cut and fold together. The downside? You're limited to the length of a sheet of plywood. Build longer beams by butting them together and covering the seam with a piece of matching molding.

RUSTIC/DISTRESSED
With reclaimed barn wood, you can achieve that authentic farmhouse look. Barn wood is much more forgiving because it already has nail holes, dents and dings, and it requires no staining or finishing.

READY-MADE FAUX BEAMS
A few companies manufacture beams of all styles using high-density foam. These beams are lighter than wood, easier to install and realistic. Barron Designs customizes ultra-realistic beams in any length, width and height, and can even cap beams with a decorative scrolled end.

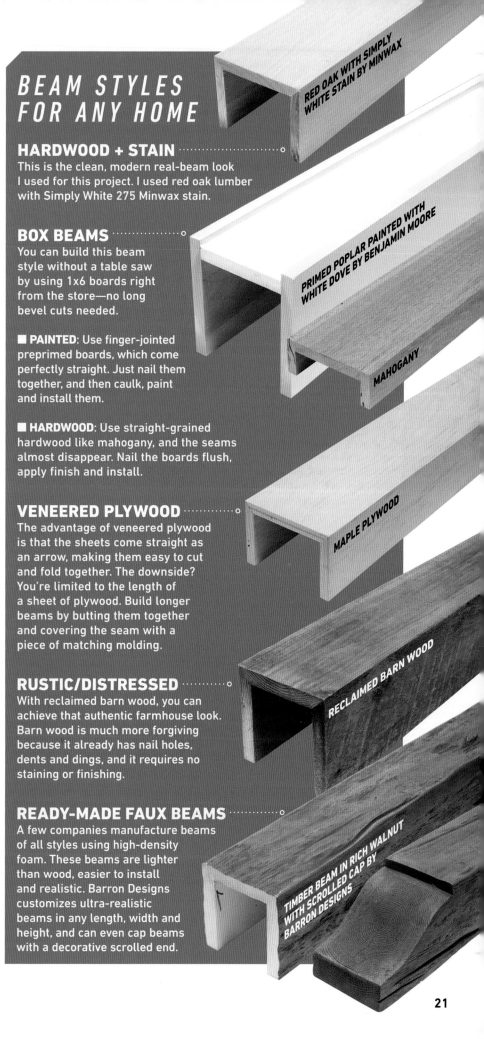

RED OAK WITH SIMPLY WHITE STAIN BY MINWAX

PRIMED POPLAR PAINTED WITH WHITE DOVE BY BENJAMIN MOORE

MAHOGANY

MAPLE PLYWOOD

RECLAIMED BARN WOOD

TIMBER BEAM IN RICH WALNUT WITH SCROLLED CAP BY BARRON DESIGNS

WHAT IT TAKES

TIME	COST	SKILL LEVEL
2 days	< $300	Beginner

TOOLS
6- and 10-in. taping knives, putty knife, mud pan, 9-in. paint roller, 3-in. taping knife, Venetian plaster trowel, sponge, drill/driver, basic hand tools

BY MIKE BERNER

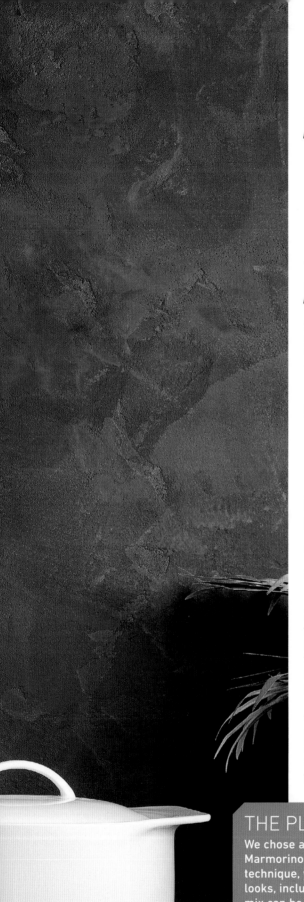

REAL VENETIAN PLASTER

HERE'S HOW TO ACHIEVE THIS MARBLE-LIKE FINISH YOURSELF

Venetian plaster, a beautiful and durable texture that mimics natural stone, is believed to date back to fourth-century Rome. Creating it is a skill that takes years to master; however, there's room for artistic license. Modern tools and materials put the technique within the grasp of a DIYer.

Venetian plaster is a great choice for a kitchen backsplash. It may seem as though it would be difficult to clean, but when the texture is burnished and sealed, cleaning it is no more difficult than cleaning grouted tile. Of all the projects the *Family Handyman* team completed in a particular kitchen remodel, this Venetian plaster wall had a huge impact on the entire look and will be the most friendly to beginning DIYers.

This was my first try at a plaster wall, and I'm not even very good at finishing drywall. But with guidance from PlasterCenter's Drew Beninati and a little practice, I felt confident enough to tackle it. After you read this, I hope you will too!

THE PLASTER

We chose a type of Venetian plaster called Marmorino. Depending on the application technique, you can achieve a variety of finished looks, including polished, matte and satin. The mix can be customized with different size aggregate for rough and smooth textures, and prepped in custom colors. We had our supplier mix a batch with larger aggregate in a beautiful charcoal color.

1 REMOVE CABINETS

The kitchen wall we chose to plaster had a few cabinets that we planned to replace with open shelving, so our first step was to tear them out. If you're plastering a wall that holds cabinets you plan to keep, you can plaster right up to them.

2 REPAIR WALL DAMAGE

It's best to start a plastering job with a smooth wall. Removing the cabinets damaged our drywall in some areas. And while we were removing the glass tile backsplash, chipping it away a tile at a time, we decided it was safer and easier to remove the backsplash as a unit by cutting out the drywall it was attached to. Then we patched in the new drywall, smoothed it out with a few coats of joint compound and repaired all the dents with surfacing compound.

3 PRIME THE WALL

After sanding the repaired wall smooth, we sealed it with a special primer that has "tooth" to hold plaster, which is thicker and heavier than paint. Texturline Sharktooth Primer rolls on just like any other primer but dries with a grittier surface, which is key to creating a good bond for the plaster. Let the primer dry for three to four hours.

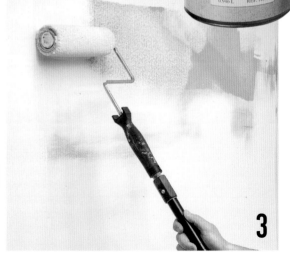

MEET THE EXPERT

DREW BENINATI owns and operates the PlasterCenter in Minneapolis, MN. He has been a plaster contractor for 40 years and has run his training center for 20 years. Go to *plastercenter.com* to learn more.

4 TROWEL ON THE FIRST COAT

Apply the first coat evenly across the entire wall. Use a 3-in. taping or similar knife to scoop the plaster onto your trowel. Then, start from one end and work your way across the wall, applying a thin coat, troweling the plaster in different directions, then smoothing it out.

To avoid trowel marks in plaster that has been smoothed, spread the plaster from the bare wall into your previous strokes. If you're going for lots of texture, make many small strokes; make longer strokes for larger smooth areas.

5 SKIP-TROWEL THE SECOND COAT

The second coat is lighter than the first and is meant to smooth out the ridges created by the first coat. I started on the opposite side of the wall and worked my way across, putting plaster on my trowel, applying it to the wall and smoothing it out toward the previous strokes. I intentionally left some areas uncovered, letting the first coat show through in small patches.

TROWEL INTO THE PLASTER

4

5

PRO TIP

We taped the counters and walls to protect those surfaces. Be sure to remove the tape while the plaster is slightly wet and replace it with new tape before the next coat. I kept the initial tape on throughout the project and ended up having to patch the edges where removing the tape chipped the plaster.

6

BURNISH THE PLASTER

6 Before the second coat was completely dry, I burnished the entire wall with a clean trowel. Starting on the same side of the wall as I did for the second coat, I slid the trowel across the plaster, holding the trowel at an angle and using moderate pressure.

Burnishing closes the pores of the plaster, creating a smooth and more water-resistant surface. The technique is also what gives Venetian plaster its unique shine. Burnishing makes the texture created by the first coat come alive.

WAX THE PLASTER

7 After the second coat, wait 48 hours to let the plaster dry completely, then apply the protective wax. I used Cera Wax to brighten up the wall, protect it from moisture and make it soft to the touch. I applied this liquid to the wall with a sponge in a circular motion. Apply two or three thin coats to complete the wall.

7

READY-TO-ASSEMBLE RANGE HOOD

DO IT YOURSELF—SIMPLIFIED!

BY BRAD HOLDEN

I f you can't find an off-the-shelf range hood that suits your kitchen, you can build your own—or you can take an easier route, as we did. Archways & Ceilings offers many range hood designs that you can size perfectly for your space.

Once you've chosen your design and supplied the dimensions (following the instructions on the company's website), Archways & Ceilings cuts all the parts for your range hood kit and ships it to your door. You assemble the hood and then finish it as you wish. On the next pages, we'll walk you through the steps to install it.

BOTTOM BOX ASSEMBLY

1

1 ASSEMBLE THE BOTTOM BOX

Gather your parts and assemble the hood's bottom box with construction screws. All the parts have precut joinery for foolproof assembly.

2 ASSEMBLE AND HANG THE TOP

Put the top of the hood together, and then hang it in place above the range, driving construction screws into the studs and joists. You could assemble the whole hood and install it as a unit, but it's easier to do it piece by piece, even with a helper.

3 ADD THE BACK

Slip the dovetailed back panel into its mating part in the top assembly, and then secure it to your wall studs.

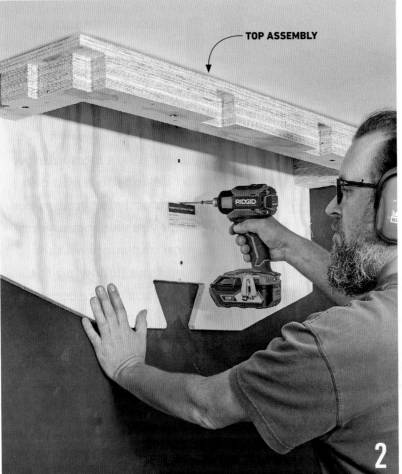

TOP ASSEMBLY

2

BACK

3

SIDE

HANG THE BOTTOM

4 Lift the bottom box into position, connecting it to the back panel via a precut dovetail. Fasten the bottom box to the wall studs with construction screws.

ADD THE SIDES

5 Fasten the sides to the assembly with screws or finish nails.

ADD THE FRONT RIBS

6 Slip the curved ribs into their indexed slots on the top and bottom boxes. Fasten the ribs with finish nails or screws.

MEET THE BUILDER

BRAD HOLDEN, DEPUTY PROJECTS EDITOR, HOPES TO SOON FIND TIME FOR HIS OWN KITCHEN UPGRADE.

RIB

7 INSTALL THE FAN

With the framework secured to the wall, install the fan according to the manufacturer's instructions. Before you attach it, you'll need to add any cleats and filler pieces needed to mount it and likely drywall the underside of the hood. After installing the fan, make the ductwork and electrical connections.

8 SKIN WITH DRYWALL

We chose to cover the hood with drywall for painting. For the curved front, dampen both sides of the drywall and carefully bend it onto the form, fastening as you go. We used two layers of 1/4-in. drywall here to meet fire code, and 1/2-in. drywall for the flat parts.

9 TAPE, MUD AND SAND

Apply flexible corner bead and joint compound to the curved edges. We used the flexible bead on all the joints for uniformity. Once the joint compound is dry, sand it smooth. This typically requires more than one coat. If you're installing the hood on a finished wall, mask off the surrounding surfaces; this is a messy job.

10 PAINT THE HOOD

When the last coat of joint compound is sanded smooth, apply a drywall primer. When that's dry, roll on your paint and you're done!

DAMPENED DRYWALL

FLEXIBLE CORNER BEAD

10

MATERIALS & SUPPLIES

- Range hood kit
- Exhaust fan insert
- Drywall
- Joint compound
- Joint tape
- Flexible corner bead
- Construction screws or finish nails

BELLA

MODERN

ARCADIAN

TUSCAN

BELL CURVE

CRAFTSMAN

CUSTOMIZE YOUR HOOD

Archways & Ceilings offers an array of possibilities for customizing range hoods. Bella, the style we chose for our kitchen, is just one option.

The company also makes curved framing kits for archways, ceilings and walls, or "your hard-to-build stuff."

CHOOSING A COUNTERTOP

THREE KEY FACTORS: PRICE, MAINTENANCE AND APPEARANCE

BY BRAD HOLDEN

Today's kitchens and countertops are used for more than just cooking. The kitchen is a living room, study, dining room and entertainment area rolled into one, which calls for a countertop surface that meets a lot of needs. Here, we will weigh the pros and cons of the most popular materials. They all have their strengths and weaknesses, and they all require maintenance and care.

Wondering what's on top? Plastic laminate still reigns for its affordability and color/pattern options.

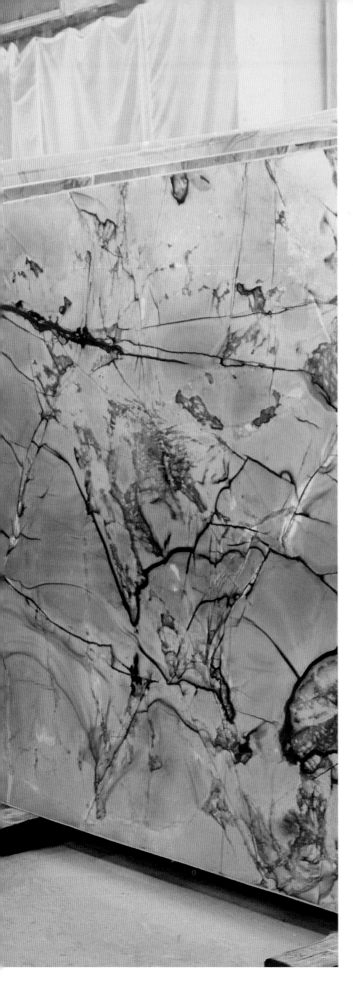

HOW TO CHOOSE

To help you select a countertop, answer these three questions:

- How much can you spend?
- How much maintenance are you willing to do?
- What material do you most like to touch, see, show off and work on?

PRICE

You can spend $2 to $250 per sq. ft. for countertops. Surprisingly, few choices fall between inexpensive laminates and pricey stone and solid-surface tops. Wood and tile tops fall in the middle, but of all the tops we looked at, these had the most critics. Regarding price, kitchen specialists follow a few rules of thumb:

- The length of time you plan to stay in a house should help your choice—the longer, the more durable and upscale the selection. The "cost per year" becomes a bargain as the years pass.
- Tops and installation usually compose 10 to 15% of a kitchen remodel budget. Tops that fall outside this range may not look as if they fit.
- Put your money where your heart is—especially when you're on a budget. If you love high-tech appliances or custom wood cabinetry, spend your money there.

MAINTENANCE AND USE FACTORS

Maintenance on most countertops is minimal. There is preventive maintenance, such as mopping up spills, using hot pads and working on cutting boards. And there's long-term maintenance, which usually involves regularly applying a sealer or finish. Ask yourself: How careful—*really*—are you and your family? What do you expect your top to look like in five years? Does it make more sense to stick with laminate until the kids are out of grade school?

AESTHETIC AND TACTILE FACTORS

If budget and maintenance aren't decisive factors for you, how the top looks and feels are the true deal makers. Both you and your countertop have personalities; select one that you can get along with. Texture, aesthetic, glossiness, "warmth," how natural the material looks and feels, and how it fits in with the design of your kitchen and home are all part of the final equation. One of the beauties of today's trend toward multiple countertop surfaces is when torn between two tops, you can install them both!

PLASTIC LAMINATES

Plastic-laminate tops still account for 75% of the market. They are inexpensive as well as durable, come in lots of colors and can be installed by do-it-yourselfers.

Plastic laminates are multiple layers of resin-soaked kraft paper topped by a patterned sheet of melamine that's subjected to heat and pressure. The resultant 1/16-in.-thick laminate sheet can be made into countertops in two ways:

■ It can be post-formed at a fabrication plant to create tops with a rounded "unibody" backsplash and nosing. Post-formed tops can be purchased off the shelf at home centers in limited colors or special ordered. This style top is the least expensive, easiest to clean and quickest to install.

■ It can be custom fabricated into an extraordinary range of styles. Laminate sheets are glued to particleboard, then edged with laminate, wood, even solid-surface strips.

Plastic laminates resist grease and stains and are easily cleaned with soap and water. Laminate is durable, and if you ever want to change your color scheme, it won't cost an arm and a leg.

On the downside, laminate tops can be damaged by hot pans and sharp knives; abrasive cleaners can dull the finish; and if water penetrates seams, the substrate can expand and the laminate bulge. Surface damage is difficult to repair. But all these problems can be avoided through proper installation and use.

THINGS TO KNOW BEFORE YOU BUY

■ Darker solid colors and glossy finishes tend to show scratches more readily than patterned or matte surfaces.

■ Tops where the laminate overlaps the edging, rather than butts to it, are more resistant to water damage.

■ New technology in printing has improved the clarity and depth of patterns. Many wood grains and stone patterns are amazingly crisp and realistic.

■ Special kits are available to allow installation of undermount sinks with laminate.

SOLID SURFACE

DuPont introduced the first solid-surface countertop, Corian, to the world in 1971, and the category continues to thrive. Currently, more than a dozen manufacturers offer countertop materials in hundreds of colors and designs.

Most, if not all, solid-surface tops are handled by trained pros who have been certified to fabricate and install the specific product.

Solid-surface tops are usually 1/2 in. thick and made of acrylic or polyester (or blends of the two) along with fillers. Edges are built up with two or three layers of material for a thicker appearance. These tops are nonporous, making them ideal for food preparation. They're difficult to stain and can be formed into nearly any size and shape.

Because they're a uniform material throughout, light scratches can be buffed, deep scratches and burns can be sanded, and severely damaged areas can literally be cut out, replaced, then blended to be nearly invisible. Sinks can be undermounted and backsplashes can be integrated into the top, making them seamless.

Most potential problems with the tops can be avoided by proper installation—and companies are increasingly selective about whom they'll certify to do their fabricating. There are some negatives, however. These tops are expensive. Cutting on them will leave scratches, and those that are solid color or have a high-gloss finish can be especially revealing. Some people object to their homogenous look and cold feel.

THINGS TO KNOW BEFORE YOU BUY

■ The key to a trouble-free solid-surface top is installers who know their stuff. Seams should be offset 1-1/2 to 3 in. from inside corners, inside corners should be radiused, and joints should be reinforced.

■ Know where your seams are and take precautions not to use electric cooking pots, griddles and hot plates in those areas. The expansion and contraction during the cool-down cycle can cause cracks.

■ Have a pro resand and repolish the top every five to seven years for a hard-to-tell-it's-not-new look.

GRANITE

Although granite has been around for millions of years, it's still considered the new kid on the block. Not long ago, granite fell into the "exotic" or "extravagant" category. Today it's become more accessible and affordable. Shipping is easier (more than 90% comes from overseas), and new technology and thinner blades allow it to be cut with less waste and cost.

In its natural state, granite resists most stains, and when it's sealed, it becomes tougher yet. Many edge styles can be crafted: Most common are bevel, radius, half-radius, ogee and square. Granite comes in a wide range of natural colors, patterns and depths. Each top is unique. Sinks can be undermounted. And it can handle hot pans.

On the downside, neglected granite can be stained by hot grease. It's hard and cold. It can be scratched by extreme abuse. Cutting on it will more likely dull your knives than damage your top, but repeated cutting in one area can eventually affect the sheen. Seams are more evident with granites that have a strong pattern or grain. And since working with granite requires special tools, it's not a do-it-yourself material, and on-site repairs are difficult to make.

THINGS TO KNOW BEFORE YOU BUY

■ Most slabs are 9 x 5 ft. The fabricator will often factor in a "waste charge" for the portion of the slab not used. Keep this in mind. For instance, don't spec out a 10-ft. island when a 9-ft. one will work.

■ If possible, visit the granite "boneyard" and select the actual slab your top will be made from. The look of a large slab can differ greatly from a small sample.

■ Dark and solid-colored granites show dings and spills more readily.

■ Granite with a gloss finish will have more depth and liveliness than one with a matte finish, but it will also show scratches much more readily.

ENGINEERED STONE

Blend the functional benefits of solid-surface material with the aesthetic attributes of natural stone and you get a new class of countertop materials called engineered stone. These materials are composed of more than 93% crushed natural stone bound together by acrylic or polyester resins. The tops gained popularity in the U.S. market in the 1990s.

Like solid-surface materials, they're nonporous and nearly impossible to stain. Most never need sealing. They have excellent scratch resistance and have more "give" than granite. Because they're composed of stone, they can have a natural look. But because they also have resins and fillers, they can also be tinted to create colors not found in nature.

They're expensive, with most falling between solid-surface and natural-stone prices. And while manufacturers say the materials can stand up to hot pans better than solid-surface materials, engineered stone tops can crack and even change color if subjected to extreme temperatures. And they share some of granite's negative qualities: They're slippery, cold to the touch and unforgiving with a tipped glass.

THINGS TO KNOW BEFORE YOU BUY

- Manufacturers of the quartz-based products claim zero sealing is required—ever.
- The composites made of marble (Compac) and limestone (Tere-Stone) are best suited for bathrooms.
- Cambria offers a transferable full lifetime warranty.

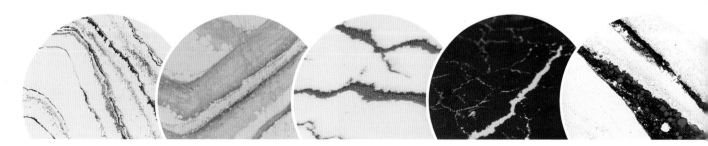

WOOD

Wood is the original solid-surface countertop; it's uniform throughout, and damage can be repaired by sanding and recoating.

Most wood tops are created from glued-up strips of maple, although other species are available. End-grain maple tops—the true "butcher block" with cut ends forming the cutting surface—are usually 4 or more inches thick and proportionately expensive.

If you're intending to use wood as a primary top, finish it with a penetrating oil so cuts and dings can be touched up by wiping in a little oil. If you intend to use the surface as more of an eating area, tops with a varnish finish can be ordered.

Moisture is the No. 1 enemy of wood tops. Seams and areas around sinks are particularly vulnerable. And a wood top can, and will, expand and contract.

THINGS TO KNOW BEFORE YOU BUY

- In heavy-use areas, wood will need regular refinishing.
- It is not heat-friendly or moisture-friendly.
- Water, grease or other spills can stain wood counters.
- Some wood species will darken as they age.

TILE

Tile has many virtues. It's inexpensive, do-it-yourself-friendly and available in an astounding variety of materials and colors; it also offers design flexibility. But it has equally strong drawbacks: It's exceptionally hard, the piecemeal nature means surface unevenness, and grout lines are vulnerable to staining.

Not all tiles are created equal. Granite, porcelain and glazed tiles are the least porous and are quite durable. Marble, unglazed clay or limestone tiles are absorbent, soft and usually not recommended for kitchens.

Grout is another part of the equation. Epoxy grout is more durable but harder to install and may yellow. Standard cement grout must be sealed often and well.

The tile base or substrate must be solid and watertight. Backer board over plywood is the most do-it-yourself-friendly base. Many pros will form and build a "mortar bed" for laying their tile.

THINGS TO KNOW BEFORE YOU BUY

- High-gloss and solid-color tiles show scratches.
- Select flat tile instead of tile that has a slight pillow effect.
- Larger tiles leave fewer grout lines that need to be sealed and maintained.

STAINLESS STEEL

If all the great restaurants of the world use stainless steel tops, why don't you see them more in homes? Well, they're expensive and it's difficult to find fabricators. Critics also point out that they show fingerprints and water spots (especially when new), and they readily show nicks, dents and scratches.

On the upside, they are antimicrobial, provide a good heatproof surface and are easy to clean.

THINGS TO KNOW BEFORE YOU BUY

- There are different grades and thicknesses of stainless steel. Make sure you know what you are paying for.
- Make certain the stainless steel is wrapped completely around the edges of the substrate to protect it.

EXOTIC SURFACES

MARBLE

Marble can be used for kitchen countertops, but its porosity and fragility make it best suited for bathrooms, where it's less likely to be damaged by knives, acidic foods and impact.

Marble is undeniably gorgeous; it has more natural graining than most stone and is available in a wide range of colors.

SOAPSTONE

Soapstone has proven its durability in chemistry labs over the last 100 years. It has natural veining and a rugged natural look. Although the material is relatively soft, an application of mineral oil will disguise most scratches. Heavier damage can be sanded out. Sinks can be seamlessly integrated into the top, and it can be worked with carbide tools. Most sections are limited in length to 6 ft.

RICHLITE

Richlite is composed of more than 60% paper, but it looks and acts more like stone or wood and has a warm, soft look and feel. It has been used in commercial kitchens and food-processing plants for decades. According to the manufacturer, the phenolic wood material resists heat, stains and scratches, and it "lasts a lifetime." It can be installed by do-it-yourselfers; costs start at about $25 per sq. ft. for the material.

CONCRETE

Concrete countertops are expensive, are prone to staining (even with a lacquer finish), can chip easily and are as hard as, well, concrete. So why would anyone install one? "They're fun!" explained one fabricator. You can form them into any shape, embed stuff in them and dye them. And they're durable and heat resistant. But only those committed to a fair level of maintenance should consider them.

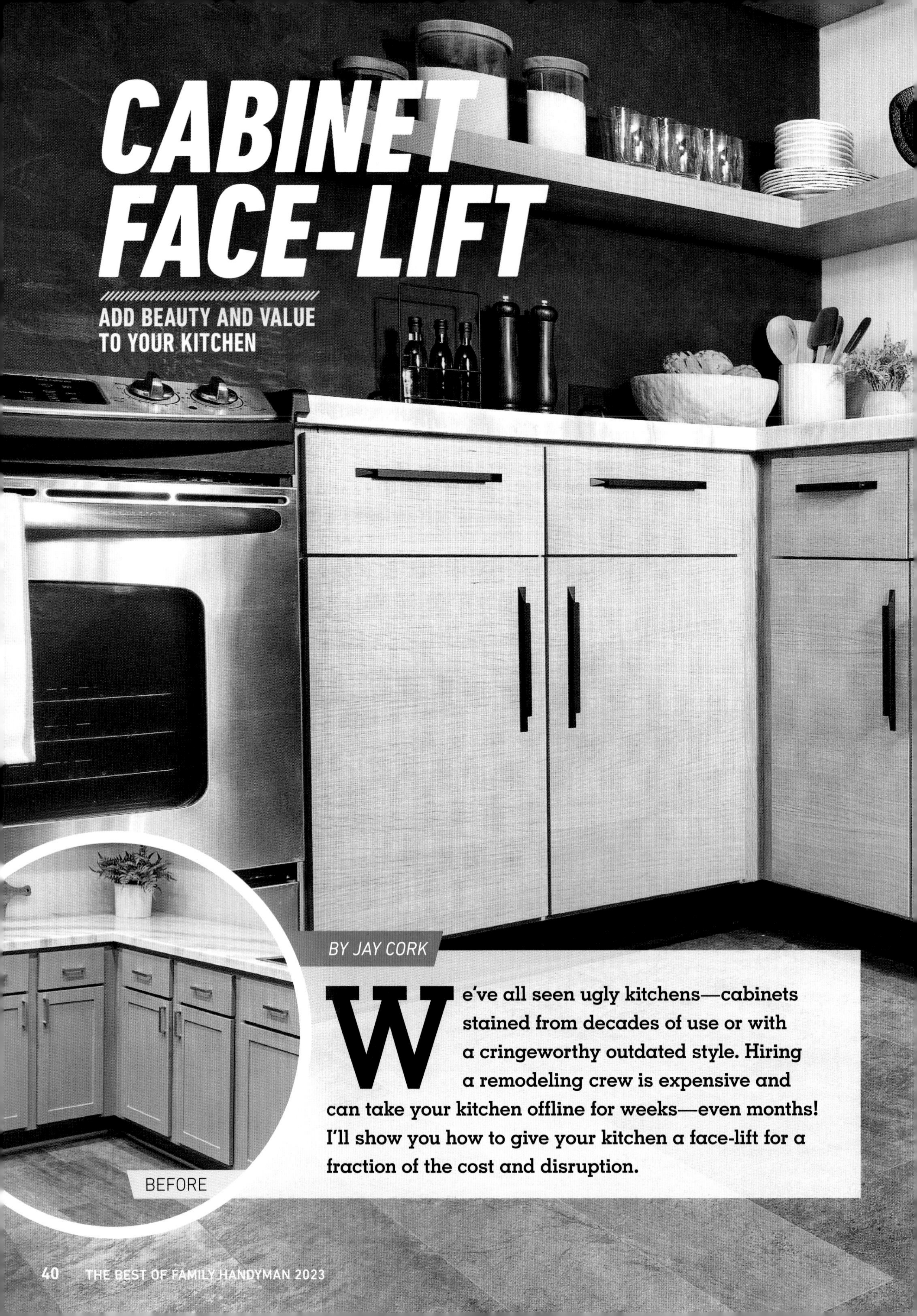

CABINET FACE-LIFT

ADD BEAUTY AND VALUE TO YOUR KITCHEN

BY JAY CORK

We've all seen ugly kitchens—cabinets stained from decades of use or with a cringeworthy outdated style. Hiring a remodeling crew is expensive and can take your kitchen offline for weeks—even months! I'll show you how to give your kitchen a face-lift for a fraction of the cost and disruption.

BEFORE

SPECIAL TOOLS

These tools are designed to make refacing cabinets easy.

SEAMING TOOL
This tool from FastCap makes seaming veneer joints a snap. Find yours for about $50 on Amazon.

MARKING KNIFE
This flat-backed marking knife is perfect for trimming edge banding.

VENEER CUTTER
The Virutex laminate strip cutter costs about $150, and it's worth every penny.

1 STRIP DOWN THE CABINETS
Remove all the doors, hinges and drawer fronts. Label all the parts for reference later. I used numbers, but you can use anything that helps you remember what goes where.

2 TAKE MEASUREMENTS
Take accurate measurements of each rail and stile to determine the overall size of each cabinet. I drew all my cabinets in SketchUp, but you can use graph paper. Next, measure all doors and drawer fronts, and give each one a name or designation.

3 SAND THE FACE FRAMES
Normally I want to roughen a surface that's being glued, but not with PSA-backed veneer. For pressure-sensitive adhesive, you want the substrate smooth. I sanded the painted surface of the rails and stiles with 320-grit sandpaper—not to sand off all the paint, only to make it smooth.

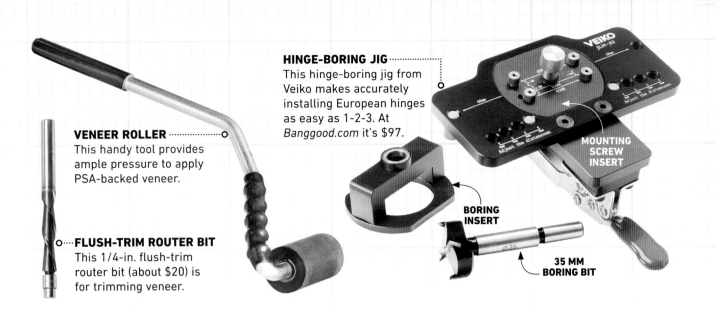

VENEER ROLLER
This handy tool provides ample pressure to apply PSA-backed veneer.

FLUSH-TRIM ROUTER BIT
This 1/4-in. flush-trim router bit (about $20) is for trimming veneer.

HINGE-BORING JIG
This hinge-boring jig from Veiko makes accurately installing European hinges as easy as 1-2-3. At *Banggood.com* it's $97.

MOUNTING SCREW INSERT

BORING INSERT

35 MM BORING BIT

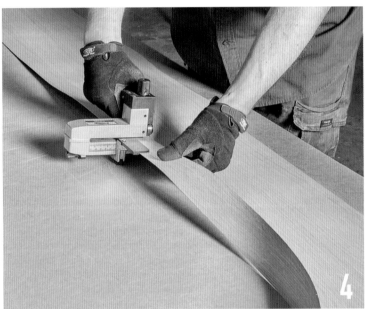

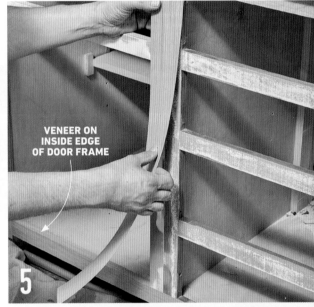

VENEER ON INSIDE EDGE OF DOOR FRAME

STILE

RAIL

4 CUT VENEER STRIPS
Using the Virutex veneer cutting tool, cut the strips for the face frames 1/8 in. oversize; any more would be wasting material.

5 VENEER THE STILES
Start by veneering the inside edges of the door frames, which creates the look of solid wood when the door is open. Next, apply veneer to the front of the stiles. Trim it flush with a compact router and flush-trim bit.

6 VENEER THE RAILS
Using the FastCap seaming tool and a marking knife, trim the stile veneer flush to the rail. Apply veneer to the rail. Using the seaming tool again, trim it to fit.

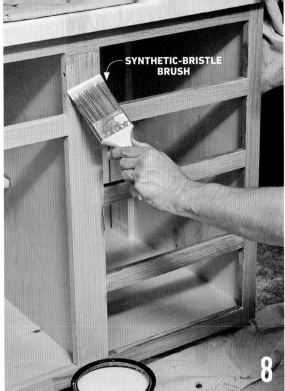

SYNTHETIC-BRISTLE BRUSH

3/4" VENEERED MDF

1/4" SPACERS

7 SAND THE FACE FRAMES

Sand the face frame veneer to 180 grit. I used a random orbital sander to avoid directional sanding scratches.

8 APPLY FINISH

For this kitchen, I wanted to showcase the quarter-sawn white oak in its natural beauty. I chose a water-based urethane because it dries quickly and won't turn the oak amber over time. To ensure good protection, I applied three coats of finish.

9 CUT THE NEW PARTS

Many shops will cut doors and drawer fronts for you. If you don't have a table saw (or the time), this is a good way to go. Because I was after a continuously oriented horizontal grain pattern, I chose to make the parts myself. Label each part accordingly as you cut it.

10 VENEER THE FACES

Lay veneer face down on a flat work surface. Set the doors and drawer faces into position one at a time. I used 1/4-in. spacers to help position them. Once the faces are all set, press down firmly on the backs. Cut them apart with a utility knife, making sure to run the blade down the center of each gap.

VENEER ROLLER

11

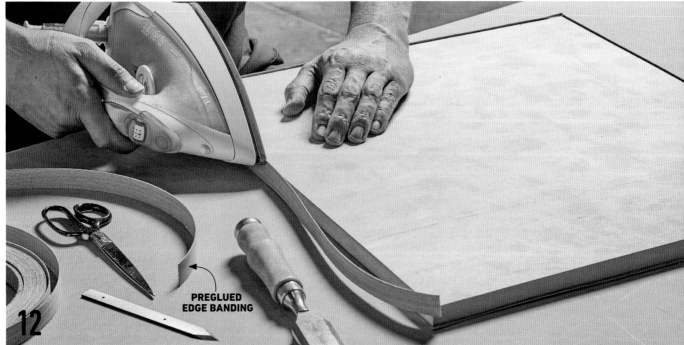

PREGLUED EDGE BANDING

12

11 ROLL THE VENEER
After the parts have been separated, flip them over and use a veneer roller to apply pressure to the faces. Pressure-sensitive adhesive needs to be activated—press hard!

12 APPLY THE EDGE BANDING
Before trimming the veneer on the face, iron on the edge banding, starting with the bottom. I used a sharp chisel to trim the ends of the edge banding. Next, do both sides, and then finish with the top. Doing it in this order helps hide the seams on the corners.

13 TRIM THE EDGE BANDING
With the part face down, trim the edge banding with a knife. I used a flat-backed marking knife for this purpose because it keeps the cutting edge flat to the surface.

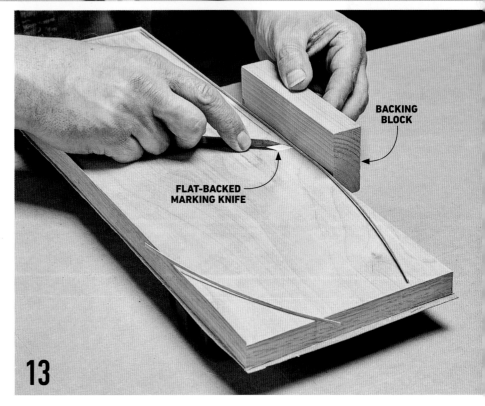

BACKING BLOCK

FLAT-BACKED MARKING KNIFE

13

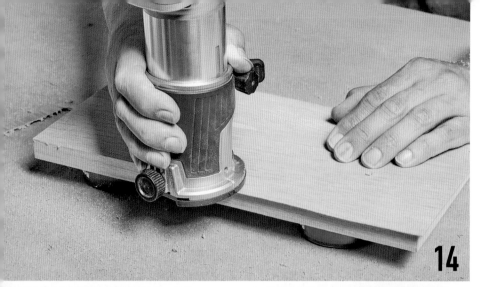

14

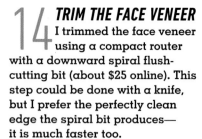

TRIM THE FACE VENEER

I trimmed the face veneer using a compact router with a downward spiral flush-cutting bit (about $25 online). This step could be done with a knife, but I prefer the perfectly clean edge the spiral bit produces— it is much faster too.

15 DRILL FOR CUP HINGES

I chose to replace the existing hinges with European soft-close hidden hinges. Using the handheld hinge-boring jig from Veiko (see p. 43), I drilled the 35 mm holes for the cup hinge 4 mm from the edge. The jig automatically places the holes 68 mm from the top and bottom of each door.

16 SAND THE PARTS

Using a random orbital sander, sand the doors and drawer faces up to 180 grit. After sanding the faces and edges of all the parts, ease the corners by hand with a used sanding disc.

17 APPLY THE FINISH

Apply three coats of water-based urethane, lightly sanding with 320-grit sandpaper between coats. For the larger flat surfaces, it's OK to use a foam roller to spread the urethane. Smooth out the finish by dry-brushing in the grain direction.

HINGE-BORING JIG

15

16   **17**

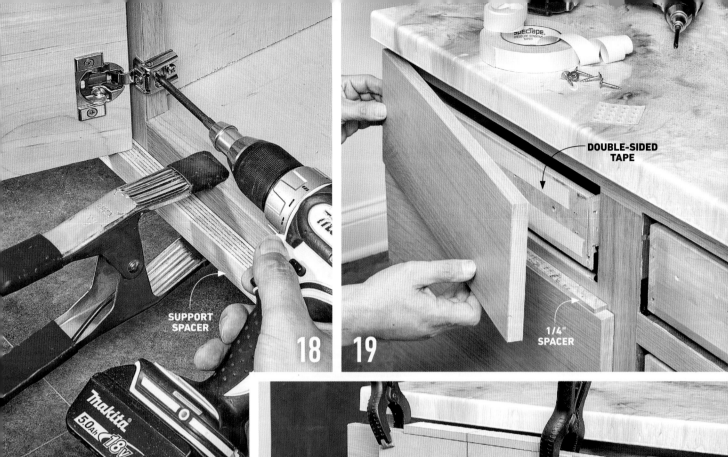

DOUBLE-SIDED TAPE

SUPPORT SPACER

18 **19**

1/4" SPACER

HARDWARE MOUNTING JIG

HARDWARE MOUNTING JIG

20

18 INSTALL THE DOORS FIRST

With the hinges attached to the doors, hold them up to the cabinet faces. I used a support spacer clamped to the bottom of the cabinet to help me position every door the same. Attach the hinge plates to the face frames with 3/4-in. No. 6 screws. Adjust all the doors so they look square to the face frame.

19 ATTACH THE DRAWER FRONTS

Once the doors are adjusted, line the drawer fronts up with the tops and bottoms of the doors. Use double-sided tape to hold the drawer fronts in position, then attach them to the drawer boxes with 7/8-in. drawer mounting screws through 1/4-in. holes in the drawer box.

20 INSTALL THE PULLS

Using a shop-made hardware drilling jig (see Sept. '22 issue p. 77 for help), drill holes for the handles and drawer pulls with a 5/32-in. drill bit.

NO-MYSTERY UPHOLSTERY

REPAIR YOUR OWN CUSHIONS AND COVERS

USE THE RIGHT NEEDLES FOR THE MATERIAL
Choosing the correct sewing needle for your material eliminates frustration and breakage. Nate uses 140/22 needles for most of his vinyl projects. Leather and denim require thicker, stronger needles.

BY JAY CORK

Ever wonder how pros sew buttons onto pillows or get their cushions so perfectly straight and smooth? Unwrap the mystery of upholstery, and stitch together some skills to sew small projects and make repairs. I spent a day with Nate Van Hofwegen at his shop, talking about his upholstery magic and what tricks he could teach us.

MEET THE EXPERT

NATE VAN HOFWEGEN HAS BEEN AN UPHOLSTERER FOR 20 YEARS. HIS FAVORITE PROJECTS ARE VINTAGE VAN AND MOTORCYCLE SEATS.

MAKE YOUR PLEATS NEAT

Making rounded corners and edges look consistent is not easy. Here are the steps Nate takes to achieve the same look around the entire seat cushion.

First, he gathers the material tightly around the corner and spaces the staples evenly.

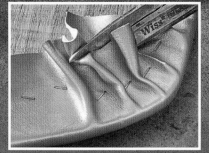

He then trims the excess material, snipping the crowns off the pleats.

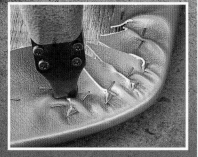

Finally, stapling about 1/2 in. from the edge, he fastens the loose tails so they lie flat.

REPLACE, DON'T REPAIR

We've all seen the upholstery repair kits that claim to "work like magic." The problem is, they don't. Often it's easier to just replace your item; sometimes you can't beat new.

CHOOSE THE RIGHT FABRIC

Use the right material for your project—outdoor cushions need fabric designed to withstand the elements. There are even special types of vinyl designed to make upholstery easier.

WHAT IS A YARD?

Commercially available upholstery material is typically 54 in. wide. At a fabric store, you may find some material that's not this wide, but no matter how wide the material is, a yard of fabric is always 3 ft. long.

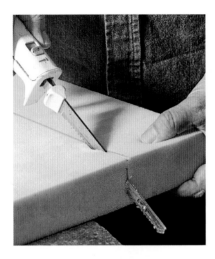

CUTTING FOAM

Nate has a saw designed to cut foam. An everyday alternative to this pro tool is an electric bread knife. A bread knife's serrated edges easily cut through thick foam, and the knife is also lightweight and easy to control.

STIFFEN EDGES WITH BATTING

Polyester batting stiffens a cushion and eliminates wrinkles, making a cushion cover taut and smooth. Glue the batting to foam with a spray such as 3M Headliner & Fabric Adhesive ($25).

← LOCK STITCH

LOCK YOUR STITCH

Backstitching locks a stitch in place, ensuring it won't unravel. Start by going in reverse about an inch, and then go forward over that bit of stitching. This locks in the thread at the beginning of the seam. Do the same at the end of the seam.

MAKE A PATTERN

When you're going to make more than one of anything, a pattern is essential. Nate suggests making patterns that account for the seam allowance, so you don't have to remember to offset the line every time you trace the pattern. Nate uses chalk, not markers, for marking his lines. Chalk isn't permanent, and markers tend to bleed.

SHOPPING FOR MATERIALS

Most materials needed for an upholstery project—even foam—are available at local fabric and hobby stores.

USE A SPECIAL FOOT FOR ZIPPERS

Zippers and piping often require stitching closer to an edge than a regular foot will allow. For these operations, Nate uses this special foot on his sewing machine.

LEAVE THE PIPING FOR THE PROS

Piping adds a significant level of style to any cushion and also a significant amount of difficulty. Piping requires the use of a special foot on the sewing machine (as shown above), and the machine itself must be able to handle thick material.

REPLACE A MISSING BUTTON

The buttons on a tufted cushion often come loose, get damaged or disappear. Nate showed me how easy it is to replace them. With a long needle called a regulator and a simple knot, you can replace a button on any cushion.

UPHOLSTERER'S SLIPKNOT

BUTTON

SLIDE

NATE'S TOOLS OF THE TRADE

Here are the essential tools Nate uses every day in his upholstery shop.

REGULATOR
A regulator is the needle used to replace tufting buttons. Expect to pay about $10 for one.

STAPLE REMOVER
This essential tool for removing staples costs about $30 online.

FOAM-CUTTING SAW
For large pieces of foam, this purpose-built saw is indispensable.

PNEUMATIC STAPLER
A pneumatic stapler is probably the most-used tool in Nate's shop. He uses 1/2-in. staples. Expect to pay $80 for a good one.

NEEDLES
A great assortment of needles will serve you well. Find them at your local fabric, hobby or leatherworking stores.

SOFT TAILOR'S TAPE
Essential for measuring curved surfaces, these flexible tapes are available at fabric stores for about $5.

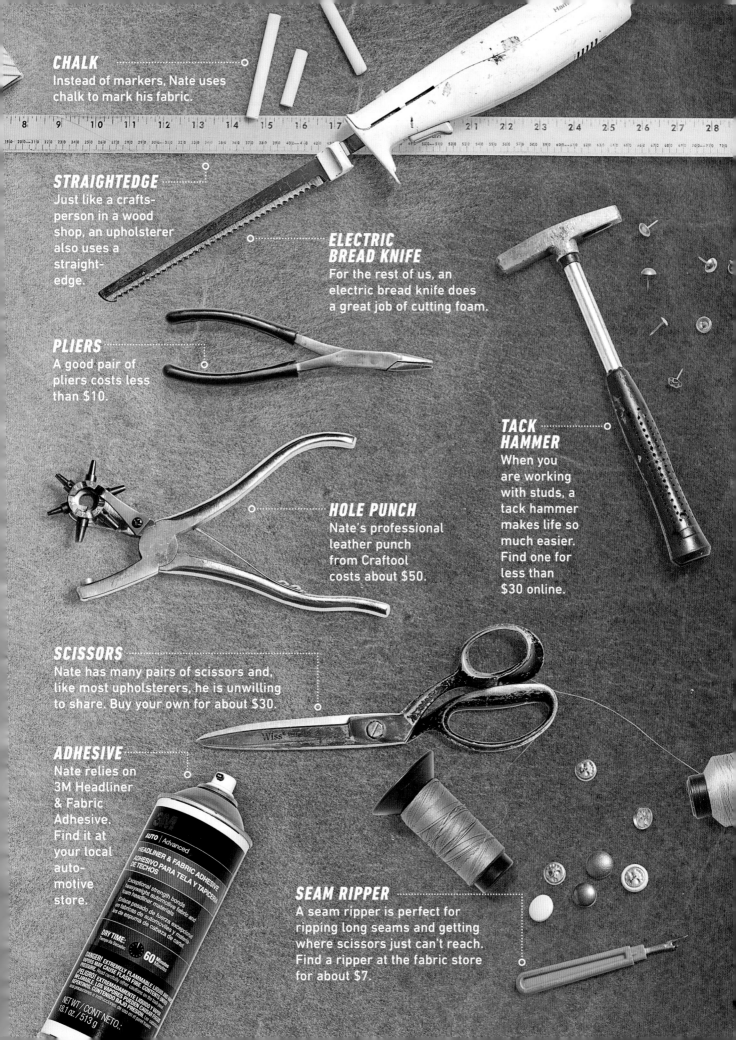

CHALK
Instead of markers, Nate uses chalk to mark his fabric.

STRAIGHTEDGE
Just like a crafts-person in a wood shop, an upholsterer also uses a straight-edge.

ELECTRIC BREAD KNIFE
For the rest of us, an electric bread knife does a great job of cutting foam.

PLIERS
A good pair of pliers costs less than $10.

HOLE PUNCH
Nate's professional leather punch from Craftool costs about $50.

TACK HAMMER
When you are working with studs, a tack hammer makes life so much easier. Find one for less than $30 online.

SCISSORS
Nate has many pairs of scissors and, like most upholsterers, he is unwilling to share. Buy your own for about $30.

ADHESIVE
Nate relies on 3M Headliner & Fabric Adhesive. Find it at your local auto-motive store.

SEAM RIPPER
A seam ripper is perfect for ripping long seams and getting where scissors just can't reach. Find a ripper at the fabric store for about $7.

HOME INSPECTION LESSONS

A CRASH COURSE IN HOUSE HEALTH

LEAKING WINDOWS

EVIDENCE OF WATER DAMAGE

ROOF DAMAGE

LIGHTS NOT WORKING

BAD WEATHERSTRIPPING

BY JAY CORK

When you're buying or selling a home, it helps to have an ally. Hiring a home inspector can help you avoid surprises at the closing table. I talked to Chris Meis of Honest Home Inspection to discover the most common issues he finds and what advice he has for buyers and sellers alike.

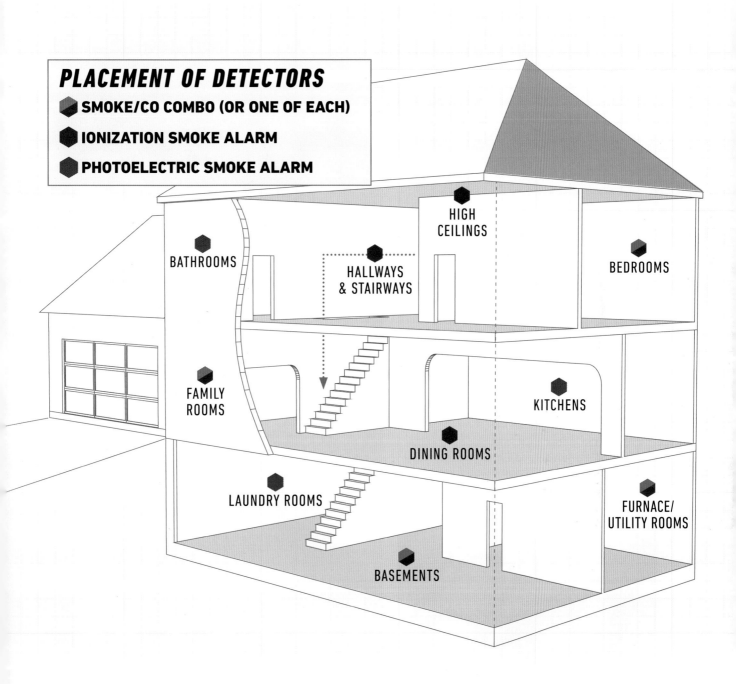

PLACEMENT OF DETECTORS

- ⬡ **SMOKE/CO COMBO (OR ONE OF EACH)**
- ⬡ **IONIZATION SMOKE ALARM**
- ⬡ **PHOTOELECTRIC SMOKE ALARM**

HIGH CEILINGS

BATHROOMS

HALLWAYS & STAIRWAYS

BEDROOMS

FAMILY ROOMS

KITCHENS

DINING ROOMS

LAUNDRY ROOMS

FURNACE/ UTILITY ROOMS

BASEMENTS

INADEQUATE SMOKE AND CO DETECTORS

Chris often finds that houses have inadequate smoke and CO detectors. Your home needs a smoke detector in every bedroom and on every floor of the house. And you must have a CO detector within 10 ft. of every bedroom.

MEET THE EXPERT

AFTER CAREERS IN CONSTRUCTION, AUTOMOTIVE MECHANICS AND CABINETRY, **CHRIS MEIS** FOUND A PROFESSION WHERE HE CAN APPLY AND SHARE ALL HIS KNOWLEDGE.

NUISANCE PLUMBING LEAKS

Ceiling stains mean there's a leak somewhere, but it might not be directly above the stain. Sinks, toilets and tubs are all potential sources of water leaks. If not repaired, leaks become water stains, rotten floors and mold.

ROOFING

The roof is the single most important protective element for any house, and Chris finds plenty of problems here. Vents, chimneys and flashing are all potential weak spots. Keep a close eye on a tile roof for storm damage or wear.

EXTERIOR WATER MANAGEMENT

The most common problem Chris encounters is poor exterior water management. When full of debris, gutters will overflow and water will find its way right into the basement. If you keep your gutters clean and intact, you're one step closer to a dry basement and a healthy house.

CHRIS'S ADVICE FOR BUYERS & SELLERS

DON'T SKIP THE INSPECTION!
Unless you're a housing professional with the ability to spot and take care of any and all issues yourself, skipping an inspection is a dangerous game. Don't do it!

ASK ABOUT INSURANCE
Housing inspectors may not be required to keep Errors and Omissions insurance in your region. If they don't have insurance and they miss something that turns out to be significant, you may have no recourse. Always ask about this upfront and make an informed decision.

NO REPAIR? BE READY TO ASK FOR A LOWER PRICE
It's important for buyers to understand that a seller may choose not to fix the problems highlighted in the inspection report. This is the buyer's opportunity to negotiate a better purchase price for taking on the repairs.

WHICH ISSUES DO YOU NEED TO TACKLE FIRST?
Once you've closed on your new home, the real work begins. Chris likes to help his clients formulate a plan to address the issues discovered in the inspection. You don't need to fix everything at once. Chris suggests prioritizing projects and creating a repair plan that fits your timing and budget.

DIY ... OR HIRE A PRO?
Determine which issues you're able to fix yourself and which ones are best suited for an expert. Roofing, electrical and plumbing are best left to the professionals.

BE PROACTIVE
Even if you're not in the market to sell, having an inspection is a fantastic way to gauge the health of your home.

DO A PRESALE INSPECTION
Position yourself for a quick and happy sale by doing a prelisting inspection. It highlights any issues upfront and avoids surprises at the closing table.

CHECK FOR MOLD
Selling a home with mold is difficult; mold may even be a deal breaker. Mold is most commonly found in attics, basements and bathrooms. If you think your home has mold contamination, Chris recommends scheduling a comprehensive mold inspection right away to find out if there is a problem and how big it might be. It's always best to deal with this issue before listing for sale.

RECEPTACLES AND SWITCHES
Chris commonly finds dropped grounds or swapped wires in electrical outlets and switches. His circuit tester quickly indicates problems with GFCI and normal receptacles. Buy your own tester, or hire a pro if needed.

PET STAINS
It's not uncommon for sellers to have the carpets cleaned just before they begin showings. A freshly cleaned carpet may mask pet stains from our eyes, but it may still be hiding dirty little secrets. Chris uses a black light to find evidence of pet stains. Eww!

MASK
Home inspection is often a dirty business. Chris protects himself with a Rikon half mask respirator ($50).

FLASHLIGHT
This rechargeable lithium-ion flashlight from Milwaukee ($80 online) has served Chris for years.

BLACK LIGHT
Even after carpet cleaning, pet stains can still be detected with a black light. Not for the faint of heart.

RADON MONITOR
This RadStar monitor ($1,400) allows Chris to test for radon, but it also gives him insight into other environmental variables.

CAMERA
Chris and his crew document everything. A digital camera is essential for this.

RADSTAR α
CONTINUOUS RADON MONITOR 516

START TEST

END TEST

DELAY MODE

OFF ON

EK7000
4K Ultra HD
Wi-Fi
AKASO

COLLAPSIBLE BUCKET Chris never knows when he may need a bucket. This one fits in his toolbox.

LASER THERMOMETER A laser thermometer can help Chris determine whether in-floor heating is working. Expect to pay about $45 for one.

SCREWDRIVER Basic? Yes. Indispensable? Absolutely!

MOISTURE METER If water damage is hidden, a Protimeter moisture meter ($400 and up online) will find it.

REPORT APP With an app on his phone, Chris is able to provide detailed reports to his clients via email.

WATER PRESSURE GAUGE This Rain Bird water pressure gauge gives Chris an accurate reading of water pressure throughout the house.

OUTLET TESTERS This outlet tester reveals whether an electrical outlet has a dropped ground or swapped lines. You can find testers at any hardware store.

Sections
- Inspection Details
- Roof
- Exterior
- Heating
- Cooling
- Plumbing
- Electrical

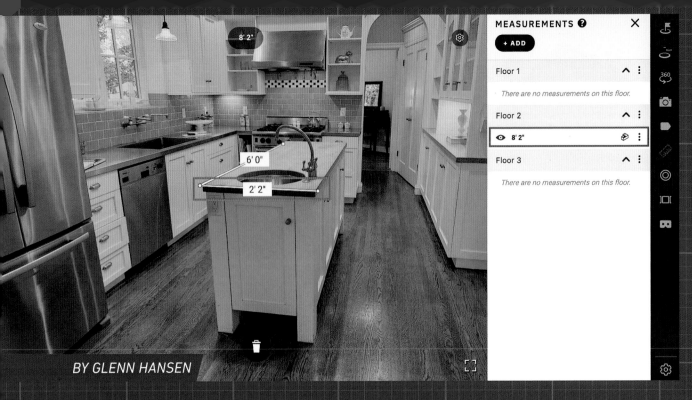

BY GLENN HANSEN

A 3D TOUR CAN HELP YOU SELL, RENT OR REDESIGN YOUR HOME

High demand and a comparatively low supply of existing homes helped make 2021 a big year for home sales. Homes moved fast in high-priced markets. The activity slowed in 2022, and if you're considering selling a home, you need to be aware of all the new tools available in the real estate market.

"As a home seller, you want as many eyeballs on your property as possible," says Mike Velez of BLDG Realty in Chino Hills, California. "Realtors used to send postcards to show homes locally, but today's audience is the whole world, especially during COVID with remote work letting people live nearly anywhere. I sold a home in Southern California to a couple from South Carolina, and they didn't set foot on the property until they owned it. I'm not the only one doing that."

One of Velez's favorite tools is a 3D tour. Using the Matterport 360-degree camera and 3D-tour technology (*matterport.com*), agents and home sellers can show a home's features beyond just wall colors and floor coverings. A 3D tour lets shoppers see a home's interior from every angle, giving

room measurements, window sizes and specifics of kitchen countertop materials, appliance features and much more.

"Good photography is the foundation of every home sale," says Velez. "Every buyer wants information about room sizes, materials and feature details." Realtors like Velez pay the cost of Matterport's 3D-tour service, and the video can be captured using one or more cameras. For owners of vacation rentals or Airbnb properties, the same 3D-tour features can help promote property rentals.

Matterport might also be a worthwhile tool, literally, in a home-remodeling project. When paired with a software such as RoomSketcher, Matterport can help you visualize new flooring, select and place different furniture, or even move walls and resize rooms. Along with the 3D visualization features, you can create two-dimensional floor plans with room-size specifications, which can be helpful for estimating prices of carpet or hardwood flooring.

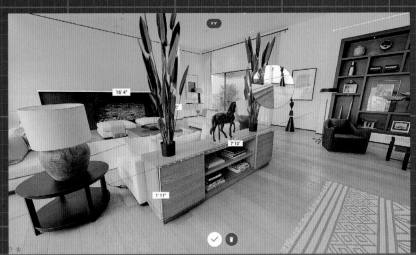

GREAT GOOFS®

🔶 LAUGHS AND LESSONS FROM OUR READERS

FIRE IN HIS BELLY

In an attempt to be neat while taking down the backsplash in my kitchen, I covered the counters, stove and sink with newspaper. I was leaning over the stove to get at the backsplash behind it, and my belly turned on a burner. The newspaper started burning while I was trying to figure out what that clicking noise was. I saved the house but learned a lesson: Keep combustibles away from sources of fire and always know where the faucet is, especially if it's covered up!

KEITH HETRICK

PLASTER— IT'S WHAT'S FOR DINNER

My parents were turning the attic space directly above our dining room into an extra bedroom. The space had no flooring, which was one of the first jobs they wanted to tackle. One evening, they set out dinner and went upstairs to work while we ate. Suddenly, we heard a scream and a crash, and then we saw Mom's foot come through the ceiling! She'd forgotten about the lack of flooring and stepped right through. She wasn't hurt, but the soup that night was pretty crunchy—with the plaster dust and all.

ELLEN SAMUEL

2 HVAC, PLUMBING & HIGH-TECH

CLEANING AIR DUCTS

Man wrestles octopus, trains it to clean houses. OK, that's not really true. Actually, Adam Bonine, a professional duct cleaner, used that black and yellow tube—an extra-large vacuum hose—to suck all the dust and dirt from my home's ductwork. I hired him recently because the air ducts in my 15-year-old house had never been cleaned. Here's how he tackled the job.

BY GLENN HANSEN

MEET THE EXPERT

ADAM BONINE OWNS AND OPERATES FRESH AIR VENTS, A DUCT-CLEANING SERVICE IN MINNESOTA.

First, Adam cuts access holes (he patches them later) in the main supply and return ducts near the furnace. He then connects the vacuum hose to pull out dust and dirt before it can get into the furnace and blower fan.

Should all homeowners have their home's air ducts cleaned?
"Yes. If a house gets dirty, then its ducts get dirty too," Adam said. Fresh Air Vents, his residential and commercial cleaning company, is based in St. Paul, Minnesota.

How often should air ducts be cleaned?
"That is a personal preference—different people have different sensitivities. The National Air Duct Cleaning Association recommends duct cleaning every two to four years. I believe this might be overkill, and more often I suggest that homeowners have their ducts cleaned every three to five years. A large family living in a smaller home or a household with several pets should have the ducts cleaned more often."

What are indicators of dirty ducts?
"If your furnace filter gets dirty more often than usual, your ducts are probably dirty. Remove a return vent cover and look inside using the flashlight on your phone. These unfiltered ducts can collect dirt."

What tools do you use?
"My main tool is a giant vacuum. It has a 31-hp engine attached to a fan to pull dirt and dust into a bag outside of the house. The vacuum moves 7,000 cfm (cubic feet per minute) of air and creates negative air pressure in the home while I'm cleaning. Meanwhile, we agitate and disrupt the ducts. We snake tools with compressed air "whips" on the end into the ducts. The vacuum continues to pull out as we agitate inside. I also use a HEPA-filtered backpack vacuum for precleaning."

What should homeowners expect from clean ducts?
"People ask me, 'Is my house going to be dirty after you're done cleaning?' No, not at all. It will look cleaner and feel cleaner, with a noticeable reduction in dust."

Plus:
- Duct cleaning can help your furnace work more efficiently.
- Cleaning only some ductwork does no good.
- Be wary of services marketing chemical biocide treatments.
- Hire a pro who will explain the process and tools.
- Average cost? $450 to $1,000.
- Change the furnace filter often!

With rubber cords at the end of a compressed air hose (left), the whip system goes into ductwork and agitates the dirt and dust to be vacuumed out.

With a smaller shop vacuum (below), wall spaces behind return air grilles are cleaned by hand.

VOCs IN YOUR HOME

From vinyl flooring to plug-in air fresheners, different products in your home might emit harmful vapors. We talked to four experts to better understand how to lessen our exposure to volatile organic compounds (VOCs).

WHEN DID VOCs BECOME A PROBLEM?

VOCs have been around for a long time, though it's been only in the last couple of decades that science has discovered the extent of their dangers. Yet our exposure to them continues to grow.

"For one, we now spend more than 90% of our time indoors," says Oyvind Birkenes, CEO of Airthings air quality monitors. "Also, over the last couple of decades, scented products such as candles, room sprays and even garbage bags have become extremely popular, especially in westernized countries such as the U.S., which has contributed to the prevalence of VOCs."

While the EPA has banned extremely toxic chemicals such as methylene chloride, it lacks the authority to regulate VOCs in indoor products that can off-gas for hours, months or even years. Fortunately, there are ways to minimize your exposure to VOCs.

BY KARUNA EBERL

WHAT COMMON HOUSEHOLD ITEMS CAN OFF-GAS VOCs?

Nearly any interior finish that isn't glass, ceramic, concrete, metal or stone can off-gas, but alternative products are available with low- or no-VOC content. When buying building materials, look for certifications such as SCS Indoor Advantage Gold, FloorScore, Green Seal and Greenguard.

PAINT

"VOC off-gassing is highest during and immediately after application, but paints can continue to off-gas for longer periods," says Nina Hwang, lead environmental scientist at Green Seal, a nonprofit that certifies eco-labeling. Purchase certified low- or no-VOC paint and keep the work area well ventilated until the paint dries. Note: Solvent-based paints contain higher VOCs than water-based coatings.

RUGS AND CARPETS

"Most VOCs from carpets come from the backing and the adhesive," says Docia Boylen, owner of Handyman Connection of Golden, Colorado. For low VOCs, look for a Green Label or Green Label Plus certification for carpets and adhesives, and air out the space for at least 72 hours after installation. "A woolen carpet with a natural-fiber backing is also a great choice, since wool is naturally flame and stain resistant," says Boylen.

FURNITURE

Composite wood products, as well as the foam found in mattresses, cushions and padding, contain resins and adhesives that can include formaldehyde and other VOCs. "Emissions are highest when products are new and slowly drop over time," Hwang says. "However, off-gassing may continue for years."

Look for furniture that has been VOC tested by the California Department of Public Health or certified by SCS Indoor Advantage or Greenguard. "Or buy secondhand furniture that has had more time to off-gas," says Hwang.

INSULATION

Building insulation is usually made from fiberglass, polyurethane or polystyrene, then treated with fire-retardant chemicals. "These products can leak VOCs into your air, especially during excessive heat," says Boylen. She recommends a formaldehyde-free brand, mineral wool insulation or sprayed foam products.

FLOORING

Because of their large surface areas, flooring products such as vinyl tile can be big contributors to VOCs in your home. "Fortunately, there is a large majority of flooring that has been tested and certified," says Karen Righthand, vice president of corporate sales at SCS Global Services, which monitors third-party environmental certifications.

"VOC emissions from vinyl flooring are highest immediately after installation, but lower levels may continue for years," Hwang says. Also, use a low- or no-VOC adhesive if you can.

CLEANING PRODUCTS

For many, cleaning products offer especially high VOC exposure. Choose fragrance-free products or those certified by a reputable eco-label like Green Seal or Safer Choice.

"These chemicals are unfortunately all around us," Birkenes says, "but with education, monitoring and intervention, they can be mitigated successfully."

HOW CAN I LIMIT HARMFUL VOCs IN MY HOME?

- Ventilate. "Open your windows regularly to infuse fresh air into your living space," says Birkenes.
- Regularly replace air filters in indoor fan and HVAC systems, and create alerts to remind you to change them.
- Choose products certified low- or no-VOC and building materials like stone and tile that are naturally safer.
- Don't store products or buy in bulk. Buy only what you need, since VOCs can leak from containers such as old paint cans and bleach bottles. If you must store them, put them in a garage or shed separate from the house.
- If you can't open windows, use air purifiers with active carbon and HEPA filters.
- Stop using air fresheners. "They have been targeted as a key source of VOCs in your home," says Boylen.
- Air out your clothes after picking them up from the dry cleaners.
- Get an air quality monitor that tracks VOCs and can alert you if your levels cross certain thresholds. "It can also provide insight into the exact times when your VOCs may be highest," Birkenes says, "which can provide context for what may be contributing to the problem based on your activity or where the device is located."
- Lastly, use common sense. "Listen to your nose," says Birkenes. "When something smells, it is more than likely emitting VOCs!"

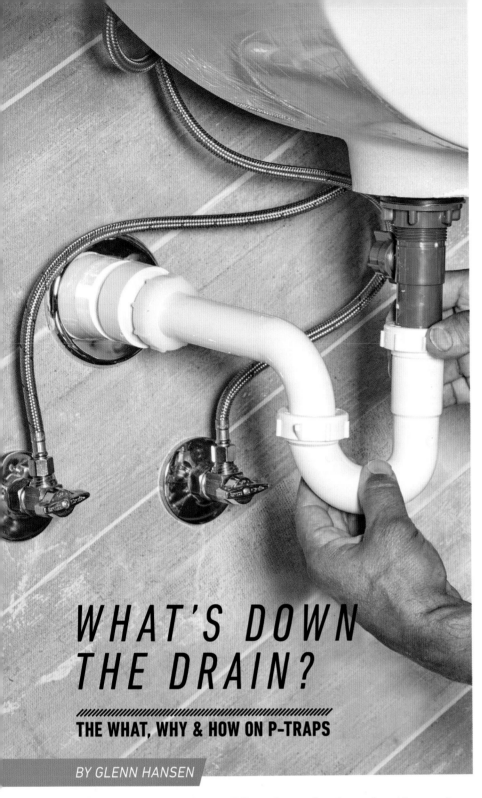

P-trap pipes are available in different materials, but the assemblies are similar. Your P-trap can be polypropylene (white or black), ABS (black), PVC (white) or 18-gauge brass (either chrome-plated or natural). Plastic traps come in inside-diameter sizes of 1-1/4 in. (for a standard bathroom sink), 1-1/2 in. (for a laundry sink, bathtub or standard kitchen sink) and 2 in. (for a shower or floor drain).

If your bathroom sink drains slowly, you may have a clog of hair around the stopper below the drain. Those clogs can usually be removed with a long wire hook.

If the clog is deeper than that, it could be inside the P-trap. The same design that traps water can also trap hair, food and diamond earrings. To clear the first two, try a plunger; block the sink overflow or other openings before plunging. Drain cleaners can damage fixtures and pipes. A plumbing snake can also clear the trap, but it won't retrieve that diamond earring. For that, you may need to disassemble and reassemble a P-trap in your kitchen or bathroom. Here's how:

If you're lucky, your sink's trap has a cleanout nut located on the lowest portion of the bend. You can remove that and clear many clogs. Grab an empty bucket and place it under that nut, then remove the nut and let the contents drain out. If your trap doesn't have a cleanout nut, you can easily disassemble the trap and find that earring; you might not even need tools.

The P-trap is connected to the tailpiece at the sink end and the drain line (also called the waste line) at the opposite end. Those connections use slip nuts and beveled cone washers. An older home with metal P-traps might use squared and thick rubber washers with accompanying flat metal washers. Either way, if

WHAT'S DOWN THE DRAIN?

//

THE WHAT, WHY & HOW ON P-TRAPS

BY GLENN HANSEN

t's shaped like a "P" and can be found under sinks, tubs and showers. A simple device, a P-trap holds just enough water to create an airtight seal that prevents sewer gas from backing up into your home. As you run water down a drain, you're continuously refilling that trap. This plumbing masterpiece has been in use for about 250 years. Here's what you need to know about it.

you're taking apart your P-trap to remove a clog, be sure to pay close attention to the placement of the washers and reassemble them the same way.

If you're tackling this job because the P-trap is leaking, it's best to buy a new PVC P-trap. It will last longer than metal and costs only about $10. If your plumbing is visible—underneath a pedestal sink, for example—you can purchase decorative P-traps.

REMOVE THE P-TRAP

If your P-trap was installed properly, you should be able to remove it using only your hands, but a V-jaw tongue-and-groove pliers, sometimes called a water pump pliers, will give you a good grip on slip nuts.

First, grab some rags and place an empty bucket below the trap. Slowly loosen the nut connecting the P-trap on the outflow side. Pay attention to the placement of the washers inside, and be ready for water to come out. You might find the clog in the trap or the union joint. Clean those areas with water and a brush, and replace the slip nut washers if the connection shows any sign of leakage—and I hope you found the diamond earring.

REASSEMBLE THE P-TRAP

To reassemble the P-trap, start by replacing the drain line end, then reconnect the tailpiece to the sink. Keep any slip nut connections loose for now. Connect the sink side of the P-trap to the tailpiece and position the drain line end to align with the drainpipe. That drainpipe slides into the wall with some adjustability for length, easing the final connection to the P-trap. Each beveled washer is placed so that the large end contacts the slip nut. When tightened, a slip nut eases the washer into a leak-free connection.

Do not use plumbing tape or putty on any of these connections. Some plumbers use plumber's grease on threaded connections, but that's not necessary. Tighten all the connections by hand. If you overtighten them, you risk distorting the washer or cracking the pipe.

Once all the fittings are secured, run two tests. First, turn on the tap and run water through the sink while inspecting the P-trap connections for leaks. Second, fill the sink basin with a couple of inches of water, then remove the drain plug and let the water flow through the trap.

If you have a leak, you'll need to simply loosen the slip nut where the leak appears, inspect the placement of the washers, and then reinstall. Most leaks happen because a washer is installed incorrectly or because a slip nut is threaded improperly or overtightened.

P-TRAP OPTION   P-TRAP

Designed to make installation even easier, the Insta-Plumb from Keeney costs about $15 at home centers and hardware stores. Its hero features are the push-connect fittings where this P-trap connects to the sink and the drain. They eliminate the need to align a cone washer or properly thread and tighten a slip nut. Inside each fitting there's an O-ring and a locking ring. A release collar at the top of each fitting secures the connection. To undo a fitting, compress the release collar and disconnect the pipes. No tools necessary.

The Insta-Plumb is available in 1-1/4-in. and 1-1/2-in. P-trap sizes. For small cabinets with hard-to-reach pipes and P-traps, it can ease installation and service work. The system is approved in most plumbing codes, but check in your area. The Insta-Plumb is for use with drainpipes, not for pipes under pressure or potable water pipes.

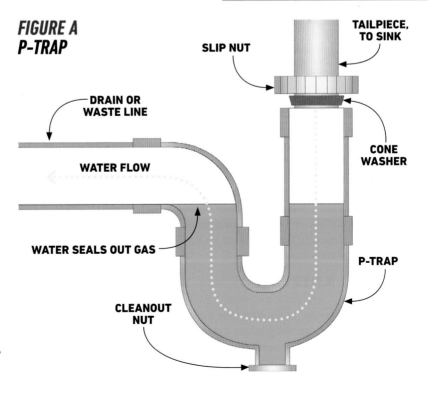

FIGURE A
P-TRAP

TAILPIECE, TO SINK

SLIP NUT

DRAIN OR WASTE LINE

WATER FLOW

CONE WASHER

WATER SEALS OUT GAS

P-TRAP

CLEANOUT NUT

WHY CAULK A TOILET BASE?

BY GLENN HANSEN

We posted this question on our Facebook page some time ago, and the comments were ... well, it was Facebook. Here is the argument *against* caulking a toilet base: If the toilet develops a leak, the caulk will prevent you from noticing that leak until it's too late, and the damage will worsen out of sight. But that argument doesn't hold water. Toilets rarely leak from the base onto the floor. Instead, they generally leak below, and the evidence appears on the ceiling underneath. The argument *for* caulking is much stronger. Here's why:

CAULK KEEPS WATER OUT

Caulking a toilet base prevents water on the floor from seeping under the toilet. Whether from tub splashes, a soaking-wet mop job or an errant potty trainer, any spills that get under your toilet will cause smelly messes. Some installers leave a small section uncaulked at the back of the toilet.

CAULK SECURES THE TOILET

Yes, your toilet is secured to the floor with bolts, but if your floor is uneven at all (most floors are), caulk will provide a cushion of support around the entire base. Grout can do an even better job of securing and stabilizing the toilet, and you can add clear silicone over the grout to protect it.

CAULK LOOKS BETTER

A gap between the toilet base and the floor that's been filled with a color-matched caulk looks more finished.

IT'S REQUIRED

The International Plumbing Code and the Uniform Plumbing Code both require a watertight seal (408.2 2000 UPC): "Where a fixture comes into contact with the wall or floor, the joint between the fixture and the wall or floor shall be made watertight." Many home inspectors also list this as a requirement in purchase processes.

SMART, POWERED WINDOW SHADES

//

BY GLENN HANSEN

Smart technology is applied to a whole lot of things in your home that really don't need smarts. An internet-connected trash can or juicer? A smart salt shaker? I don't understand.

Smart window shades, however, are one of the smartest ideas out there. You can power a bedroom's shades for bedtime or as a wake-up call. Add privacy to any room when desired, even if you're not in it. And make large or hard-to-reach window coverings respond to your needs. Smart and powered window shades let you take control of your home. That's smart.

The shade part of powered window shades is easy; the power part takes some thinking. Windows don't have electrical outlets, and nobody wants an extension cord running from the top of the window to the nearest outlet. Two electrical engineers from Missouri started a company in 2017 called PowerShades to make that hard part easy.

PowerShades window shades are available in dozens of colors, textures and fabrics and include styles for both residential and commercial buildings. What makes these shades unique is the power source capability. These shades can run on AC or DC power, batteries, solar power or PoE power. That last one is Power over Ethernet and means that a standard Cat 5 or Cat 6 ethernet cable can power these shades. The company calls this TruePoE, and the shades require only 5 watts of power. Of course, you still need to get most of these power sources to your windows, but having more options available can ease the installation, and it's simple for any new construction.

I tested the rechargeable-battery-powered PowerShade on a large window in my home that's tall enough to make using a traditional manual-operation window shade difficult. After months of use and daily operation to open and close the shade, I have not needed to charge the battery. Doing so will require that I reach the shade's drive motor to plug in a charger, and the manufacturer claims the charge should last six months or more. That's easier than running full-time power to the shade.

As for smart capabilities, PowerShades can be programmed to run on any schedule you choose. They will also work with smart-home networks and voice-control devices such as Google Home and Amazon Alexa. You can manipulate multiple shades in one program, giving users such as office managers control from a distance.

PowerShades makes indoor and outdoor shades and sells through many retailers nationwide. Visit *powershades.com*.

CLEANER AIR & HELPFUL DATA

Even with the relatively clean air in Minnesota, I wonder about my home's indoor air quality. Smoke from wildfires hundreds of miles away, fumes from construction projects, chemicals sprayed on neighboring yards, my own drywall project—who knows what's in the air I breathe? What I do know are the potential harmful effects of air pollutants, from a nagging cough to asthma symptoms to long-term lung conditions.

BY GLENN HANSEN

You can do two things about air pollution immediately. First, increase your awareness of indoor and outdoor air conditions, and second, clean the air inside your home. I've been testing the Aura Air purifier device in my home for several weeks. Once plugged in, the device goes to work immediately to clean the air and to inform me about the quality of the air I'm breathing, and that's one of the manufacturer's main goals.

"We want to inform and provide a solution," says Roei Friedberg, CEO of Aura Air. "As we work to build a new standard for indoor air quality, we know that information is an important element of the process."

To clean indoor air, the Aura Air purifier uses a system of filters, sensors, a UVC LED light and a recirculating fan. The device's prefilter snares large particles such as dust, pollen and even pet hair.

The purifier's larger ray filter targets the contaminants you can't see. This filter—which is about the size and shape of an old automotive air cleaner—includes a high-efficiency particulate air (HEPA) filter, a carbon filter to absorb volatile organic compounds (VOCs) and foul odors, and a zinc-lined copper fabric filter with virus-killing properties.

The UVC LED light works to kill pathogens in the air; this technology is increasingly common in air-cleaning devices. The Aura Air's Sterionizer element converts oxygen molecules into positively and negatively charged atoms, which can reduce the spread of airborne pathogens.

In clinical trials performed in Japan, the Sterionizer reduced the levels of influenza H1N1 virus in the air by 92% after just 30 minutes of exposure and 98.9% after 60 minutes.

The Aura Air wall-mounted cube weighs about 12 lbs. and measures about 15 in. across. I mounted it on the wall outside my bedrooms and home office, and I was able to secure it easily with the included hardware. Then I plugged in the unit, downloaded the app and connected the device to my home network.

Once I entered my Wi-Fi password, the small light on the Aura Air turned green and it began to work. I know it did because I could hear it. I mean, I could definitely hear it. Louder than I expected it to be, the Aura Air's fan works hard to pull air through all its filters. The sound reminded me of a small window air-conditioning unit.

But while I explored the app and the unit's settings, I noticed the Aura Air became quieter, as if it shifted down a gear or two. With the unit in Auto Mode, it will cycle as needed from low to high. I discovered I can manually set it to any mode (including Silent Mode) and program a Night Mode to quiet the device and turn off the indicator light.

With the app and my connected Aura Air, I have access to loads of data about indoor and outdoor air quality. Information about particulate matter, VOCs and the overall air quality index is important to those suffering with asthma or allergies. The Aura Air monitors CO and CO_2 indoors, and it reports on nitrogen oxides, ozone and sulfur dioxide in the outdoor air. It also works as a smoke detector.

The Aura Air is designed to handle about 600 sq. ft. of living space and retails for about $500. There's also an Aura Air Mini, a battery-powered portable unit, for use in hotels or smaller workspaces. If you're curious about the air quality where you live, enter your ZIP code at *airnow.gov*, a site created in part by the U.S. Environmental Protection Agency.

A SMART, ECONOMICAL LIGHTBULB

Its flickering cry for help caught my attention before it flashed its final light. That was the last incandescent lightbulb in my house, and it went dark. Elated, I quickly screwed in a new smart bulb and now feel as if my home has left the 20th century behind. Dramatic? Maybe, but the shift from heated wire filaments to LED bulbs that we can talk to is as big as it sounds. To replace that last old-school bulb, I twisted in a new Solana smart LED bulb from Bulbrite, a company that has been in the lightbulb business for more than 50 years.

Bulbrite's Solana smart bulb lineup includes standard bulbs in a range of lumens; globe, chandelier and reflector-style bulbs; and Edison-style bulbs with visible filaments. We tried a Bulbrite color smart bulb in the A19 size with a 60W equivalency. When buying smart bulbs, look at "brightness" measured in lumens (a measure of the visible light). Most manufacturers note the wattage equivalent on the packaging. A single bulb is about $20; that's on the middle-to-low end of smart-bulb pricing.

Installation is just a bit more difficult than screwing in a lightbulb. Download the Bulbrite app to your phone and then spend some time learning how to make the bulb work best for you. No additional accessories are required; no remote or smart-home connection is needed. The Solana bulbs don't work with IFTTT actions. You can, however, easily set schedules for a Solana bulb with the easy-to-use app, and you can create scenes within those schedules. The bulb generates colors in a pleasing array for fun scene opportunities, and the scheduling options add convenience that makes these bulbs well worth the price.

GLENN HANSEN *DEPUTY EDITOR*

SMART LEAK DETECTION AND WATER CONTROL

Copper pipe remains the standard for plumbing in as many as 85 percent of homes in the United States. But copper is prone to corrosion over time from overly acidic water supplies. When California began adding chloramine to its water supply to help kill bacteria, homeowners saw an increase in pinhole leaks developing in copper plumbing. These and other failures in copper pipes are often difficult to detect until significant water damage has occurred.

To be fair, polyethylene (or PEX) piping isn't perfect either. Leaks can develop in PEX piping or at fittings, and they may go undetected as well. The solution? Leave all your plumbing exposed indoors so that you can easily identify leaks. Or install a device that does this for you.

My home has copper main lines and plumbing manifolds that lead to PEX supply lines for fixtures and appliances. I can see much of the plumbing in my unfinished basement, but I still want more information and the security of a "smart" system. I installed the Flo by Moen smart water valve, which is part of the manufacturer's Smart Water Security System.

Installation on your home's main line—3/4- to 1-1/4-in. pipe diameter—is fairly simple if you have some experience working with copper pipe, or it's quick work for your plumber. Depending on the location and strength of your router, the Flo by Moen connects easily to Wi-Fi. It works with Alexa and Google systems, but it doesn't require a smart-home hub.

When installed on the main water supply line, this valve monitors water flow rates and pressure in real time. It then reports the data through an app on your phone. During setup, the app asked me about my water use, such as whether I have a sprinkler system. Then over seven to 10 days, the system learned my water-use habits. The valve was in Sleep mode then and not protecting me, but it was monitoring.

After its first day in Learning mode, it reported a 632-gallon usage for my sprinkler system. When the learning was complete, the device continued to monitor for changes in pressure and flow rate. If there's a catastrophic failure such as a burst pipe or if the water is left running, I get an alert and can shut off the water from anywhere. I can set it up to shut off the water automatically as well.

If I'm planning to use an unusually large amount of water, maybe to fill a new hot tub, I can put the system in Sleep mode and it won't think there's a leak somewhere. The app will also notify me of situations such as a running toilet or a faucet not completely closed.

Preventing major water damage is the main benefit of this Flo system. I had a pipe burst once because it froze in the winter. I don't want to go through that again. I can also use this smart water valve to measure and

FLO BY MOEN SMART VALVE

MOEN SMART WATER DETECTOR

rethink my family's water usage, saving money as well.

The smart valve system runs daily Health Tests on my plumbing. It closes the main valve for a bit to test for changes in pressure. The system will schedule this test for a time when we don't use water. Water use at the time will override the test. I can also schedule these tests myself.

The Flo by Moen smart valve is designed to work on its own, no subscriptions needed. You can also add Moen's Smart Water Detector devices, which you place at individual plumbing fixtures or appliances. They'll communicate with the smart valve directly or work through the Moen app. Moen does offer a monthly subscription service called FloProtect, which includes an extended warranty, additional customer support and money toward an insurance deductible. Your insurance company may provide you with discounts for any of these services.

GLENN HANSEN *DEPUTY EDITOR*

FINGERPRINT ACCESS FOR YOUR HOME

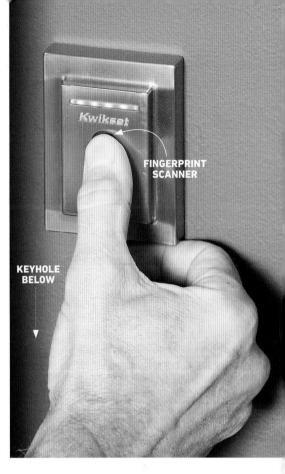

Yes, I got a traditional key with this Kwikset Halo Touch door lock. And there is a keyhole for it. But I'm hoping to never use it. (I did use it once during installation so I know it works.) The actual key is my fingerprint. Or my wife's. Or that of whomever I want to access my house.

This smart lock from Kwikset is a complete replacement for your existing door hardware. Even though I needed to grab a chisel and a drill to make the set's new strike plate fit my door, the whole installation took about 30 minutes. And that included downloading the Kwikset app, creating an account and scanning some fingerprints. For most installations, the job requires just a screwdriver.

The Kwikset Halo Touch has a circular fingerprint scanner just above the keyhole. On the inside of the door, a rectangular housing holds a motor, a few inches of wiring and a case for the four AA batteries.

To lock the door, simply place any finger on the scanner. No fingerprint security is needed to lock the door. Or activate the lock from the phone app or using Alexa or Google Assistant. We wish this Kwikset lock had an IFTTT interface. Feeling nostalgic? You can use the key.

Unlocking the door requires a saved fingerprint—up to 50 fingerprints (people) can be saved in your account. The app lets you limit access to any of those fingerprints by date or time of day. And you can shut off fingerprint access whenever you want. There is also a detailed history of who entered by fingerprint and when.

For its easy installation, attractive style and incredibly smart control interface, this Kwikset Halo Touch lock is a new favorite feature at my house. The lock shown costs about $250 online and at home centers.

GLENN HANSEN *DEPUTY EDITOR*

FINGERPRINT SCANNER

KEYHOLE BELOW

The Kohler H2Wise provides whole-home protection by monitoring household water usage. It sends real-time alerts to your smart device if the system detects changes in water pressure.

Easy for DIYers to install, the H2Wise connects to under-sink water lines. It's compatible with 3/8-in. water lines and threaded angle stops.

WATER ASSISTANT

With one smart plumbing device under your kitchen sink, you can monitor all your home's plumbing fixtures and water usage. When you connect the new Kohler H2Wise device to your hot and cold water pipes, it monitors water pressure, learns your water-use habits and looks for unusual changes through the day.

The Kohler device uses technology developed by Phyn, a subsidiary of consumer electronics giant Belkin International. Phyn developed a leak-detection technology that uses ultrasonic sensors to sample a plumbing system's pressure 240 times every second. The goal is to empower homeowners with information that can help them reduce water use and prevent major damage if a leak occurs.

As the Kohler H2Wise runs its diagnostic tests, it can alert you of water leaks—even small ones. It can also inform you of blockages and send you freeze warnings so you can protect your pipes. The H2Wise system ($300) is simple to install under a kitchen sink as long as a dedicated electrical outlet is nearby. Kohler's H2Wise+ system ($500) is a device that a plumber installs on your home's main water line. It also monitors water use and can shut off the water to your home in an emergency. Both products are available online and at home centers.

GLENN HANSEN *DEPUTY EDITOR*

INDOOR GARDEN

The best part of gardening is being around growing things. I love watching plants, flowers, fruits and vegetables grow—and, of course, eating food that I've grown myself—so it only made sense for me to bring a garden right into my kitchen. I enjoy being greeted each morning by something fresh and fragrant, and as a lifelong vegetarian, having access to fresh produce during the winter months is a real perk.

Many manufacturers make indoor gardens of all sizes, designs and functionality, but I was drawn to the sleek, modern look of Rise Gardens. I love vertical gardens, but I didn't want that in my small kitchen, so I opted for a countertop model.

I was very happy with the compact size of the Personal Rise Garden (18 in. long, weighing a mere 10 lbs.) and how easy it was to set up. The kit includes a base, grow lights, a water pump, a garden nursery, a variety of seeds, eight net cups and a bottle each of Sprout, Thrive and pH balance.

You can't choose the veggies and herbs that come in the initial package, but what they provided worked for me. You can always order individual seedpods directly from the site if you want something different. Rise Gardens sells everything from microgreens to beets.

The Personal Rise Garden is a hydroponic garden—it doesn't use soil. Agriculturists consider this to be one of the most eco-friendly gardening methods because it requires little water or space.

Since indoor hydroponic gardens are in a controlled environment, they can also produce higher yields than more traditional gardening methods. The keys to hydroponic gardens are their use of a water pump and the manual addition of specific nutrients (included with the Rise Garden). These help supplement nutrients that plants would normally get through the soil.

This was my first hydroponic garden, so I was a little intimidated at first. How does it work? What if the pump breaks? What if the plants aren't growing?

Once I started setting it up, I realized that this was going to be easy. After you wrap your head around testing the pH level in your tap water (using the kit provided) and manually adding nutrients (Thrive, Sprout and pH balance—all provided in your kit), it's a total breeze.

At $349, the kit provides great value. I haven't done the math to see if I save money on fresh veggies or herbs by growing them at home instead of buying them at a grocery store. But that's tricky to calculate given each user's consumption habits and access to fresh produce.

The kit also includes an app, which is its biggest difference from outdoor gardening. You can download the Rise Gardens app, create an account and connect your garden to your home's Wi-Fi. I had trouble with this at first because the garden app wouldn't work on our 5G network, so I had to choose a different network, and it took me a few minutes to figure out the issue.

You don't need to connect to the internet to use the garden, but there are some real benefits of doing so. The app will notify you when it's time to add nutrients or water, and you can also use the app to control the lights and the water pump.

A few lights on the front of the garden also alert you when it requires care. The garden tells you when to harvest your veggies or herbs, based on what you're growing and when you planted it. You can buy the Rise Personal Garden online from Rise Gardens.

AMY NOVAK *CONTENT DIRECTOR*

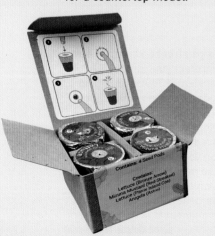

GREAT GOOFS

EVER-FLOWING WATER HEATER

When the plumber replaced one of the heating elements in my electric water heater, I watched carefully, knowing the other element would eventually need replacing too. Sure enough, a year later the other one went. I checked it with an ohmmeter, confirmed my diagnosis and headed to the plumbing supply store.

When I got home, I killed the power supply at the box and at the wall switch. Feeling proud and confident, I dragged the garden hose into the house, connected it to the heater and ran it into the floor drain to empty the heater—just as the plumber had done. Then I sat and waited for the water to stop flowing. After about an hour of a good, steady flow, it occurred to me to SHUT OFF THE WATER SUPPLY! Fifteen minutes later and hundreds of gallons of water poorer, I replaced the element.

DIANNA TUCKER

EXPLODING TOILET TRICK

Our toilet kept running because the float wouldn't turn off the water completely. I had fixed the same problem in our old toilet by bending the float arm down a bit to increase the pressure on the shutoff valve in the tank. But since our new toilet had a plastic arm, I decided to apply some heat to soften it so that I could bend it.

First I sprayed aerosol silicone lube on everything in the tank to help things slide a bit better. Then I leaned over the tank with my lighter, clicked it and … WHOOOOMPP! The spray I had just shot into the tank exploded. Luckily, I escaped with only singed hair and eyelashes. But now my wife can't stop telling people about our exploding toilet.

RON WOODWARD

3 WOODWORKING & WORKSHOP PROJECTS & TIPS

WALNUT WATERFALL

THIS TABLE IS SO SIMPLE—THE BEAUTY OF THE WOOD DOES MOST OF THE WORK!

Live-edge wood has a natural appeal that makes it popular for a variety of woodworking projects—dining room tables, shelving and more. But where do you find beautiful 2-in.-thick slabs of walnut or maple? Certainly not at home centers. Search online for local sawmills and hardwood suppliers to find live-edge wood slabs.

At the supplier, you're sure to find DIYers and pro woodworkers combing through stacks of wood slabs looking for that perfect piece. We sourced this walnut from a local hardwood supplier and had it surfaced-planed at a local sawmill.

BY JOE CRUZ

MEET THE BUILDER

JOE CRUZ IS AN ARTISAN WHO BRINGS SIMPLE, ELEGANT DESIGN TO EVERYDAY DIY.

IMAGINATION

The artistic challenge—or opportunity!—of any woodworking project is visualizing your finished item in the piece of wood even before you buy it, let alone pick up a tool. Have general measurements in mind and bring a tape measure when you go hunting for that superb slab.

A few things to think about when looking at a slab: Start with your overall dimensions, including the thickness of the piece. Then consider how much of the live edge is exposed, the amount of sapwood and how many cracks are in the piece of wood. (You can fill cracks. Don't let them deter you from buying an attractive piece.) Determine how much machining and milling it will take to make the piece of wood usable for your project. It's the science and art of woodworking.

WHAT IT TAKES		
TIME	**COST**	**SKILL LEVEL**
Full day	$250	Beginner

TOOLS
Circular saw, straightedge, miter saw, drill/driver, rubber mallet, orbital sander, wood chisel, safety goggles, dust mask, measuring tape, clear packing tape

1 LAY OUT THE TOP

Before you start cutting, examine the contours of the live edge and notice the wood's grain patterns. Decide which surface will be most pleasing for the top of your table. As much as possible, leave the live edge untouched.

Lay out the size of your table frame on the underside of the piece. Draw lines where you plan to make cuts. The front edge of the top will have a 45-degree angle, with the front edge of the table frame aligning at the short point of the 45-degree angle on the underside of the top. Some of your tabletop might have straight 90-degree cuts; that depends on the slab you chose and the shape of its live edges.

2 SET UP FOR CUTTING

Secure the slab on a stable workbench or sawhorses. You can make your cuts by letting the slab hang over the edge of your work surface or setting it on top of the 2x4s. This allows room for the saw blade underneath so you won't cut into your workbench.

Next, measure the distance between the edge of your circular saw's base plate and the saw blade (inset photo). Add that dimension to the perimeter lines you'll cut. Lay a straightedge or piece of plywood as a saw guide on top of the wood slab at the line you just made, and then clamp all the pieces to your work surface.

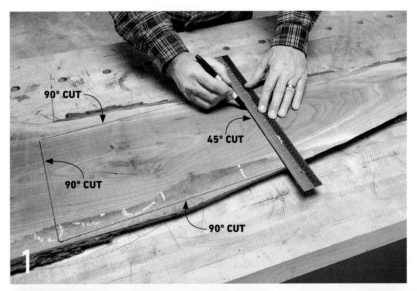

3 CUT 90-DEGREE ANGLES

Set the depth of your saw blade so it's slightly deeper than the thickness of your wood slab. Make all your 90-degree cuts first.

4 CUT 45-DEGREE ANGLE ON WATERFALL

Next, set your saw blade back to full depth and tilt the circular saw base plate to a 45-degree angle. Make your first 45-degree angle cut. The long point of the 45-degree angle should be the front edge of your waterfall.

5 CUT 45-DEGREE ANGLE ON TABLETOP

To cut the angle on the table-top, move your plywood saw guide to accommodate the next cut, clamping it to your work surface. Cut another 45-degree angle in the opposite direction along the line of the short point of the 45-degree angle.

6 EXPOSE THE LIVE EDGE

Using a chisel or multi-tool, carefully remove the bark to expose the natural edge—in some cases, the bark will pull off easily. Of course, you can always leave some of the bark on for a natural and rustic look.

NOTE:
The distance between the edge of your circular saw base plate and the saw blade changes when you tilt the table base to 45 degrees.

7 SAND THE PARTS

Once you've removed the bark, use an orbital sander with 150-grit sandpaper to smooth the surface and knock off any sharp edges. Always wear a dust mask when sanding.

8 TAPE THE TOP

To glue the tabletop and waterfall pieces together, position them so the long points of both 45-degree angles face each other. Next, stick three or four strips of clear packing tape across the seam to join the two pieces.

9 APPLY GLUE

Carefully turn both pieces over and apply wood glue to both 45-degree angles. Lift the waterfall piece to close the gap between the two 45-degree angles and create a 90-degree angle.

10 GLUE UP THE TOP

Hold the joint together and stretch packing tape from the waterfall piece to the tabletop. Use a damp cloth to wipe away any glue that squeezes out.

CAUTION:
Wear proper
eye protection.

90° ELBOW
ASSEMBLY

FIGURE A METAL TABLE FRAME
OVERALL DIMENSIONS: 10"W x 16"D x 25"H

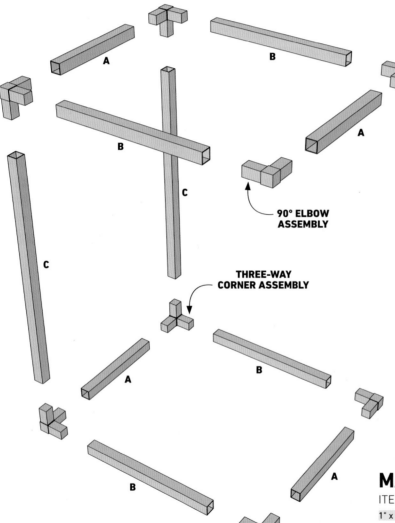

A

B

B

A

B

C

90° ELBOW
ASSEMBLY

C

THREE-WAY
CORNER ASSEMBLY

C

A

B

A

B

11 CUT THE SQUARE TUBING
Cut the square tubing using a miter saw with a carbide-tip saw blade.

12 ASSEMBLE THE TABLE FRAME
The frame of this table goes together quite easily. Start by constructing two rectangle frames using parts A and B, the 90-degree elbows and the three-way corner connectors. Then simply connect the two frames with the two uprights (C).

NO-WELD METAL TABLE FRAME

We built our table frame using 1-in. square aluminum tubing and press-fit framing connectors from *grainger.com*. Yes, we were originally eager to weld some steel for this, but then we found these materials—they're affordable, easy and strong.

You simply cut all the square tubing to length and assemble the table legs with nothing more than a rubber mallet.

NOTE: The size of your frame depends on the size of your tabletop.

MATERIALS LIST

ITEM	QTY.
1" x 1" x 12' square tubing (No. 18G632)*	1
90-degree press-fit connectors (No. 18G638)*	4
Three-way press-fit connectors (No. 18G639)*	4
1" x 12" x 36" live-edge walnut	1
Wipe-on polyurethane	
Spray paint and primer	
1-1/2" wood screws	
Wood glue	
Stick-on felt pads	4
Clear packing tape	

Available from grainger.com

CUTTING LIST

KEY	QTY.	DIMENSIONS	PART
A	4	1" x 8"	Front and back
B	4	1" x 14"	Sides
C	2	1" x 23"	Uprights

13 APPLY A FINISH

Once the glue is completely set, make another pass over the whole piece with the orbital sander. Apply three to four coats of wipe-on polyurethane to seal all the surfaces of the wood, including the bark if you chose to leave it on. Sand with 400-grit sandpaper between coats. Finish the table frame by spraying primer and paint on all sides in the color of your choice.

14 ASSEMBLE THE TABLE

To attach the top to the frame, drill two 1/4-in. holes into each of the two 14-in. square tubes (B) on the upper assembly, 3 in. from each end.

Lay the tabletop upside down so the waterfall is pointing up. Set the table frame on the underside of the top so the back of the waterfall aligns with the 23-in. uprights (C). Drill a 3/32-in. pilot hole into the underside of the top at each of the four 1/4-in. predrilled holes in the frame.

15 ATTACH THE FRAME

Attach the frame to the top with No. 8 1-1/2-in. wood screws in the four predrilled holes.

To prevent scratching an uncarpeted floor, stick four felt pads to the bottom frame assembly.

PRO TIP
Set the depth of your drill bit or use a piece of tape as a stop so you don't drill through the top. Also, double-check the length of your screws to be sure they're not too long.

ENTER IN STYLE!

THREE PROJECTS DESIGNED TO CREATE AN INVITING SPACE

SIMPLE COATRACK

MODERN SHELF

MEET THE BUILDER

JAY CORK, AN ASSOCIATE EDITOR, LOVES TO BUILD MID-CENTURY MODERN STYLE FURNITURE.

BY JAY CORK

Welcome family and friends to your home with a pretty spot to hang coats and a comfy bench to make it easy to remove shoes and boots. The eye-catching shelf is positioned here to create a stylish boundary for an open entryway, but it could grace any living space. That's the best part of this project—you can build one or two pieces, or the whole trio!

BENCH WITH STORAGE

MAKE THE ROUTING TEMPLATES
To save money, I wanted to cut the shelf legs and coatrack legs from the same boards. Routing templates make it easy to produce multiple parts consistently. I made my routing templates from 1/2-in. MDF.

CUT AND ROUT THE PARTS
After tracing all the shapes on the boards, cut close to the line but not up to it. I used a combination of double-sided tape and micro pins to secure the routing template onto the wood. Rout the parts on a router table.

PRO TIP
Rout with the grain whenever it is possible.

WHAT IT TAKES

TIME	COST	SKILL LEVEL
3 days	$875	Intermediate

TOOLS
Table saw, band saw, miter saw, palm sander, cordless drill, pocket hole jig, dowel jig, basic carpentry tools

WORKING WITH CHERRY
Cherry, a common North American hardwood, is one species I rarely stain. It naturally darkens over time and develops such a beautiful patina all on its own. On the downside, it tends to burn when milling; use sharp blades or expect to spend time sanding out burn marks.

FIGURE A
CUTTING DIAGRAMS
OVERALL DIMENSIONS OF EACH BOARD:
4/4 x 8"W x 72"L

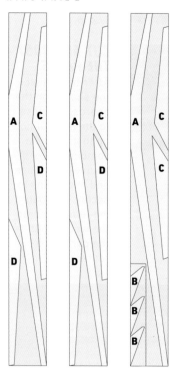

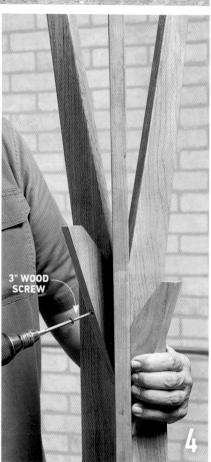

3" WOOD SCREW

1 CUT THE CENTER BLOCK

This three-legged coatrack presents a unique challenge during assembly because there's no good way to use a clamp; a combination of glue and screws will get the job done. I glued the three legs together around an inner triangle of wood. Cut this triangular block on the table saw with the blade set to 30 degrees. Each face should be the same thickness as the legs.

2 GLUE THE LEGS TOGETHER

When I can't use clamps, I use a trick called a rub joint—rubbing two pieces of wood together until the glue becomes tacky. Hide glue works well for this because it dries fast. Glue the center block to one leg first, and let it dry. Glue the other legs onto the center block one at a time, allowing the glue to dry before gluing the next leg. Use tape to help keep things from shifting around while the glue dries.

3 MAKE THE HAT HOOKS

The hat hooks will need a double bevel on the inside edge to fit between the legs of the coatrack. You'll need to make two passes on the table saw with the blade set to 30 degrees. Predrill for the assembly screw with a countersink bit.

4 PREDRILL FOR FINAL ASSEMBLY

Using thick CA glue, attach the hat hooks onto the legs, staggering each one a few inches. Let the glue set up for 10 minutes, then drill pilot holes and countersink for 3-in. screws. The combination of screws and glue will strengthen this coatrack for the heaviest winter jackets.

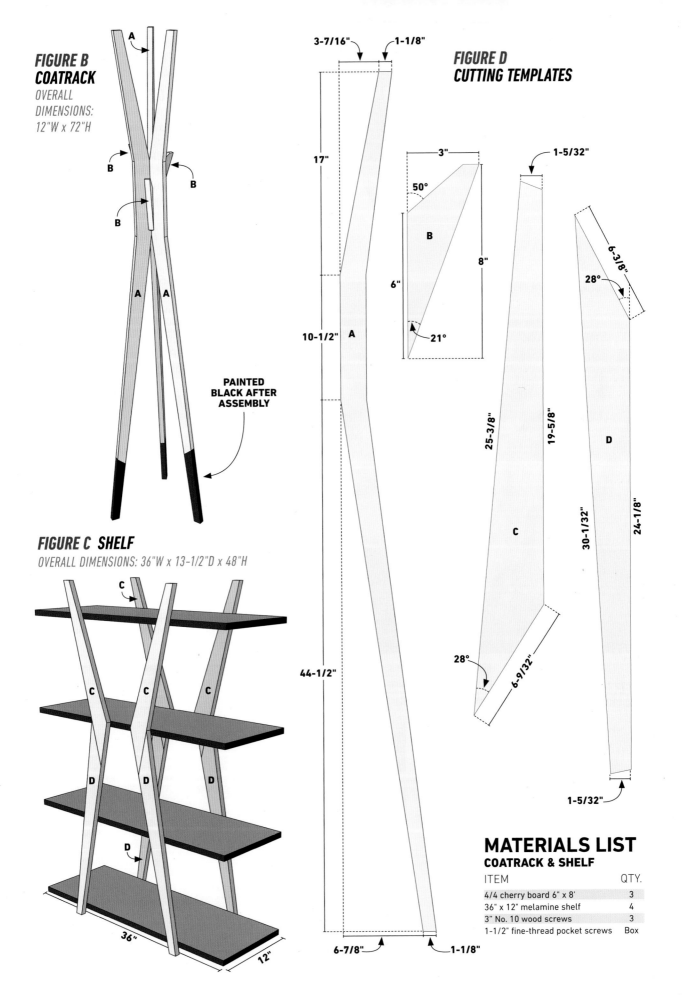

FIGURE B
COATRACK
OVERALL
DIMENSIONS:
12"W x 72"H

A

B

B

B

B

A A

PAINTED
BLACK AFTER
ASSEMBLY

FIGURE C SHELF
OVERALL DIMENSIONS: 36"W x 13-1/2"D x 48"H

C

C C C

D D D

D

36"

12"

FIGURE D
CUTTING TEMPLATES

3-7/16"   1-1/8"

17"

10-1/2"

44-1/2"

6-7/8"   1-1/8"

A

3"

50°

B

6"   8"

21°

1-5/32"

25-3/8"

19-5/8"

C

28°

6-9/32"

6-3/8"

28°

D

30-1/32"   24-1/8"

1-5/32"

MATERIALS LIST
COATRACK & SHELF

ITEM	QTY.
4/4 cherry board 6" x 8'	3
36" x 12" melamine shelf	4
3" No. 10 wood screws	3
1-1/2" fine-thread pocket screws	Box

WARM THE HIDE GLUE

THE SHELF

1 GLUE UP THE LEGS

The way these angled legs join makes using clamps difficult. Once again, use the rub joint technique, cleaning off any glue squeeze-out. Let the glue joints set up overnight before moving on to the next step.

2 MAKE THE ASSEMBLY JIG

A jig makes shelf assembly easier. Clamp the legs to a 2 x 4-ft. piece of MDF, making sure they're evenly spaced. Attach guide blocks using thick superglue and accelerator. I used 1-in. blocks for the legs and 3-in. for the shelves.

PRO TIP: Use only dabs of glue or risk gluing the legs too!

3 MARK FOR POCKET SCREWS

With two legs in the assembly jig, place the shelves in the jig and mark where the pocket holes need to go. Mark two holes per joint and drill them with a pocket hole jig.

4 ASSEMBLE THE SHELF

After drilling for the pocket holes, place the shelves back in the jig. Using 1-1/2-in. pocket screws, attach the shelves to the legs. When you've completed the first side, flip everything over and repeat the process for the other two legs.

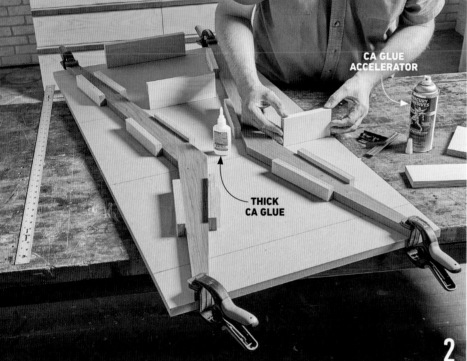

CA GLUE ACCELERATOR

THICK CA GLUE

1-1/2" POCKET SCREW

THE ENTRY BENCH

1 MAKE THE BENCH TOP

Glue the two halves of the bench top together, using dowels to help keep them aligned during glue-up.

I was lucky; my lumberyard had milled 4/4 and 6/4 cherry—the perfect thicknesses to edge-glue pieces together to achieve the width I needed. Don't be shy about asking your lumberyard if it offers milling services!

2 ATTACH THE LEGS

I found steel legs in the style I was after at *tablelegs.com* (see p. 92 for details), so I decided to save time and buy, not build. Screw the legs to the bottom side of the bench with 1-in. washer-head screws. I made a positioning jig out of scrap 1/2-in. plywood. This easy-to-make jig will ensure precise spacing and alignment of all four legs.

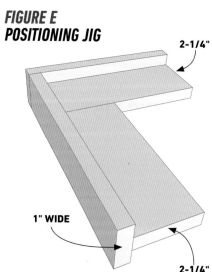

FIGURE E
POSITIONING JIG

2-1/4"

1" WIDE

2-1/4"

3 CUT SKIRTS TO SIZE AND ATTACH

Use a bevel gauge to determine the angle of the leg, and then transfer that to your table saw blade. Cut that bevel on one edge of a little more than 2 ft. of the skirt material.

With the legs attached, mark the two end pieces against the legs and cut them to length. Once those have been screwed into place, set the longer skirt pieces up against them and mark for cuts. Cut them on the miter saw and attach them with pocket screws.

TRANSFER THIS ANGLE TO THE TABLE SAW

1" WASHER-HEAD SCREWS

4 MAKE THE DRAWER CASE

The cabinet case will be made from solid cherry and will feature mitered corners. Make the 45-degree cuts using a table saw. To glue these parts together, lay them flat with the insides facing down, and tape the edges together. Flip everything over, apply glue to the joint and tape the two sides together, keeping them square.

PRO TIP: Drill your pocket holes before glue-up.

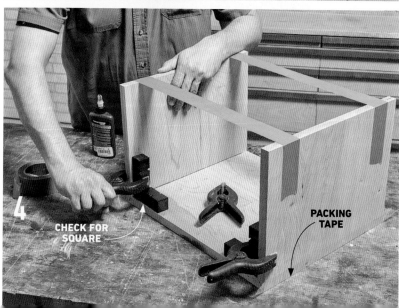

CHECK FOR SQUARE

PACKING TAPE

1-1/4" POCKET SCREWS

5

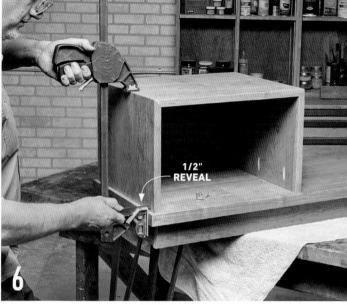

1/2" REVEAL

6

CUTTING LIST

KEY	QTY.	DIMENSIONS	PART
A	2	1-1/2" x 55" x 8-1/2"	Bench seat
B	4	7/8" x 8" x 12-1/8"	Drawer case side
C	2	7/8" x 8" x 19-1/2"	Drawer case top
D	1	7/8" x 17-7/8" x 3"	Cross member
E	1	7/8" x 11-1/4" x 3"	Drawer slide support
F	2	Cut to fit	Skirt—front and back
G	2	Cut to fit	Skirt—side
H	4	1/2" x 16" x 4-1/4"	Drawer box front and back
J	4	1/2" x 12-5/8" x 4-1/4"	Drawer box side
K	2	7/8" x 17-1/2" x 5-1/2"	Drawer face
L	2	1/2" x 16-1/2" x 12-1/8"	Drawer bottom
M	2	Cut to fit	Drawer case back

FIGURE F ENTRY BENCH
OVERALL DIMENSIONS: 55"W x 17"D x 29-1/2"H

5 FIT THE DRAWER CASE BACK
Once the drawer case is glued together, take an exact measurement and cut the back to fit. Use a few clamps to hold it in place, and secure it with 1-1/4-in. pocket screws.

6 ATTACH THE CASE TO THE BENCH TOP
The drawer case should be offset 1/2 in. from the side and front of the bench. Clamp it in place. Start with the outer side first, attaching it to the bench top with 1-1/4-in. pocket screws. Double-check for square and then repeat that process for the inner side.

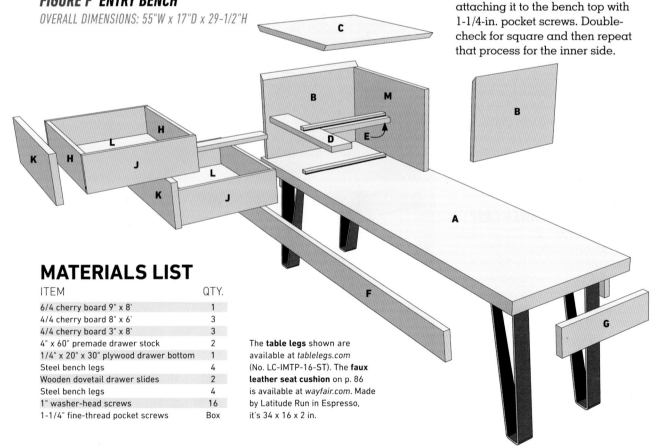

MATERIALS LIST

ITEM	QTY.
6/4 cherry board 9" x 8'	1
4/4 cherry board 8" x 6'	3
4/4 cherry board 3" x 8'	3
4" x 60" premade drawer stock	2
1/4" x 20" x 30" plywood drawer bottom	1
Steel bench legs	4
Wooden dovetail drawer slides	2
Steel bench legs	4
1" washer-head screws	16
1-1/4" fine-thread pocket screws	Box

The **table legs** shown are available at *tablelegs.com* (No. LC-IMTP-16-ST). The **faux leather seat cushion** on p. 86 is available at *wayfair.com*. Made by Latitude Run in Espresso, it's 34 x 16 x 2 in.

7 ASSEMBLE THE CROSS MEMBER

Assemble the cross member with a little bit of glue. Then screw the dovetail drawer slide perfectly centered.

PRO TIP: I cut the cross member parts a little oversize, and then cut them to fit once the case was assembled and installed.

8 COMPLETE THE CASE

Install the lower dovetail drawer slide. Then cut the cross member to fit and attach it with 1-1/4-in. pocket screws. I used a spacer block to help me position it perfectly.

7/8" SETBACK

5 5/16"

9 MAKE THE DRAWERS

Assemble the drawers using 1-in. pocket screws. Notch a space in the drawer back for the center-mounted drawer slide. Using a small square, make sure the slide is square to the box, then glue it in place.

PRO TIP: Premade drawer stock saves a lot of time—it's preslotted for the drawer bottom and comes prefinished. Woodcraft sells 60-in. lengths.

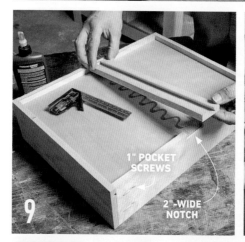

1" POCKET SCREWS

2"-WIDE NOTCH

10 ATTACH THE DRAWER FACES

I used wood spacers to help me achieve a 1/8-in. reveal around the drawer faces. With the drawer box inserted, place two dabs of hot melt adhesive on the back of the face then press it against the drawer box. After the glue sets, secure the drawer face with 1-in. washer-head screws.

1/8" SPACER

11 INSTALL THE DRAWER PULLS

Center and mark the holes for the drawer-pull mounting screws on the drawer face. Using a 5/16-in. drill bit, drill completely through the drawer face and the drawer box. Mount the drawer pulls with the supplied mounting screws.

PRO TIP: Make your marks on a piece of tape on the drawer face. Your marks will be easier to see, and you'll protect the wood while it's being drilled.

CENTERING RULER

CONSOLE STEREO REVIVAL

VINTAGE STYLE, MODERN SOUND!

This 1960s console stereo had so much potential. We weren't going to let a little water damage and outdated electronics doom it to a landfill. Using simple woodworking techniques, we refurbished this console and added to its high style. Then we filled it with 21st-century audio goodies. The best part? We'll show you how to do the same.

BEFORE

WHAT IT TAKES

TIME	COST	SKILL LEVEL
3–4 days	$600	Intermediate

TOOLS
Table saw, band saw, random orbital sander, router, basic woodworking tools

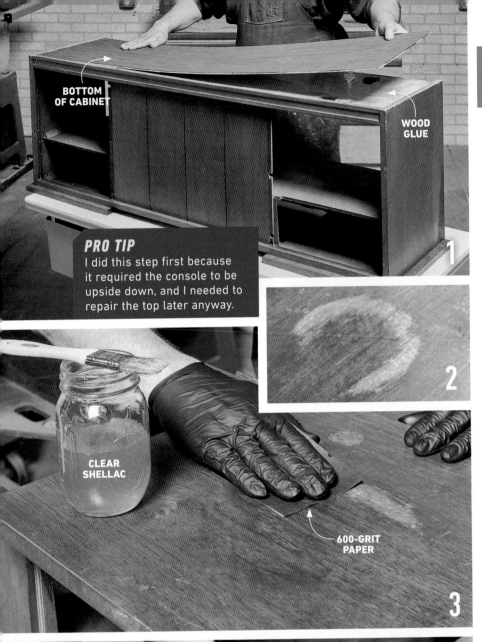

BOTTOM OF CABINET

WOOD GLUE

PRO TIP
I did this step first because it required the console to be upside down, and I needed to repair the top later anyway.

CLEAR SHELLAC

600-GRIT PAPER

FIX COSMETIC DAMAGE

1 FIT A NEW BOTTOM PANEL

When I found this console, it was in rough shape. The legs had broken through the particleboard bottom, so first I attached a new plywood base. I predrilled 16 holes in 1/4-in. Baltic birch plywood and spread the glue evenly with a glue spreader. Then I screwed the plywood to the old bottom with 3/4-in. wood screws.

2 INSPECT WATER STAINS

I got lucky with this water stain; only the finish was damaged—the underlying particleboard wasn't swollen and the wood veneer was only slightly discolored from UV light.

3 RUB SHELLAC INTO THE DAMAGED AREA

A little shellac helps restore the natural tone in the damaged wood where the finish is gone. With a piece of 600-grit wet/dry sandpaper, work a small amount of shellac into the damaged area. Wipe off any excess with a clean cloth dampened with denatured alcohol. This rejuvenates the natural tone of the damaged wood and fills in the grain.

4 ADD STAIN TO EVEN OUT THE COLOR

I let the shellac dry for an hour, then artistically applied the first layer of stain to blend out any evidence of damage. Let this stain dry for at least a day.

CLEAR GEL TOPCOAT

GEL STAIN IN ANTIQUE WALNUT

MATERIALS LIST

ITEM	QTY.
6/4 x 9" x 48" sapele	1
3/4" x 10" x 60" mahogany	1
Sapele veneer	4 leaves
3" No. 10 washer-head screws	10
3/4" No. 8 wood screws	16
Hide glue	Bottle
Cold press veneer glue	Bottle
White craft glue	Bottle
Gel stain, Antique Walnut	Pint
Gel stain, Java	Pint
Oil-based semigloss topcoat	Quart
Speaker cloth	1 yd.
QuikWood Epoxy Putty	2 oz.

5 FILL CHIPS AND NICKS WITH WOOD PUTTY

Before you apply the final coat of stain, repair surface flaws. I used QuikWood Epoxy Putty ($10 online) blended with a bit of artist's oil paint (burnt umber) to match the existing color, and I filled the nicks along the edges. Let the putty dry, then use alcohol-based markers to match the surrounding wood.

6 STAIN AND TOPCOAT THE ENTIRE CONSOLE

After repairing damage with wood putty, I applied the first coat of stain to the water spots. When it was dry, I applied a final coat of stain to darken the entire console by about one shade.

REBUILD THE FRONT PANEL

The center panel needed to be covered in place. I chose a four-way bookmatch pattern, with sequence-matched leaves of figured sapele veneer. The speaker cloth was faded, so I replaced it with classic black ($18 per yard, *parts-express.com*) and designed new slats to lay over the top.

1 PREPARE THE VENEER

I determined the size of each quadrant and cut two blocks of 3/4-in. plywood 2 in. longer and 2 in. wider. Stack four leaves of veneer and use the plywood as a guide to cut all four at once using a utility knife.

Figured veneer needs to be flattened before glue-up, so I sprayed the leaves with Veneer Tamer ($14 at Woodcraft) and laid pieces of craft paper between the leaves. Stack everything between the two pieces of plywood and place heavy weights on top. Replace the paper once a day to help draw out all the moisture. Do this until the veneer is completely dry.

MEET THE BUILDER

JAY CORK HAS GUTTED HIS SHARE OF VINTAGE STEREO CONSOLES; A SLEDGEHAMMER IS HIS FAVORITE TOOL FOR THIS.

220-GRIT SANDING PAD

ALCOHOL-BASED BRUSH MARKER

SPRAY LIBERALLY

PLYWOOD BLOCK

2 CUT THE VENEER TO SIZE

Drill small pilot holes along two edges and drive short screws through the stack. Make sure the screws won't go through the other side! Now, cut the block to width on a table saw, and then cut it to length on a miter saw.

3 VENEER THE PANEL

Spread a thin layer of veneer glue on the back of each veneer leaf and lay it face down (Photo 3A). The veneer may curl slightly as the glue dries, but don't worry, it'll lie back down. Spread a layer of glue on the substrate and allow everything to dry overnight.

Once the glue is dry, spread one more thin coat of glue on all surfaces and allow that to dry for about an hour. Perfectly center one leaf on the substrate, and with a household iron set to cotton, run the iron slowly and firmly over the entire leaf (Photo 3B). This briefly reactivates the glue, joining the veneer to the substrate. Once the first leaf is complete, repeat this process for the remaining three.

4 MAKE NEW BAFFLES

I used 1/4-in. Baltic birch to make the speaker baffles. To accommodate the new speakers, I cut a rectangular hole with rounded corners 1-1/2 in. from the bottom and 1 in. from the sides. Check for fit and paint the baffles black with water-based paint.

5 APPLY THE SPEAKER CLOTH

Spread white craft glue evenly on the painted baffles. Pay attention to the lines in the speaker cloth; make sure they stay straight and square as you place the cloth on the baffle. Place plywood on top to provide even pressure as the glue dries. Trim the speaker cloth with a utility knife.

COLD PRESS VENEER GLUE

SECOND COAT OF GLUE

3A

KEEP THE IRON MOVING

3B

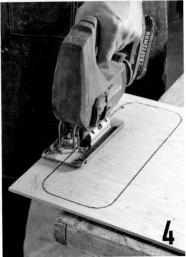

4

WHITE GLUE

5

CAUTION:
Use your safety guard. We removed ours for the photos.

FLAT-TOP RIPPING BLADE

6A

6B

6C

CUT THE SLAT PARTS

Cut 2-in. x 16-1/2-in. blocks from 3/4-in. mahogany. This console needs eight. First, mill the rabbet on the ends of the stiles. Place the blank in the center portion of the jig (Photo 6A) and with a flat-top ripping blade set to 1/2 in. high, make multiple passes to cut the full width of the rabbet.

Next, make the first two angled cuts (Photo 6B) on each block. Clamp the stile blank in the jig. Make one cut and flip the blank over (Photo 6C) to make the second. Flip the sled 180 degrees and make the second two angled cuts (Photo 6D) on each block, creating a slender chevron shape.

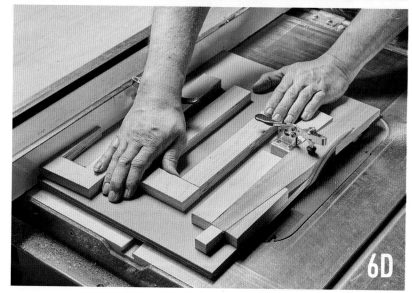

6D

1/2" x 1" RABBET

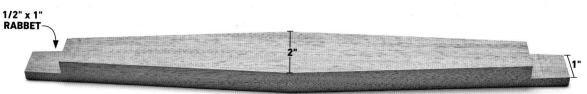

2"

1"

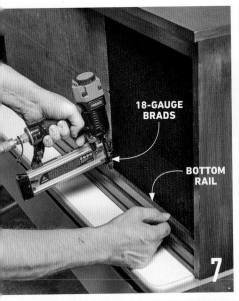

18-GAUGE BRADS

BOTTOM RAIL

7

23-GAUGE PINS

8

7 INSTALL THE SPEAKER BAFFLES

To ensure a good fit, I made the speaker baffles slightly smaller than the opening and attached them with glue and brad nails to mounting blocks on all four sides of the opening.

8 ASSEMBLE THE SLATS

I trimmed two slats flat on one edge and placed those on the left and right sides first, then attached the full slats that cover the joints between the veneered face and the speaker baffles. Finally, evenly space the inner slats and pin them in place.

MAKE NEW LEGS

I chose sapele for the console's new legs because it was a good match for the veneer on the front panel. Sapele looks like mahogany and is similar to work with, but it often has a pronounced ribbon figure, which I love. I found 6/4 sapele at a local lumberyard.

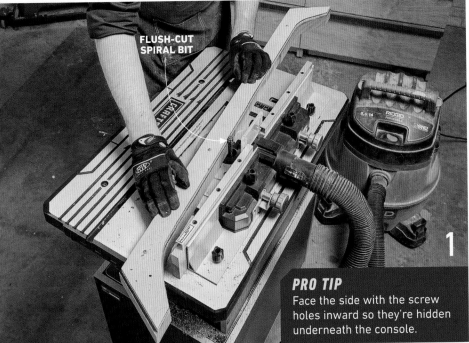

FLUSH-CUT SPIRAL BIT

1

PRO TIP
Face the side with the screw holes inward so they're hidden underneath the console.

1 CUT AND ROUT THE LEGS

Make a routing template from 1/2-in. MDF. Drill four evenly spaced holes in the template. Trace the template on the sapele and rough-cut the leg with a band saw, staying about 1/8 in. away from the line. I attached the routing template to the leg blanks with four small screws and cut it flush on the router table.

2 ATTACH THE LEGS TO THE CONSOLE

Using a 5/8-in. Forstner bit, drill 1/8-in.-deep holes. This is the countersink for the washer-head screws. Finish predrilling through the leg with a 5/16-in. drill bit. I centered each leg on the bottom of the console using a centering rule and set them 2 in. back from the front and back edges.

3" WASHER-HEAD SCREWS

2" SETBACK

2

FINISHING THE CONSOLE
I stained the slats with gel stain in Antique Walnut. To topcoat the entire console, I applied six coats of General Finishes Arm-R-Seal semigloss wipe-on varnish.

UPGRADING THE
AUDIO COMPONENTS

How you handle the audio upgrade can be simple or complicated. I chose simple. I removed the original bits, then found a turntable ($200 at uturnaudio.com) to fit inside the narrow console, a Bluetooth-capable tube amp and a pair of bookshelf speakers from Dayton Audio ($150 and $130 respectively at parts-express.com). Then, I removed the old components and added a panel to hold the new pieces. And it sounds great!

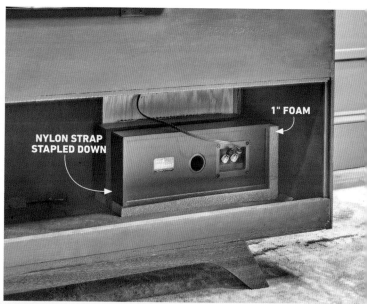

NYLON STRAP STAPLED DOWN

1" FOAM

ROUND & AROUND

//

THE SHELVES SPIN TO HIDE, OR SHOW, WHAT'S INSIDE

"One step at a time, you CAN build this." I repeated that mantra through each phase of this project. I try to stretch the limit of my skills every time I build something new. This round cabinet with revolving shelves stretched, and even bent, my skills. And I had so much fun!

If you are up for a challenge and want to learn new skills and create unique furniture, this is for you. Yes, it made my head spin. But once I started, I knew I could build this piece; you can too. Let me show you how.

WHAT IT TAKES

TIME	COST	SKILL LEVEL
Several days	$600 to $900*	Advanced

TOOLS
Table saw or circular saw, router, narrow crown stapler, 18-gauge brad nailer, 23-gauge pin nailer, basic hand tools
*Depends on your veneer. Our total cost was $900.

BY MIKE BERNER

THOSE THAT BEND TOGETHER STAY TOGETHER

BENDABLE PLYWOOD

PAPER-BACKED VENEER

BENDABLE PLYWOOD is available in different thicknesses, with the thinnest version able to bend into a circle as small as 15-in. diameter. The 1/4-in. sheets I used easily bent into a 21-in. circle. The sheets are made to bend in one direction; an 8 x 4-ft. sheet will make a 4-ft.-tall column, a 4 x 8-ft. sheet will make an 8-ft.-tall column.

PAPER-BACKED VENEER is easy to cut with a utility knife, and you adhere it with contact cement, which bonds two coated surfaces instantly. I was concerned that activating adhesive on PSA (pressure-sensitive adhesive, aka peel-and-stick) veneer would require more force than the thin bendable plywood could handle. I used paper-backed quarter-sawn curly maple veneer.

BUILD THE FORMS

The bendable plywood needs a structure to hold its shape. I built two forms: one for the inner shelf unit and one for the cabinet unit. I'm using pairs of plywood discs at the top and bottom of each cylinder.

1 TRACE ALL THE CIRCLES

This cabinet consists of 10 plywood discs in four sizes. To draw perfect circles on plywood, I made a compass with a 1/4-in. plywood scrap. I drove a finish nail through one end and then measured from the nail to mark the radius of each of the four circles. I drilled holes at each mark to fit a pencil and then drove the nail into the plywood and pivoted the pencil around the nail. Then I roughly cut out all the circles with a jigsaw.

2 DIVIDE INTO THREE EQUAL SLICES

Dividing each disc into three slices (like a pie) helps align the discs when you build the forms. Draw a line through the center, then a perpendicular line through the midpoint of the radius. Connect the points on the outside of the circle to the center to outline the three equal slices.

3 CUT PERFECT CIRCLES

With a compass jig, you can cut perfect circles. To attach the router to 1/4-in. plywood, start by removing the baseplate and using it to trace the holes onto the plywood. Then drill the holes and screw the plywood to the router using the baseplate screws.

Measure from the straight bit to mark the radii of the inner discs (A and C); drive a nail at each mark. Place a nail in the center of the disc and pivot the router around the nail counterclockwise. Trim the inner discs for the revolving shelf and two of the inner discs for the cabinet.

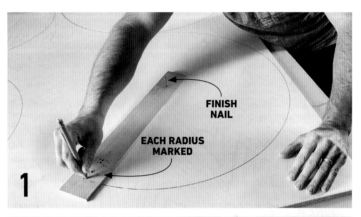

1 FINISH NAIL · EACH RADIUS MARKED

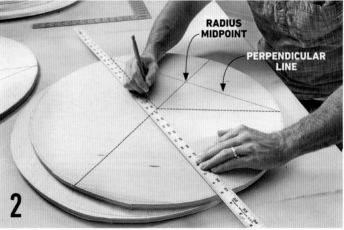

2 RADIUS MIDPOINT · PERPENDICULAR LINE

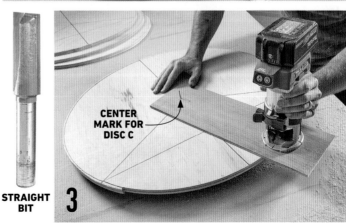

3 STRAIGHT BIT · CENTER MARK FOR DISC C

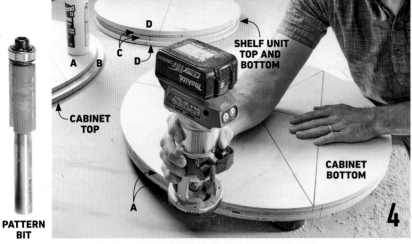

CABINET TOP

PATTERN BIT

SHELF UNIT TOP AND BOTTOM

CABINET BOTTOM

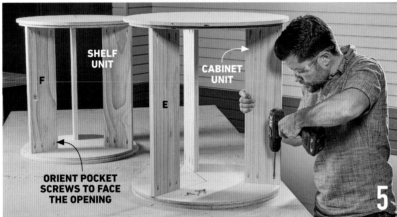

SHELF UNIT

CABINET UNIT

ORIENT POCKET SCREWS TO FACE THE OPENING

4 GLUE AND TRIM THE DISCS

Glue the inner discs to the top and bottom discs, centering them using the lines that divide the discs. The top and bottom of the shelf unit are identical, with the top/bottom discs larger by at least 1/4 in. than the inner discs. The top of the cabinet unit disc is larger than the inner discs by at least 1/2 in. Glue together the bottom discs of the cabinet unit and trim them flush with a pattern bit.

5 CONNECT THE DISCS

Join the tops and bottoms of the cylinders with form spacers. I cut three pieces (F) sized for the shelf unit and three more (E) for the cabinet unit from 1x6 boards, then drilled pocket holes on both ends. I lined them up to the dividing lines on the discs, pointing the pocket holes toward the opening (to make them easier to remove). Flush the form spacers with the outside of the discs and fasten them with pocket screws.

FIGURE A CABINET UNIT
OVERALL DIMENSIONS: 24-1/8"W x 24-1/8"D x 31"H

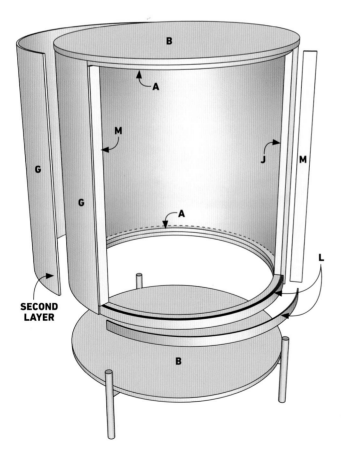

SECOND LAYER

FIGURE B SHELF UNIT
OVERALL DIMENSIONS: 21-9/16"W x 21-9/16"D x 23-3/4"H

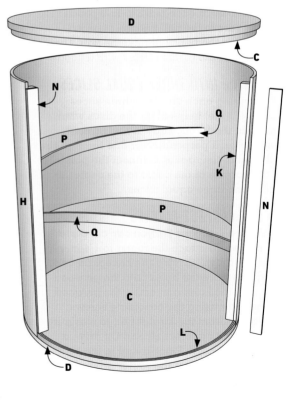

SHELF UNIT

1"

START

1"

END

BEND THE PLYWOOD

The bendable plywood fits between the top and bottom discs on the shelf unit. The plywood for the cabinet unit will be cut wide, and the bottom will be trimmed after it gets fastened.

6 CUT THE BENDABLE PLYWOOD TO LENGTH

After ripping the bendable plywood to width, determine its length. To do this, start by making marks at each edge of the opening, 1 in. inside the form spacers. Drive a nail to loop the string at the "start" mark, then wrap the string around the back and mark the string at the "end" mark. Then use the marks on the string to transfer the measurements to the plywood. You can also calculate the total circumference using the formula $2\pi r$ and then subtract the opening size.

H

6

MEET THE BUILDER

MIKE BERNER, AN EDITOR AT *FAMILY HANDYMAN*, LOVES A GOOD CHALLENGE.

CUTTING LIST

KEY	QTY.	DIMENSIONS	PART
A	3	1/2" x 11-5/8" radius	Cabinet inner disc
B	2	1/2" x 12-3/16" radius	Cabinet top/bottom disc
C	3	1/2" x 10-3/8" radius	Shelf inner disc
D	2	1/2" x 10-11/16" radius	Shelf top/bottom disc
E	3	3/4" x 5-1/2" x 23-1/2"	Cabinet form spacer (Photo 5)
F	3	3/4" x 5-1/2" x 21-3/4"	Shelf form spacer (Photo 5)
G	2	1/4" x 25" x cut to fit	Cabinet shell
H	1	1/4" x 22-3/4" x cut to fit	Shelf shell
J	2	3/4" x 3/4" x 23-1/2"	Cabinet stiffener
K	2	3/4" x 3/4" x 21-3/4"	Shelf stiffener
L	Build layers to fit	1/8" x cut to fit	Bent wood strips
M	2	1/4" x 1-1/4" x 23-1/2"	Cabinet edge banding
N	2	1/4" x 1-1/4" x 21-3/4"	Shelf edge banding
P	1	10-3/8" radius	Shelf (halve the disc and shape to your preference)
Q	2	1/8" x 1" x cut to fit	Shelf edge banding

MATERIALS LIST

ITEM	QTY.
Maple plywood 1/2" x 4' x 8'	2
Bendable plywood 1/4" x 8' x 4'	2
Maple hardwood 1/2" x 5-1/2" x 3'	1
Maple hardwood 3/4" x 5-1/2" x 8'	1
Quarter-sawn curly maple paper-backed veneer 4' x 8'	2
Table legs	3
16" heavy-duty lazy Susan	1
1/4" glass top, 24-1/8" diameter	1
18-gauge 1-1/4" brad nails	
18-gauge 3/4" narrow crown staples	
Glue	
All-purpose wood filler	
Finishing supplies	

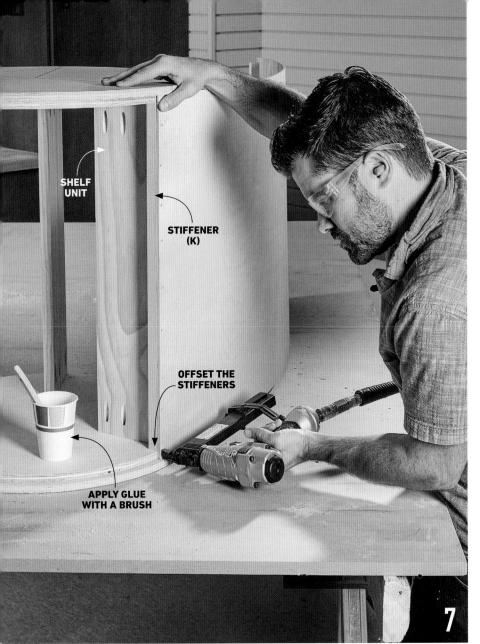

SHELF UNIT

STIFFENER (K)

OFFSET THE STIFFENERS

APPLY GLUE WITH A BRUSH

7

7 FASTEN STIFFENERS

Staple and glue stiffeners to each end of the bendable plywood. The stiffeners are cut to fit between the tops and bottoms of the shelf and cabinet units to prevent the plywood from bowing while you bend it around the forms. Be sure to offset the stiffener so the plywood fits the form, then glue and staple the plywood to the form on one side of the opening.

8 BEND THE PLYWOOD

I temporarily screwed the form to my work surface. Brush glue on the edge of the top and bottom discs. Work in small sections and flex the plywood tight to the form as you staple it to the sides, alternating between top and bottom. Keep pressure on the plywood to keep it from springing back and pulling through the staples.

9 ADD A SECOND LAYER

The shelf unit needs only one layer of plywood, but the cabinet needs to be sturdier, so I added a second. Mark the length of the second layer by clamping one end of the bendable plywood flush with the opening and bend it around to the other side of the opening. Cut it to length and spread a layer of glue on the back side. Staple it to the stiffener, then bend and fasten it around the cabinet just like the first layer.

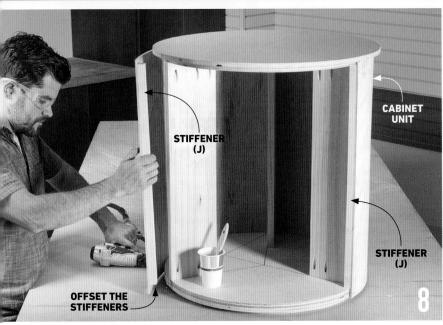

STIFFENER (J)

CABINET UNIT

STIFFENER (J)

OFFSET THE STIFFENERS

8

SECOND LAYER

9

CLAMP HERE

BENT WOOD STRIPS (L)

10 LAYER EDGE BANDING

I used a technique called "bent wood lamination" to cover the exposed plywood and build up the opening to match the rest of the cylinder. Using strips of 1/2-in. maple cut to 1/8 in. thick, I glued, bent and stapled them to the exposed edge until it was flush with the plywood. Don't worry about a perfect fit; vertical edge banding will hide gaps.

EDITOR'S NOTE:
I had trouble stapling these at first. Staples drove through and split the strips at the ends. I ended up clamping the ends of the strips against the form spacers, and then I turned the output pressure on my compressor way down and stapled the strips toward the middle.

11 COVER BENT PLYWOOD EDGES

I cut a 1-1/4-in.-wide strip of 1/4-in. maple to fit between the top and bottom and glued it to the plywood edge and the stiffener. A few 23-gauge pin nails hold it in place.

12 TRIM THEM FLUSH

When the glue is dry, use a pattern bit to trim the top and bottom discs flush to the plywood and trim the plywood on the cabinet unit. The bent laminations at the openings weren't quite flush with the bendable plywood, so I sanded and smoothed out the unevenness. This doesn't have to be perfect, but applying the veneer will be easier if it is.

13 SMOOTH IT OUT

After sanding and smoothing, fill all the staple dimples and gaps on the outside with all-purpose wood filler. Let it dry and then sand it smooth.

Once you put the shelf unit inside the cabinet unit, there's no way to finish it, so finish this part first.

14 VENEER THE INSIDE

The inside of the shelf unit is visible, so it needs to be veneered. But after cutting the veneer to width, I realized the difficulty of adhering this in one piece, so I sliced it into 12-in. lengths, keeping it in sequential order to keep the grain continuous.

To adhere the veneer, spread two coats of contact cement on the plywood inside and one coat on the paper side of the veneer. Let the contact cement dry until it's barely tacky after each coat (about 20 minutes). Then align the first piece to the plywood and press the veneer on. Butt the next pieces in sequence against the previous one. Trim the last piece and press the entire surface against the inside wall.

15 FASTEN SHELVES

From the extra inner disc (C) cut for the shelf unit, trace two curved shelves. Glue a 1-in. strip of maple edge banding along the front edge of each. I cut spacers to hold up the shelves evenly, then nailed them into place from the outside.

16 VENEER THE OUTSIDE

Rolling the veneer on the outside of the pieces wasn't the most difficult step, but it made me nervous anyway. Contact cement sticks permanently on initial contact, so I had one shot to apply it right. Here's how I did it.

- I attached a fence to my work surface to hold the veneer against, then I added a strip to that fence to act as a guide while I roll the cabinet. This gave me some wiggle room.
- I cut the veneer 1-1/2 in. wider than I needed, then spread two coats of contact cement on the plywood and one coat on the veneer.

6-1/2"

7-1/2"

SHELF SPACERS

OVERHANG VENEER

CRAFT PAPER

NERVES OF BENDABLE PLYWOOD

CRAFT PAPER

FENCE

ROLL IN PLACE

STRIP

16

- With the veneer and the shelf against the fence, I lined up the end of the veneer so it was within the shelf opening. I put craft paper at the corners to keep them from sticking.
- I rolled the shelf in place and pressed it against the fence until the outside was covered completely. I used a J-roller to ensure every inch of the veneer was adhered well.
- I used a sharp utility knife to roughly cut out the opening and to cut through both layers of the veneer at the seam. Then I removed the craft paper and pressed the veneer into the contact cement.
- Using a trim router with a pattern bit, I cut the overhanging veneer flush at the opening, top and bottom of the shelf.

17 INSTALL THE LAZY SUSAN

Flip the shelf unit upside down and fasten the lazy Susan hardware. Position the hardware as close to centered as possible; be sure the distance from the outside of the hardware to the outside of the shelf is even all the way around. Flip it upright and test how it spins—if it's off center, shift the hardware until it spins evenly. Lightly sand and apply finish to the shelf unit, inside and out.

CHECK FOR CENTER

17

BOTTOM OF CABINET UNIT

18

18 CUT OUT THE CABINET BOTTOM

To get the shelf inside the cabinet unit, cut out the cabinet bottom using the router compass jig. I set my jig to cut a 10-7/8-in. radius, which is 1/4 in. bigger than the shelf unit. I cut it out in three shallow passes. The first two passes I routed a complete circle; on the final, I made two half-circle passes, leaving the cutout attached at two points. This way, I could safely remove the router and use a saw to finish the cuts and prevent splintering as the cutout fell.

19 FIT THE INNER SHELF

Place the shelf unit inside the cabinet, then glue and nail the final disc (B) to cover the hole. Once the shelf unit is sealed inside, trim the bottom disc flush to the outside of the cabinet. Fill and sand any staple dimples, veneer the outside of the cabinet unit and apply a finish.

B

19

20 FASTEN LEGS

Flip the finished cabinet upside down and fasten three legs. I aligned the two front legs with the edges of the cabinet opening and centered the third leg at the back of the cabinet. (These legs are from *norseinteriors.com*.)

21 POSITION THE SHELF AND THE GLASS TOP

I flipped the cabinet upright and adjusted the inner shelf to move smoothly without bumping the inside of the cabinet. I ordered a piece of round glass to fit the top and set it on rubber bumpers to keep it in place.

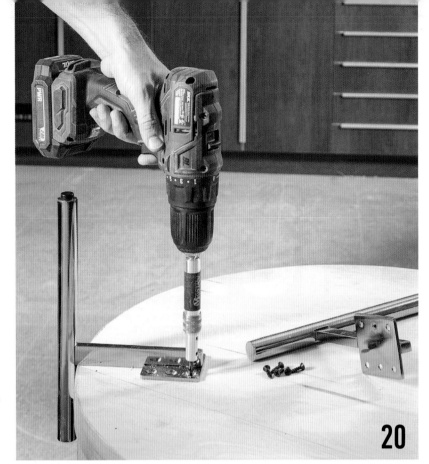

20

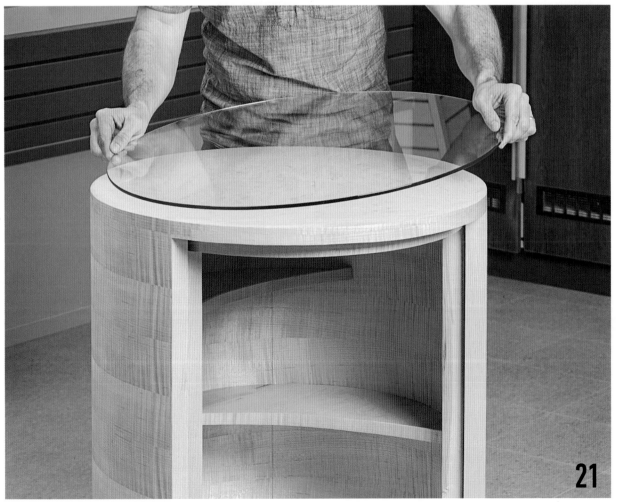

21

ART & LIGHT

MAKE YOUR OWN MASTERPIECE

BY GLENN HANSEN

I wanted a wooden floor lamp by my reading chair, but I couldn't find one at the giant light fixture retailer near me—there were no wooden lamps at all. I saw a sleek cherry lamp online, and it cost nearly $3,000. So I decided to make my own, including the lampshade.

This elegant lamp is a simple project, and it gives woodworkers creative flexibility. Make a taller floor lamp, or a table lamp. Go with more dramatic curves. Lampshade fabric opportunities abound. And the lamp cord? I'll show you how to hide it.

WHAT IT TAKES

TIME	COST	SKILL LEVEL
2 days	$400	Beginner to Intermediate

TOOLS

Table saw, jigsaw, handsaw, drill, doweling jig, router/router table, random orbital sander, wire cutter, screwdriver

THE LAMPSHADE

Make your own lampshade from nearly any type of fabric or paper. I chose Japanese shoji paper for its elegant simplicity (*eshoji.com*). You'll back the shoji with styrene, a sturdy, adhesive-backed paper that comes in rolls. Styrene adds structure and acts as a fire-resistant layer. Narrow lampshades can retain heat if you use a high-wattage lightbulb, making styrene essential here.

1 ATTACH STYRENE TO LAMPSHADE PAPER

For my 17.5-in.-tall and 8-in.-diameter lampshade, my styrene needed to be 17.5 by 25.12 in. (that's 8 in. x 3.14). The lampshade paper needed an extra 1/2 in. or less on the top and bottom to wrap around the lamp rings, and 1/2 in. on one edge to overlap the completed circle.

Lay the paper face down on a clean work surface. Set the styrene on top, adhesive side down and still covered. Peel adhesive backing from one end that's flush to the lamp paper, slowly removing the backing while pressing the styrene to the paper. Smooth out wrinkles and bubbles as you go.

2 CONNECT THE LAMP RINGS

Apply double-sided tape to both rings. With your lamp paper and styrene face down, place each ring on edge, one at the top and one at the bottom of the styrene. Slowly roll the rings along the edges of the styrene to form a lampshade drum. Binder clips help secure the styrene to the taped rings. When you complete the circle, wrap your extra paper tab over and secure it with a clear-drying glue.

3 FINISH THE SHADE

Wrap the extra 1/2 in. of lamp paper around both rings, pinching the paper carefully as you go. Fabric would be easier to work with here than delicate shoji paper. Make small cuts in the paper to wrap around any metal bracing arms.

MEET THE BUILDER

GLENN HANSEN, DEPUTY EDITOR, CLAIMS HE ONCE BUILT A MINIATURE RAFT FROM POPSICLE STICKS. NO PHOTOGRAPHIC PROOF REMAINS.

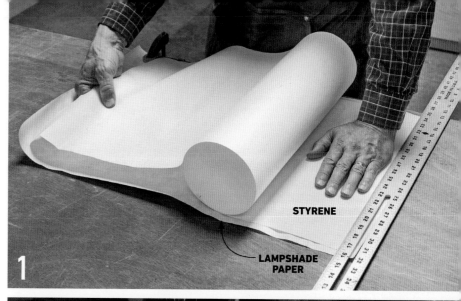

1

STYRENE

LAMPSHADE PAPER

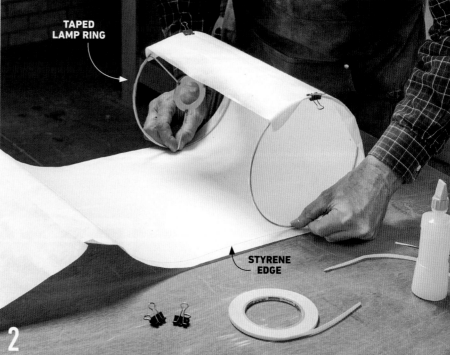

2

TAPED LAMP RING

STYRENE EDGE

3

TOP

1/2" MDF

1

NOTE:
Portable lamps are covered under UL 153, which permits a cord to pass through wood, or other insulating material, not less than 3/64 in. (1.2 mm) thick, with a smoothly rounded inner surface being equivalent to a bushing.

2

3

WIRE CHANNEL

4

THE LAMP

1 MAKE A TEMPLATE

Creating four identical legs—tall and gracefully curvy—is best done with a template. These 60-in.-tall legs are 4 in. wide at the top and 7-9/16 in. wide at the base. That makes a 16-in.-wide lamp around an 8-in. lampshade.

The outside edge of each leg has one gentle curve top to bottom. Inside, a gradual curve begins about 15 in. from the top and ends 8 in. from the bottom. The straight edges at each end will hold the lampshade (top) and act as a joining surface (bottom). Shape the curves to your liking. I used a 5-ft. straightedge, a clamp and a few nails to help establish my shapes.

2 RIP ONE LEG

Before cutting any curves in the legs, you'll rip one leg to create a channel for hiding the lamp cord, and you need the straight outside edge for that. The channel needs to be near the center of the narrowest part of the leg. I measured 2 in. from the outside edge and ripped off a 2-in. strip. You'll glue this back in place after you cut the wire channel.

3 CREATE A WIRE CHANNEL

On that ripped cherry, cut a 1/2-in. channel beginning at the bottom and stopping about 14 in. short of the top. I made a few passes on the table saw to create this channel, but you can use a router if you'd like.

The lamp cord will run through that channel from the plug end at the floor to the lamp socket end inside the lampshade. Later, you will drill a 1/2-in. hole on the side of the base to allow the lamp cord out and then another hole on the inside edge 14 in. from the top where the cord will exit to connect to the lamp socket.

4 GLUE IT TOGETHER

After ensuring the wire channel is smooth inside and big enough for the cord to easily pass through, glue the ripped strip back onto the leg so you can begin cutting the curves.

5 CUT THE CURVES

Cutting long curves into cherry takes patience. Mark your curve lines well. And prep your jigsaw to make square cuts with a sharp blade. You could use a band saw to cut these, but you'll finish with a router and sandpaper so a jigsaw works well here. Cut no more than 1/8 in. proud of the curve line. With your template and a pattern bit in a router table, you'll finish these curves.

6 PATTERN-ROUT THE LEGS

I used a few dabs of hot glue to adhere the template to each leg. Glue is easy to remove and leaves no marks. Rout in the direction of the wood grain. Using a double-bearing pattern bit, I could flip my wood over to control that direction and avoid tear-outs that can happen when you're routing against the grain.

7 ROUND THE EDGES

I wanted radiused edges on the legs. With a 1/2-in. round-over router bit, I radiused all the sharp corners. However, I left the legs square on the bottom 8 in. where the four legs will unite.

8 CUT THE LAMP CIRCLE

On a square piece of the same cherry stock, draw a 10-in. (outside diameter) circle and an 8-in.-diameter concentric circle. You're making a cherry doughnut. Use your 8-in.-diameter lampshade as a guide for the inside circle. Using a jigsaw, cut this doughnut proud of both lines, then sand the outside and inside edges to the final size. Leave the edges square.

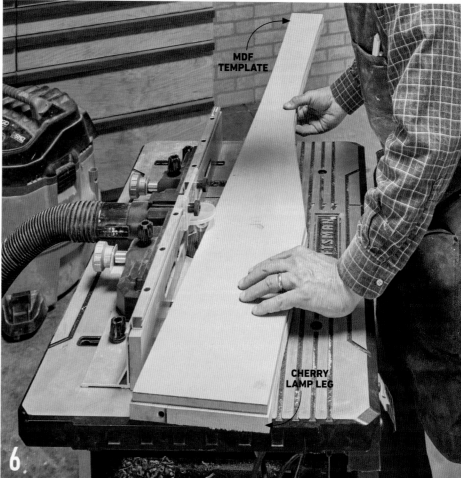

MDF TEMPLATE

CHERRY LAMP LEG

9 CUT THE NOTCHES

Use your circle to mark the four notch cutouts. Measure down from the top of each leg to ensure the circle will be level. Cut these notches by hand with a jigsaw or a handsaw. With a sharp chisel, clean up the joining surface. Test-fit the circle—you'll place it later.

10 JOIN THE LEGS

Cut a squared strip of cherry that's as thick as your finished legs and 8 in. long (or as tall as each leg's squared base). That strip will fit inside the space where the legs come together.

Using a doweling jig (Photo 10A), drill two holes on each leg. Use dowel centers to mark dowel holes around the joining strip. Offset the holes so the dowels don't hit each other. Glue two opposite legs and clamp them, then glue a third leg in place (Photo 10B) and clamp it. Don't add the final leg yet.

11 PLACE THE CIRCLE

After you've glued three of the legs at the base, place the circle inside the notched cutouts. I used a chisel to make each notch slightly concave to cleanly accept the circle. You won't need glue or nails to secure this. Then you can secure the fourth and final leg in place.

THE GEL FINISH

Sand the entire lamp, finishing with 220-grit paper. You can finish the lamp as you'd like. I chose General Finishes Gel Topcoat; I like what it does to cherry.

This oil-based product leaves a satin finish. With its thick consistency, it is easy to apply. I used a chip brush to apply the finish and then wiped off the excess with a clean, soft towel. The finish does require a long drying time, followed by light sanding in between. I repeated this process four times and was pleased with the result (but tired of sanding).

FIGURE A ART LAMP

FIGURE A ART LAMP

OVERALL DIMENSIONS:
16"W x 16"W x 60"H

THE WIRING

1 FEED THE WIRE UP THE LEG

Even though I decided to hide the cord, I bought decorative lamp cord from Color Cord Co., which has a wide range of attractive wiring options. I still want the cord to look nice as it runs from the lamp and across the floor. To fish the cord through the lamp, wrap one end in electrical tape and feed it up the channel you cut.

2 WIRE THE PLUG END

Color Cord Co. makes it easy to buy the right pieces and to connect them. Follow the instructions to create secure connections at the plug and socket.

3 CONNECT THE SOCKET END

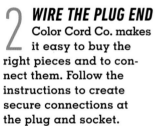

For the socket end of the wiring, I bought shade-ready sockets that fit European-style lampshade rings. If you're using a lampshade with U.S.-style rings, you'll also need to buy the saddle and harp pieces of the lampshade. A company called I Like That Lamp sells kits on *Etsy. com* and *Amazon.com*.

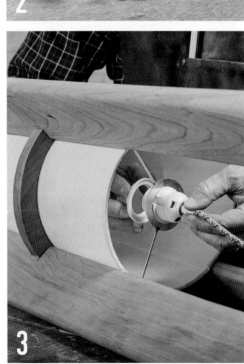

MATERIALS LIST

ITEM	QTY.
4/4 cherry	24 BF
4/4 cherry, 11" square	1
Lampshade rings, 8"	2
Styrene, adhesive-backed roll	1
Lampshade paper or fabric	
Lamp wire, socket, plug, switch	
3/8" dowels	
Rice glue (or any clear-drying glue)	
Double-sided tape	
Gel polyurethane	
Sandpaper	

CUTTING LIST

KEY	QTY.	DIMENSIONS	PART
A	4	7/8" x 7-9/16" x 60"	Lamp legs
B	1	10"-diameter circle	Cherry lampshade circle
C	1	7/8" x 7/8" x 8"	Joining strip

MILL & DRY LUMBER YOURSELF

TWO AFFORDABLE CHAIN SAW ATTACHMENTS MAKE IT POSSIBLE

If there's one thing more satisfying than building something with wood, it's building something with lumber you milled and dried yourself. You don't need a giant band saw mill to do that. All you need is a milling attachment for your chain saw. Attachments come in several styles and sizes to suit various saws and sizes of stock.

MEET THE EXPERT

CHAD BEATY IS A MASTER TECHNICIAN AND AN IN-HOUSE CHAIN SAW EXPERT AT NORTHERN TOOL + EQUIPMENT.

BY BRAD HOLDEN

WHAT IT TAKES

TIME	COST	SKILL LEVEL
1 log per day	Varies	Intermediate

MATERIALS AND SUPPLIES
Logs, 4x4s, log supports, wedges, stickers, corrugated roofing, chaps, headgear, face shield, gloves, Anchorseal, rake to keep work area clean

TOOLS

Chain saw with a 25- to 30-in. bar	$1,400
Mini edging milling attachment	$30
Frame-style milling attachment	$250
EZ Rail straightedge	$250

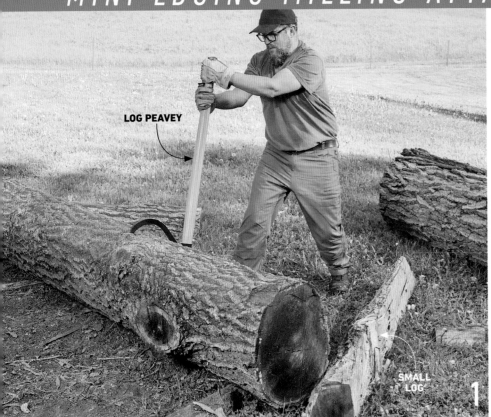

LOG PEAVEY

SMALL LOG

1

2

3

1 SECURE THE LOG

This edging attachment operates with your saw in a vertical position. Roll the log up onto smaller logs so the chain doesn't dig into the ground. Use a log peavey to roll the big logs onto the smaller ones. Wedge the log into position so it doesn't shift as you work.

2 INSTALL THE MILLING ATTACHMENT

Carefully read the instructions for your specific attachment, and then fasten the attachment to your saw's bar. Three setscrews secure this one to the saw's bar.

3 ATTACH THE STRAIGHTEDGE

For this attachment, you need to fasten only one 2x4 to the top of the log. "Use the straightest 2x4 you can find for this. The 2x4 acts as a guide, so the straighter the 2x4, the straighter your cut will be," says Chad Beaty of Northern Tool.

4 MAKE THE FIRST CUT

Start up your saw and begin the first cut. Go slowly and let the saw do the work. Since you're working vertically, it's not necessary to slip shims into the kerf unless the piece you're cutting off wants to bind. Just make sure that first cut piece will fall safely away from you.

5 MAKE SUBSEQUENT CUTS

After the first cut is done, you can now either move the 2x4 over and slice off another board, or roll the log and cut another flat side perpendicular to the first one. "Proceeding like this, you can use this attachment to make either boards or beams," Beaty says.

FLAT SIDE

FRAME-STYLE MILLING ATTACHMENT

WEDGE

LEVELING SCREW

PAWL

1 SECURE THE LOG

Start by blocking your log to keep it stationary while you're milling. A few well-placed wedges will do the trick. It is also helpful to roll the log onto sturdy blocking to make a more comfortable working height.

2 INSTALL THE MILLING ATTACHMENT

Carefully read the installation instructions for your specific attachment, then bolt it onto your chain saw. You attach this type by tightening steel pads at both ends of the bar. The attachment features a push handle and tip guard.

3 ATTACH THE STRAIGHTEDGE

A flat, straight carriage is essential to getting a flat first cut. Here we're using the EZ Rail system that has leveling screws and pawls to hold it in place. Now is the time to get some wedges ready to keep the kerf open while cutting.

4 MAKE THE FIRST CUT

Fire up your saw and start the cut. Go slowly and don't force it. Let the chain's teeth do the work. As the saw progresses through the cut, slip wedges into the kerf on both sides. This keeps the slab you're cutting from pinching your chain and bar.

5 MAKE SUBSEQUENT CUTS

Remove the slab you just cut, as well as the EZ Rail. Now you've got a flat surface for the milling attachment to ride on. Continue cutting slabs, using the same techniques you used for the first pass. "The slabs will be rough, and not dried, so be sure to leave extra thickness for drying and final milling," Beaty says.

WEDGE

Once you've cut your logs, it's time to exercise patience. The rule of thumb for air-drying lumber is one year of drying for each inch of board thickness. Buy a moisture meter so you can check your lumber's moisture content. Kiln-dried lumber is dried to about 7% moisture content. For air-dried lumber, look to get down to 12% or less. At that point, you can let it acclimate in your house or shop for a couple of weeks before further dimensioning.

1 CREATE A BASE

Make a base using 4x4s. Beaty says, "The stack doesn't need to be perfectly level, but use mason's line to ensure that the 4x4s are in the same plane."

2 START THE STACK

Place the first layer of boards. Set "stickers" on top, spacing them no farther than 12 to 16 in. apart, to help prevent your boards from bowing as they dry. Stickers can be made from any dry lumber. The gap created allows airflow between the boards.

SEALER

STICKERS

3 CONTINUE STACKING

Stack subsequent layers the same way: a layer of boards followed by a layer of stickers. The ends of the boards dry out the fastest. To help keep them from cracking, paint them with Anchorseal to slow the drying.

4 COVER THE STACK

Now you need to put a roof on the stack. A piece of corrugated roofing or other sheet metal works well for this. You want it to curl down a bit so it sheds water but doesn't inhibit airflow. Weight the roof with lumber scraps so it doesn't blow off.

WHAT CHAIN SAW DO YOU NEED?

You're going to need a commercial-quality saw, not a typical residential saw. This means a saw that's capable of extended running time and an engine with at least 50cc displacement. "If you're underpowered, you'll just destroy the saw," says Beaty. He also recommends always running two-cycle engines at full throttle. "Part-throttling some two-cycle engines can starve them of the fuel/oil mix they need for good performance." The saws don't come cheap. But if you're milling lumber that you can turn around and sell, you'll recover the initial cost in no time.

The bar length depends on the diameter of the logs you're cutting, but 25 to 30 in. is usually sufficient. This type of cutting—cutting with the grain—is called ripping. Most chains are made with teeth designed for crosscutting—typical chain saw work. To mill lumber, you'll need a special chain with teeth designed for ripping.

Northern Tool supplied all of the equipment. Find your setup at northerntool.com.

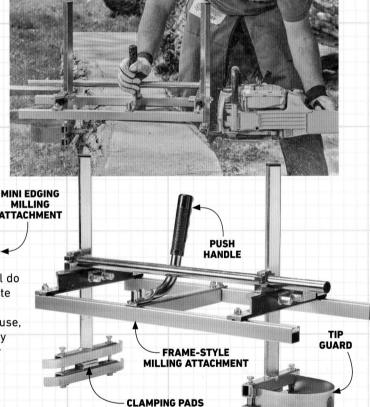

MINI EDGING MILLING ATTACHMENT

PUSH HANDLE

FRAME-STYLE MILLING ATTACHMENT

TIP GUARD

CLAMPING PADS

WHICH STYLE ATTACHMENT DO YOU NEED?

Whether you're making boards or posts and beams, either of the milling attachment styles shown will do the job. The frame style, however, is more accurate because the frame helps prevent bar deflection, giving you flatter, straighter cuts. For occasional use, to cut just a few posts for example, you can get by with the inexpensive mini edging attachment. For more frequent use, go with the frame style.

CHAIN MAINTENANCE

If you're throwing dust, not chips, your saw's chain is dull. You'll need a file with a guide to sharpen a chain. Count the strokes it takes to get a clean, sharp edge on the first tooth. Follow up by giving each tooth the same number of file strokes; otherwise you'll get an unbalanced chain and a curved cut.

BAR MAINTENANCE

Use brand-specific bar oil to cool and lubricate the chain and bar. "Some folks think used motor oil is OK to use, but unlike motor oil, bar oil has tack additives that help keep the oil on the bar instead of splattering all over," says Beaty. Clean the bar when you sharpen the chain, and clean the bar's groove using a special bar groove cleaning tool. "Also, remember to grease the two little holes in the sprocket nose at the end of the bar every time you sharpen the chain. This is also a good time to make sure to clean the saw's air filter."

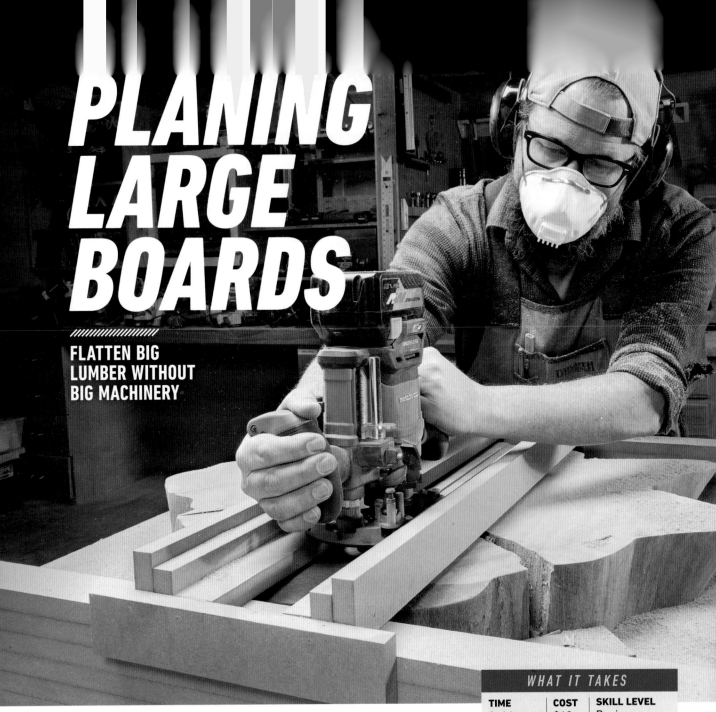

PLANING LARGE BOARDS

FLATTEN BIG LUMBER WITHOUT BIG MACHINERY

You don't need industrial-sized machinery to plane large pieces of wood. A full-size router with a 1/2-in. collet, a large-diameter bit and a simple jig will do the trick. The process will take a little longer than it would with a big machine, but the results will be just as good.

BY BRAD HOLDEN

WHAT IT TAKES

TIME	COST	SKILL LEVEL
2–4 hours	$60	Beginner

TOOLS & MATERIALS
Full-size router with 1/2-in. collet, 2-in.-diameter bottoming bit, 4 x 8-ft. sheet of 3/4-in. MDF

BIT FOR PLANING

You'll need a large-diameter router bit to speed the process along. If you have a router and a collection of bits, you might already have what you need. The bit doesn't need to be purpose-made for planing. It just needs to cut a flat surface. I used the bit shown at left that came with a door-making kit.

FIGURE A PLATFORM

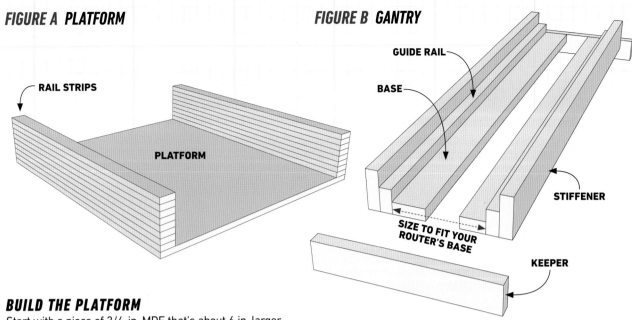

RAIL STRIPS

PLATFORM

FIGURE B GANTRY

GUIDE RAIL

BASE

STIFFENER

SIZE TO FIT YOUR
ROUTER'S BASE

KEEPER

BUILD THE PLATFORM

Start with a piece of 3/4-in. MDF that's about 6 in. larger than your workpiece, in both length and width. Build up two rails to support the gantry using 2-in.-wide strips of 3/4-in. MDF. Just stack these, tacking them in place with screws or brad nails. Then you can easily remove them as you decrease the thickness of your workpiece.

BUILD THE GANTRY

Construct the gantry as shown, using 3/4-in. MDF. Its length depends on the distance between the rails of your platform. The gantry should be just long enough to allow the overhanging keepers to slide freely along the rails.

1 SECURE THE WORKPIECE

Wedge shims underneath your stock to keep it from teetering while you're routing. Use 3/4-in. MDF blocking screwed to the platform to keep the stock from sliding.

2 FLATTEN THE WORKPIECE

Set your router's depth to remove 1/8 to 1/4 in. of material. Slide the router through the gantry, then move the gantry over a distance slightly less than the diameter of your bit and slide the router through the gantry again. This first pass may only remove a few high spots.

After cutting everything to that depth, lower the bit another 1/8 in. to 1/4 in. and proceed as above until the whole side is flattened. Then flip the workpiece over and repeat on the other side. I couldn't get enough depth for cutting with my router's dust port attached, so I had to go without. This is very dusty work, so wear a mask!

3 FINISH YOUR PROJECT

After flattening, sand your project and apply the finish. I attached hairpin legs to turn this crosscut into a coffee table.

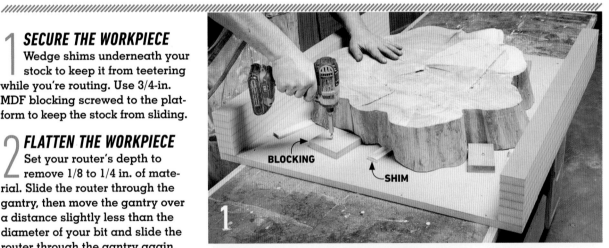

BLOCKING

SHIM

4 EXTERIOR REPAIRS & IMPROVEMENTS

KEEP SIDING LOOKING ITS BEST

MAINTENANCE AND REPAIR FOR 7 COMMON EXTERIORS

BY BRAD HOLDEN

FIBER CEMENT

WOOD

STUCCO

STEEL

ENGINEERED WOOD

BRICK

VINYL

Your home's exterior is visible to everyone, so you want to keep it looking like new. To do that, fix the little things. In doing so, you'll protect your home, keep it looking sharp, and avoid big problems requiring major work.

MEET THE EXPERT

AARON OUELLETTE IS THE PRODUCTION MANAGER AT STINSON SERVICES, A MINNESOTA-BASED ROOFING AND EXTERIOR COMPANY.

REPLACING PIECES OF VINYL AND STEEL

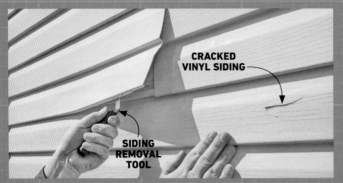

CRACKED VINYL SIDING

SIDING REMOVAL TOOL

NAILING FLANGE

TO REPLACE A piece of vinyl siding, you'll need to expose its nailing flange, which is done easily with an inexpensive siding removal tool. Working on the panel above the one you need to remove, slide the tool's hook under the panel's bottom edge to disengage the clip that holds the pieces together. Then slide the tool along the whole piece. Now you can lift that bottom edge, see the nailing flange and remove all the nails that hold the cracked piece in place.

AFTER REMOVING THE cracked piece, put the new piece in place, snapping its bottom edge onto the piece below it to lock them together. Then nail the new piece into place. Snap the bottom edge of the piece above your new piece onto the new piece, and you're done.

VINYL

The least expensive option, vinyl siding can last 30 or more years with minor maintenance needs, except for occasional cleaning. It doesn't dent or scratch but can crack if struck or hit by hail. To clean vinyl siding, wipe it down with detergent, then spray it with a hose. I don't recommend pressure-washing any exterior. If your vinyl siding cracks, it's a relatively easy fix, and a new panel typically costs less than $10. Of course, you'll need to know the exact brand and color to get a good match.

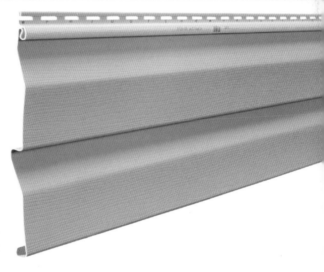

STEEL

Like vinyl siding, steel can last 30 or more years with little maintenance. Unlike vinyl, steel may need repainting. Steel siding doesn't crack like vinyl, but hail and the neighbor kid's baseball can dent it. Metal siding is installed like vinyl, but replacing a panel involves more work—you can't just lift the panel above the damaged one to get at the nailing flange because metal doesn't bend like vinyl. To get to a damaged piece, remove all the panels above it, and then replace them in order after you replace the damaged panel.

$ VINYL AND METAL SIDING: These price ranges include the removal of the old siding as well as new house wrap. The price will be impacted by both the color of the siding (light colors are less expensive than dark ones) and the length of the warranty that the contractor supplies to the property owner.

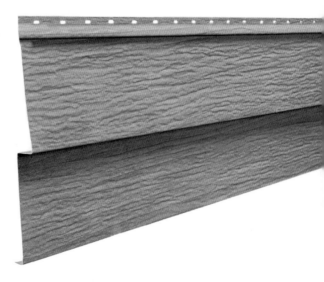

VINYL
- $700 to $1,000 per square for thin vinyl (0.042 in.)
- $800 to $1,200 per square for medium vinyl (0.044 in.)
- $900 to $1,400 per square for thick vinyl (0.046 in.)

METAL
- $1,300 to $1,600 per square

Like roofing, siding is priced by the square, which is 100 sq. ft.

REPLACING LAP SIDING BOARDS

SOMETIMES YOU NEED to remove all the boards above the damaged lap siding, but with a little ingenuity, you can usually avoid that. To remove one piece, pull all the nails securing it. If the top nails are underneath the panel above the one you're replacing, gently pry that board up to access all the nails in the damaged board. If this isn't possible, use an oscillating multi-tool to cut out the damaged piece. If the board is face-nailed as shown, cut the nails using an oscillating multi-tool.

SLIP THE NEW board into position. Make sure it's aligned with the adjacent pieces, and then nail it into place. If you've just slightly pried up the piece above it, you won't have enough access to hammer nails at the top of the new piece. In this case, face-nailing through both pieces is the only option. Fill any nail holes with exterior putty and repaint to match.

WOOD

When well maintained, wood siding can last 20 or more years. But it demands more maintenance than other types of siding—you'll need to paint or seal the wood every four to six years. Wood siding is also the least energy efficient. Being a natural material, it is highly susceptible to moisture, can get brittle as it ages, and can also cup or warp from seasonal moisture changes.

$ **CEDAR LAP SIDING:** The price range includes the removal of the old siding as well as new house wrap. The lower end doesn't include trim around windows and doors. The cedar market fluctuates quite a bit throughout the seasons.
■ $1,700 to $2,000 per square

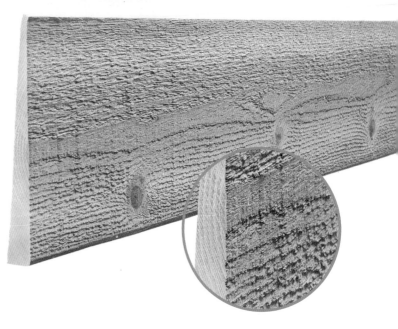

ENGINEERED WOOD

Engineered wood siding, such as LP, can last about 25 years and is one of the most durable options. If this type of siding gets scratched or dented, you don't need to replace the whole panel. You can just fill the damage with exterior putty and paint it to match.

Engineered wood siding requires minimal maintenance, except for cleaning and repainting as needed. The wood fibers have an insect repellent to prevent damage from pests. In my opinion, this type of siding is stronger than fiber cement siding when it's installed correctly, and when the corners and edges are well painted. You can easily replace a panel that's beyond repair.

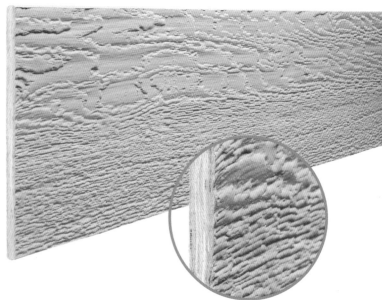

FIBER CEMENT

Fiber cement siding, such as Hardie Board, lasts about 25 years with minimal maintenance when properly installed. But it does require regular painting and is more susceptible to cracking than engineered wood siding. A cracked piece can't be repaired, so you'll need to replace it. Because of its rigidity, fiber cement siding is more difficult to replace than wood or engineered lap siding without nailing through the visible surface, but the replacement procedure is the same.

$ **ENGINEERED WOOD AND FIBER CEMENT SIDING:** The price range includes the removal of the old siding as well as new house wrap. The lower end represents primed LP/Hardie installation without trim; the higher end, prefinished siding with trim around windows and doors.
■ $1,350 to $1,800 per square

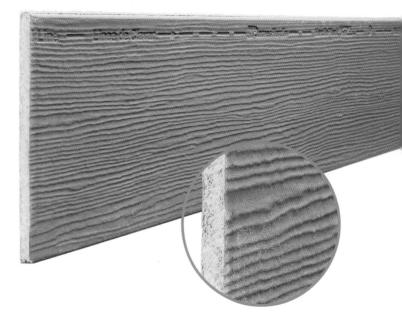

BRICK MAINTENANCE AND REPAIR

Whether your house has structural brick or brick veneer, pay close attention to the mortar joints.

As with stucco, keep a close eye on the mortar and fix little problems in mortar before they become big problems. Once things get bad, call a pro—they'll charge $25 to $30 per linear foot of mortar joints.

Fortunately, taking care of little areas is easy. All you need is a bag of mortar mix and a couple of inexpensive masonry tools.

CRACKED MORTAR

CLEAN OUT ANY loose mortar. If some areas show cracks but not loose material, use an angle grinder with a diamond wheel to remove the cracked mortar. A grinder is a better choice than a masonry chisel; the chisel creates more vibration, which can result in further cracking.

TUCK-POINTING TROWEL

MIX A SMALL batch of mortar and slide it into the cleaned joints using a tuck-pointing trowel.

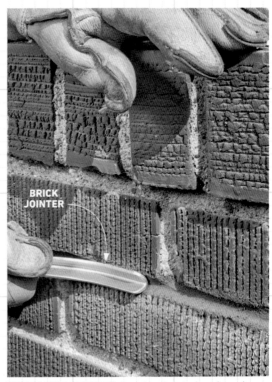

BRICK JOINTER

WHEN THE MORTAR just begins to harden, dress the joints using a brick jointer sized to suit your mortar joints. By pressing the mortar firmly against the adjacent bricks, you're making the mortar surface more impervious to moisture.

REPAIRING CRACKS IN STUCCO

Stucco can last 30 or more years, and it's the most energy-efficient option. Its longevity depends on patching holes or cracks immediately, painting regularly and cleaning. Again, I don't recommend pressure-washing any siding. Instead, use detergent and rinse it off with a garden hose.

With stucco, you need to be vigilant about checking for cracks. Even small cracks allow moisture to seep in, creating bigger problems down the road. You can fill those little cracks easily, and your work will hardly be noticeable.

I recommend using either specially formulated stucco patch, available at home centers, or closely matching caulk. Once cracks are wider than 1/8 in. or so, you'll find it difficult to hide them, and getting paint to match perfectly is hit or miss. If your stucco has lots of cracks or cracks wider than 1/8 in., call a pro.

 STUCCO:
- $2,300 to $3,000 per square

HAIRLINE CRACK

TO SEAL HAIRLINE cracks, simply apply the stucco patch or caulk. Avoid spreading the material beyond the area of the crack.

USE YOUR FINGER to press the patch material into the crack. Your finger is soft and able to press the material down into the stucco's texture, making the patch less visible.

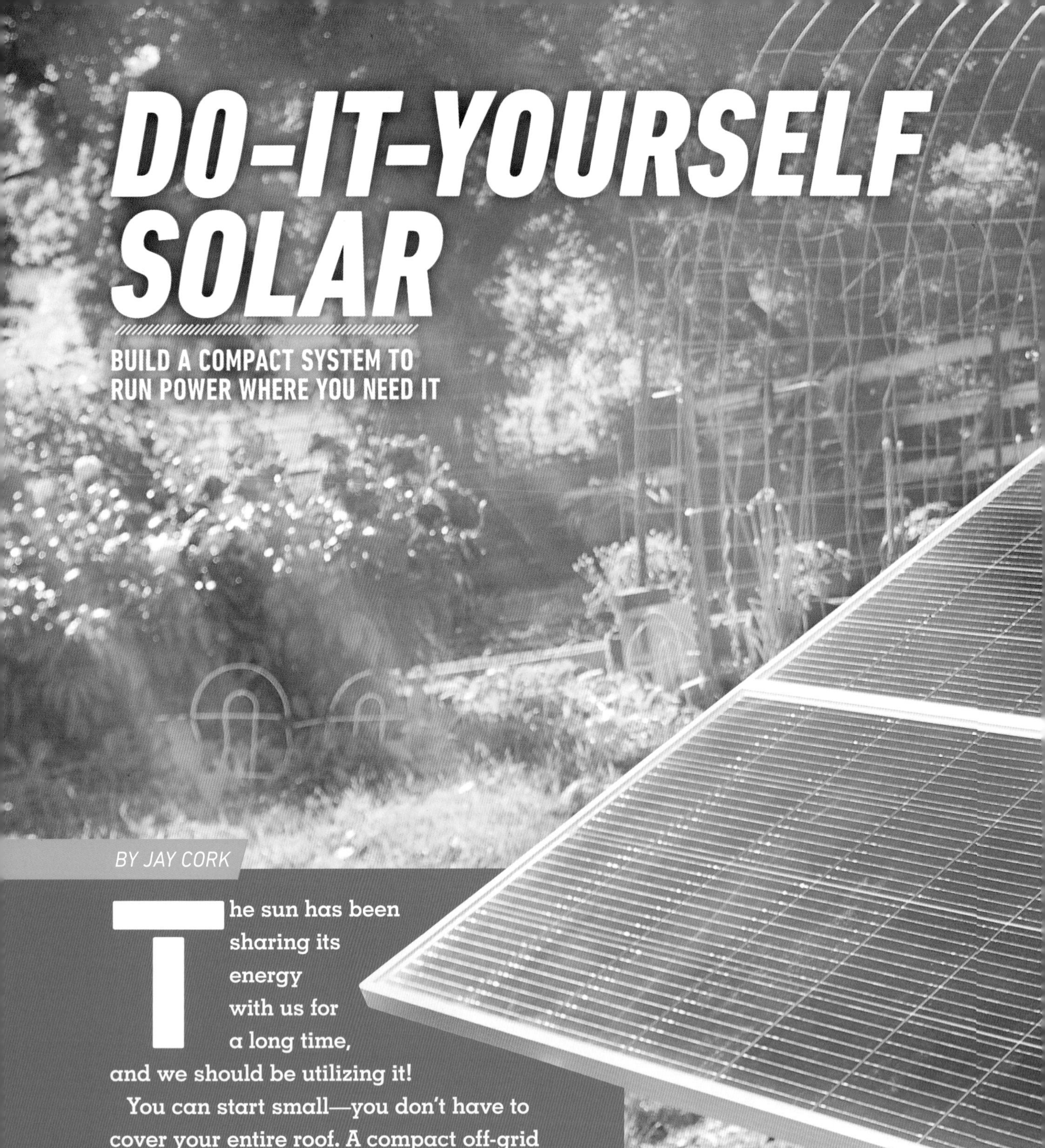

DO-IT-YOURSELF SOLAR

BUILD A COMPACT SYSTEM TO RUN POWER WHERE YOU NEED IT

BY JAY CORK

The sun has been sharing its energy with us for a long time, and we should be utilizing it!

You can start small—you don't have to cover your entire roof. A compact off-grid solar array is a fantastic solution for RVs and campers, and it can be an easy way to run power to an outbuilding. A small solar array can provide convenient power to a remote location, such as a greenhouse, and it will reduce your carbon footprint. You can even expand the array as your needs grow.

WHAT IT TAKES

TIME	COST	SKILL LEVEL
2 days	$2,000 to $3,000	Beginner

TOOLS
Cordless drill, socket set, heavy-duty lug crimpers, multimeter, basic electrical tools, specific tools for solar installation

The 200W PV panels shown above are $340 each from Rich Solar.

MEET THE EXPERT

ERIC CARTER IS A TECHNICAL SALES SPECIALIST WITH DRAGONFLY ENERGY AND BATTLE BORN BATTERIES. HE EXPLORES THE COUNTRY AND CAMPS OFF-GRID IN HIS SPRINTER VAN POWERED BY BATTLE BORN BATTERIES.

SOLAR ARRAY DESIGN

Solar power is easy to understand. First, photons emitted by the sun are absorbed by semiconductor materials in photovoltaic (PV) cells. This generates a flow of electrons, which is converted and stored as potential energy in a bank of batteries. The stored power is then made usable by an inverter. Simple, right?

CHOOSING BATTERIES

12V, 100Ah HEATED CELL $949

More sources than ever exist for batteries, but most originate overseas. I wanted strong customer support with a simple phone call, and Dragonfly Energy/Battle Born Batteries provides that and more. Based in Nevada, it offers domestically assembled lithium iron phosphate (LiFePo4) batteries. Its heated battery was a perfect choice for my greenhouse's northern location.

■ **LITHIUM IRON PHOSPHATE.** Battle Born lithium batteries have an integrated management system that protects the cells; they can't be overcharged or overdrawn. The batteries cost more, but with their high charge cycle specs (1,000 to 3,000 cycles), they still have the highest cost-to-benefit ratio.

■ **LEAD ACID.** Many types of lead acid batteries, including flooded, gel and absorbent glass mat (AGM), are available. They cost less than LiFePo4 batteries, but the drawbacks of lead acid outweigh that advantage—literally. They're very heavy, making them a poor choice for mobile installations. With their shorter life span (300 to 1,000 cycles), you'll pay more for lead acid batteries over time.

RIGHT-SIZE YOUR BATTERY BANK

USE THIS SIMPLE EQUATION TO DETERMINE BATTERY BANK SIZE.
List all AC loads in watts (W) in the table below and calculate the total watt-hours (Wh) per day. Multiply that number by the days of autonomy (DoA)—that is, the average number of days you expect to have complete cloud cover. Then divide that number by the voltage (V) of the system. This is the number of amp-hours (Ah) your battery bank should have.

OUR GREENHOUSE

AC Load	W	x	Hrs./Day	=	Wh/Day	x	DoA	=	Total Wh
14' wall fan (2)	132	x	2	=	264				
Ventilation fan	50	x	2	=	100				
LED lights (24)	15	x	2	=	30				
					394	x	3	=	1,182

FIND THE TOTAL Wh
394 Wh/Day x 3 DoA = 1,182 Total Wh

FIND THE NECESSARY Ah
1,182 Total Wh / 12V = 98.5Ah

Based on these equations, our battery bank needs 99Ah to accommodate this simple system. I chose to double this number to allow for growth.

OFF-GRID VS. GRID-TIED SYSTEMS

True off-grid systems aren't connected to the power grid, so they need a bank of batteries. Outbuildings, campers and RVs are perfect candidates for an off-grid system. A grid-tied system allows the energy generated from the solar array to power your home, but when the sun goes down, the power grid takes over.

The benefit of a grid-tied system is if you generate more power than you use, it gets shunted back to the power grid and the utility company pays you for it. The downside: If the power goes out in your neighborhood, you lose power; these systems automatically shut off in the event of a power failure to protect the line workers.

MAKE THE POWER DISTRIBUTION CENTER

I configured the panel in my workshop first, attaching all the elements on a small plywood panel that I sealed with oil-based paint. I used 3/4-in. washer-head screws to mount the solar charge control module, power inverter, shunt, bus bars and fuse block.

POWER INVERTER
Choose a power inverter that will give you plenty of room to grow. Pure sine wave inverters provide a power signature that is even cleaner than the power grid. Modified sine wave inverters may cause issues with delicate electronics such as computers; it's best to avoid this type.

BATTERY SHUNT
A battery shunt allows you to monitor the health of the battery charge. The shunt needs to be connected to the negative lead between the battery and the inverter.

FUSE BLOCK
In-line fuses protect the system from overloads and power spikes. I used a standard fuse block with a 200-amp fuse mounted directly in line with the positive side of the system.

CHARGE CONTROLLER
I chose to use the EPEVER 40-amp solar charge controller. It has an integrated heat sink design (which keeps things cool) and heavy-duty wire terminals. It's completely programmable for use with any type of battery.

BATTERY SHUTOFF
A kill switch for the batteries and on/off switch for the power inverter together provide a quick way for you to safely work on the system.

BUS BARS
Terminal blocks organize the cables and allow for expansion.

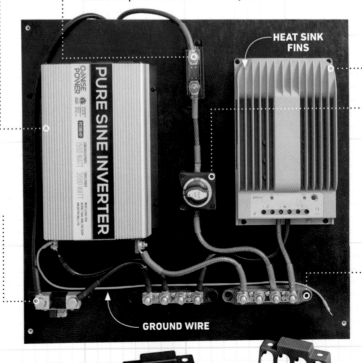

HEAT SINK FINS

PURE SINE INVERTER

GROUND WIRE

ELECTRICAL TOOLS
Specific to installing solar power systems

LARGE-GAUGE WIRE STRIPPERS

MC4 CONNECTOR TOOL

CRIMPER FOR MC4 PLUGS

THICK-GAUGE WIRE CUTTERS

LUG CRIMPER

SERIES VS. PARALLEL

Wiring batteries in series doubles the voltage while keeping the capacity the same. Alternately, wiring the terminals in parallel keeps the voltage the same while doubling the stored capacity.

AMP-HOUR RATINGS

Battery capacity, measured in amp-hours (Ah), refers to the amount of energy a battery can store. For example, a 100Ah battery can deliver 100 amps for one hour or 25 amps for four hours or 50 for two. You get the idea.

MAKING CABLES

Battle Born supplied me with premade battery interconnects, but every solar power installation will be different, so don't count on premade cables working for you. Eric Carter suggests using 1/0-gauge cable for connecting the batteries to each other. Here's how to make your own.

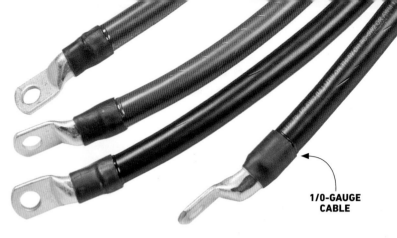

1/0-GAUGE CABLE

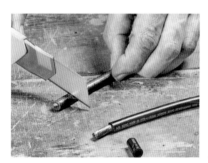

STRIP THE CABLE

Automatic wire strippers make quick work of smaller-gauge cables, but they won't work with these larger cables. Using a utility knife, I rolled the cable on the benchtop just enough to score the insulating jacket. Don't press too hard; you'll cut the copper.

CRIMP THE CABLE LUGS

To crimp the heavy-gauge lugs, I used these large lever-action crimpers ($40 online) and a quick jig I made to hold the cable steady. The best way to do this was to lightly crimp, rotate and repeat. Trying to crimp all at once often produced an ugly result.

PROTECT THE ENDS WITH HEAT SHRINK TUBING

To protect the crimped ends of my cables, I used double-walled adhesive-lined 3:1 shrink tubing. Cut the tubing to 1-1/2 in. long and heat it until it fully shrinks around the crimped cable end.

HEAT GUN

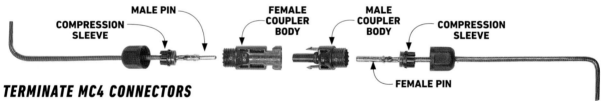

COMPRESSION SLEEVE · MALE PIN · FEMALE COUPLER BODY · MALE COUPLER BODY · COMPRESSION SLEEVE · FEMALE PIN

TERMINATE MC4 CONNECTORS

MC4 connectors are the standard for photovoltaic panels. They are rated IP67 waterproof and are easy to terminate with the right tools. Crimp the contacts to the cable and assemble the MC4 housing.

MOUNT THE PV PANELS

■ FIND A SUNNY SPOT

I had planned to mount the PV panels on the roof of our greenhouse, but because the structure faced almost perfectly south, I decided that wasn't necessary and mounted them near the ground.

■ MOUNT ON A STAND

I mounted the adjustable bracket stand ($160 via *Amazon.com*) to the foundation wall of the greenhouse and did my best to angle the panels to the sun's position in the midday sky. The optimum angle will change seasonally, and this bracket is designed to make those adjustments easily.

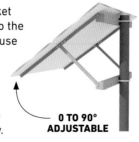

0 TO 90° ADJUSTABLE

■ RUN WIRE

I used 10-gauge cable to connect the 12V, 400W array to the power distribution panel—only 20 ft. away. To avoid power loss, longer runs need heavier-gauge cable. Cable length/gauge charts are readily available online.

MAKE THE FINAL CONNECTIONS

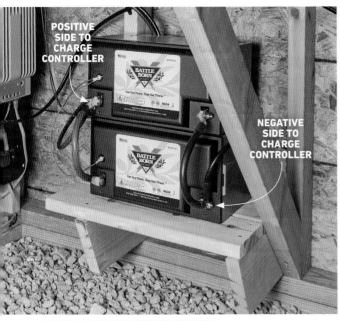

POSITIVE SIDE TO CHARGE CONTROLLER

NEGATIVE SIDE TO CHARGE CONTROLLER

NEGATIVE

POSITIVE

MAKE THE BATTERY STAND

Because there is no liquid in lithium batteries, you can lay them in any position. This makes it easy to configure multiple batteries. I stacked two batteries near the power hub on a small ledge made from scrap wood.

ATTACH THE CABLE ENTRY PLATE

I mounted a pass-through box designed for MC4 connectors on the exterior of the building. This allows the panels to be easily disconnected from the structure if needed. On the interior side, run the 10-gauge cable to the solar charge controller.

DETERMINE POLARITY

Before plugging the leads from the PV array into the entry plate, check the polarity of the cables using a multimeter. The positive lead should connect to the positive side of the entry plate and that should follow all the way to the positive terminal on the solar charge controller.

PROGRAM THE SOLAR CHARGE CONTROLLER

To program the charge controller, connect the batteries to it and plug in the MT50 remote interface. Consult with your battery manufacturer to determine the settings for your batteries.

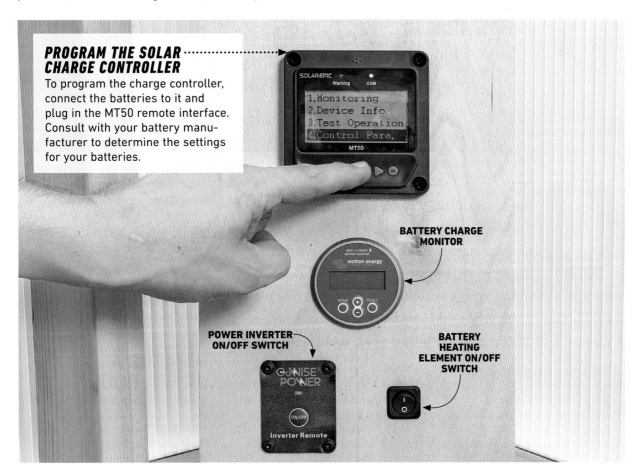

BATTERY CHARGE MONITOR

POWER INVERTER ON/OFF SWITCH

BATTERY HEATING ELEMENT ON/OFF SWITCH

BRING YOUR ROOF TO LIFE

BY KARUNA EBERL

Green roofs have been around since at least the time of the Vikings, who laid birch bark and sod on top of boards to keep drafts out of their homes. The modern incarnation of these roofs began in 1960s Europe. Now they are sprouting up everywhere, thanks to their aesthetics, sustainability and long-term cost savings. Is a green roof, also called a living roof, right for you?

"Germany started looking at green roofs as a way to cut down on the spread of wildfires," says Jim Mumford, president and resident horticulturist at Good Earth Plant Company in San Diego. "And then it came across the Atlantic."

Today, Europe is still the leader in green roofs. But several U.S. cities are embracing the benefits and giving incentives to homeowners to install them. New York, Portland, Denver and Nashville require them in new construction of a certain size. Even the world headquarters of McDonald's, located in Chicago, sports a fuzzy, green top.

"One of the things I really like about it is the addition of biodiversity," says Mumford. "I've got milkweed all over mine, so I see butterflies all the time, and birds and bees. It's a nice little wild spot."

WHAT IS A GREEN ROOF?

Green roofs feature plants growing on top of a manufactured structure. They include a hefty waterproofing layer, soil or other growing medium, and usually a root barrier, plus drainage and irrigation systems.

"What we build most is what I call an eco-roof," says Mumford. "It's got 4 to 6 in. of soil and native plants, so the roof uses as little water as possible."

Green roofs can be quite pricey, especially if you're retrofitting your house to accommodate one. But if you have the means, they pay off economically, environmentally and aesthetically.

"I think the number one reason homeowners get them is the cool factor," says Mumford. "Would I rather look at an ugly garage roof from my second-story bedroom window, or a green roof that's obviously sustainable?"

Developers and contractors can also benefit by installing green roofs. If a development requires green space, a green roof may qualify, allowing more surface room for parking and other needs. Green roofs can also ease compliance with stormwater retention codes.

BENEFITS OF A GREEN ROOF

- Possible heating and cooling savings of 20 to 25%. The plants insulate the building and cool the air.
- Durability. Green roofs last 45 years or more, two to three times longer than a regular roof. That's because they protect the roof's waterproofing layer from windblown debris, UV radiation, and expansion and contraction.
- Wildlife habitat creation. A green roof helps pollinators and birds, and adds biodiversity to the neighborhood.
- Food self-sufficiency. It's possible to grow your own food on a green roof.

In addition to the benefits above, a green roof can reduce:
- Stormwater runoff, erosion and pollution. A green roof can hold 60 to 80% of rainfall, then release it slowly while filtering and cleaning it.
- Sound transmission and reflection.
- Landfill waste, because green roofs last longer.
- The spread of wildfires.

WHAT YOU NEED TO KNOW

How Much Maintenance Is Required?
Green roofs do require regular maintenance, such as removing weeds and checking drains to ensure no water is pooling. Mumford's company performs maintenance four times a year. "I think a homeowner actually has better roof maintenance as a result of us being up there on a semi-frequent basis," he says. "Otherwise, nobody goes on the roof."

Where Can I Have a Green Roof?
"Pretty much anywhere but Antarctica," says Mumford. However, depending on your location, it may be more complex. In drier places, green roofs need irrigation. And in Florida, they must be designed to withstand hurricanes. They're especially popular in the Pacific Northwest and Canada.

Does a Green Roof Have to Be Flat?
No. In fact, they need a slight slope so water doesn't pool. On pitched roofs they feature retention systems, although they typically aren't installed on roofs with more than a 40% slope. "Once the angle rises enough, it becomes a living wall instead," says Mumford, laughing.

Can I Convert My Traditional Roof to a Green Roof?
Yes. But it's probably going to be expensive, because it requires adjusting your home's structural load capacity. A green roof with 4 in. of soil adds about 30 lbs. per square foot when it's fully saturated. Don't forget to factor in the costs of installing green-roof–specific waterproofing and hiring an engineer, as well as the green roof itself.

What Does a Green Roof Cost?
If your house is already engineered to accommodate a green roof, it'll probably cost $30 to $50 per square foot to have one professionally installed. The range can be as wide as $20 to $200 per square foot, with the high end more likely for an apartment rooftop park with trees, walkways and seating.

Typically, homeowners will put a green roof on only a portion of their house or garage. Mumford estimates a green roof for a two-car garage might run about $25,000. If you decided to cover your 2,500-sq.-ft. house, it might cost $75,000 to $100,000.

Can I Install a Green Roof Myself?
Yes, especially on smaller structures such as a shed. That's if you have the patience for research and planning, plus a good set of construction and gardening skills. Mumford says to plan on about $30 per square foot, which puts the total for an 8 x 10-ft. shed at about $2,500.

Mumford cautions against installing a green roof yourself on anything bigger than a shed. "You really don't want to risk your roof caving in," he says. "It's just too catastrophic. And you don't want a leak. Fixing a leak on a green roof is pretty easy, but finding the leak is another story. If you go for it, call me. Maybe I can coach you through it," he says.

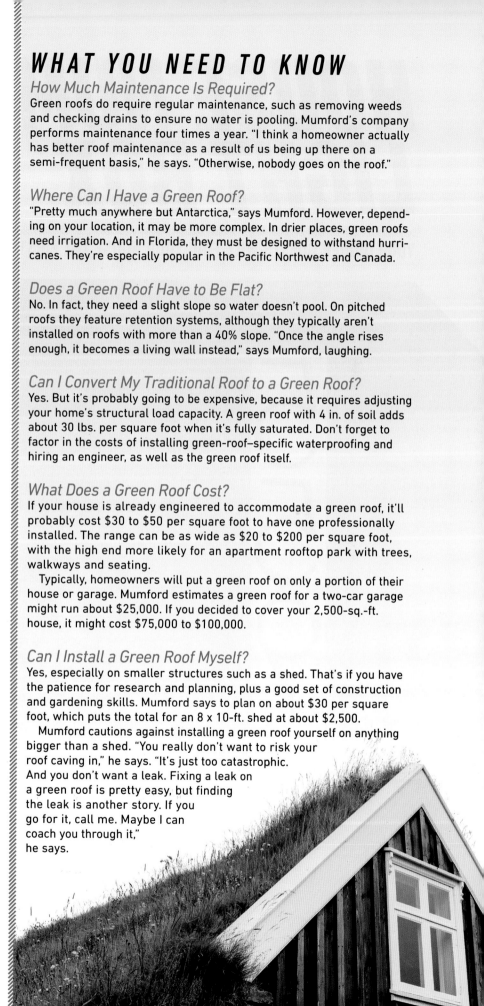

HOUSE NUMBER LIGHT BOX

YOUR DINNER GUESTS WILL FIND YOUR HOUSE THE FIRST TIME!

ONE-DAY PROJECT

BY JOE CRUZ

This solar-power LED light box can illuminate your address to make it pop! And you can build it in an afternoon with only a few tools. Place the box in an area of your front yard that gets at least four hours of direct sunlight.

WHAT IT TAKES

TIME	COST	SKILL LEVEL
1/2 day	$20–$50	Intermediate

TOOLS
Drill/driver, 1/2" drill bit, 18-gauge brad nail gun, measuring tape, miter saw, table saw

1 CUT A GROOVE

With your pieces cut to size according to the Cutting List, make a 1/8-in.-wide x 1/4-in.-deep groove 1/2 in. from the edge of both sides for the glass to fit into.

2 ASSEMBLE THE BOTTOM BLOCKS

Join the two bottom blocks with wood glue and 3/4-in. nails, keeping the blocks flush on four sides. Next, also using wood glue and 3/4-in. nails, attach a glass stop block to the bottom blocks, keeping it flush on three sides. Attach a front to the bottom blocks, leaving a 1/8-in. gap for the glass.

3 ATTACH THE SIDES

Before you attach the sides, draw a line on the inside of both sides, 1 in. from the top. You'll need it later. Apply wood glue to the left side of the bottom block assembly and position it with the front facedown. Now, attach the left side to the bottom block assembly with 1-1/4-in. nails. Be sure the left side is flush at the front and bottom of the bottom blocks, and the 1/8-in. grooves on each piece align. Attach the right side the same way.

4 ATTACH THE UPPER GLASS STOP BLOCK

Drill a 1/2-in. hole in the upper glass stop block. Attach the block to each of the sides, just below the 1-in. line and behind the 1/8-in. groove, using wood glue and 1-1/4-in. nails. Attach a front to both sides, leaving a 1/8-in. gap between the inside of the front and the stop block. The front should be flush with the front edge of both sides.

5 CUT THE ACRYLIC SHEET

Cut a piece of 1/8-in. acrylic sheet to 4-5/16 x 23-1/2 in. Test the fit by sliding the acrylic sheet into the 1/8-in. slot at the top of the box.

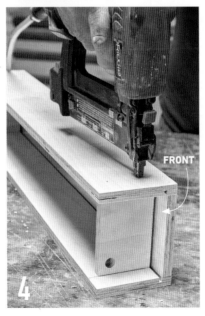

FIGURE A
HOUSE NUMBER LIGHT BOX

OVERALL DIMENSIONS:
4-7/8"W x 3-3/4"D x 25-1/2"H

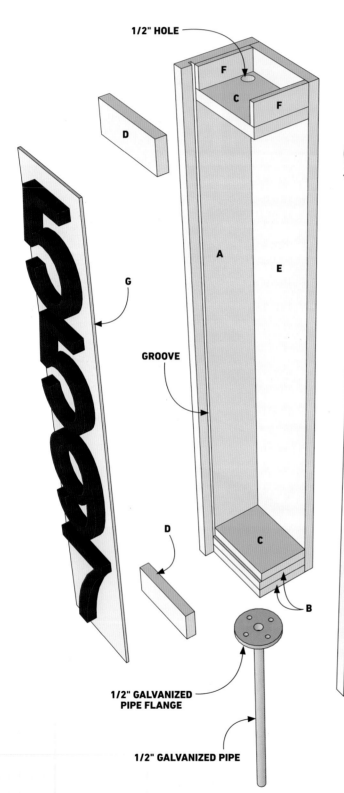

1/2" HOLE

CUT 1/2" FROM EDGE

GROOVE

1/2" GALVANIZED PIPE FLANGE

1/2" GALVANIZED PIPE

CUTTING LIST

KEY	QTY.	DIMENSIONS	PART
A	2	1/2" x 3-3/4" x 25-1/2"	Sides
B	2	1/2" x 2-3/4" x 3-7/8"	Bottom blocks
C	2	1/2" x 2-5/8" x 3-7/8"	Glass stop blocks
D	2	1/2" x 1-1/2" x 3-7/8"	Front
E	1	1/2" x 3-7/8" x 25-1/2"	Back
F	2	1/4" x 1" x 2-5/8"	Spacers
G	1	1/8" x 4-5/16" x 23-1/2"	Acrylic sheet

MATERIALS LIST

ITEM	QTY.
12" x 36" x 1/2" Baltic birch plywood	1
1/8" acrylic sheet 12" x 24"	1
Solar LED light strip	1
1/2" galvanized pipe flange	1
1/2" x 12" galvanized pipe	1
1-1/4" 18-gauge brad nails	
1-1/4" wood screws	
3/4" 18-gauge brad nails	
Acrylic latex exterior paint	
Plastic wood filler	
Waterproof wood glue	

CHOOSE YOUR NUMBERS

You can use peel-and-stick number decals, or attach flush-mount numbers to the acrylic sheet. You can also paint numbers freehand or spray-paint using stencils.

For flush-mount numbers, position the numbers in the center of the acrylic sheet so there are equal gaps between each number and from each side. (Some numbers come with templates.) Mark all the holes for the numbers and drill 3/8-in. holes at each mark. Slide the acrylic sheet out of the box and set it off to the side.

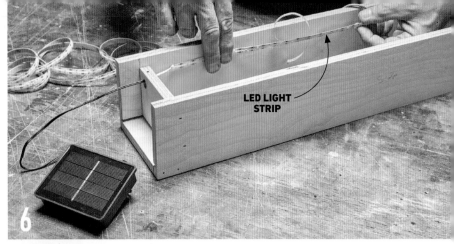

6 INSTALL THE LED LIGHT STRIPS

Through the 1/2-in. hole in the upper glass stop block, feed the solar LED strip lights until all the lights are inside the box. Peel back a few inches of the tape from the back of the LED strip. Stick the LED strips to the inside of the box, starting at the top, working your way down one side, then across the bottom and up the other side. Peel the tape as you go.

LED LIGHT STRIP

7 INSTALL THE NUMBERS

Peel the protective paper from both sides of the acrylic sheet and slide the sheet into the box. Attach your numbers. (If you're using screws, be careful not to overtighten them; you may crack the acrylic sheet.)

8 INSTALL THE BACK

Position the box with the front face down. Slide the back between the two sides, keeping it flush with the top of the sides. (If the back is too tight, trim it a bit.) Drill two 3/16-in. holes through the back into the bottom blocks and two 3/16-in. holes through the back into the top glass stop block, 1-1/4 in. from the edge of both sides. Drill two more 3/16-in. holes through the middle of each side into the back, 1/4 in. from the back edge. Secure the back by driving six 1-1/4-in. screws into your predrilled holes.

9 FIT THE SOLAR PANEL

Each solar panel is a little different; you may have to custom-fit yours into the box. You could add spacers to the inside of the solar panel compartment or notch out the back, depending on the size of your solar panel. Be sure the solar panel fits snug before gluing the two spacers to each of the sides in the solar panel compartment. Loop any excess wire and store it under the solar panel. Be sure to press the ON button before fitting the solar panel into the box.

10 FINISHING TOUCHES

Finish off the box by filling all the holes with plastic wood filler. Sand all the surfaces with 150-grit sandpaper. Seal the box with exterior spar urethane or paint it to match your house trim. Attach the pipe flange in the center of the bottom blocks with four 1-1/4-in. screws. Thread the pipe into the flange and tighten.

LIGHT YOUR PATH

BUILD BOLLARD LIGHTS TO CREATE A STYLISH GLOW

BY GLENN HANSEN

You might be familiar with those short, stout posts used around buildings, as roadway dividers, or in harbors to moor large vessels. They're called bollard posts because, as the story goes, they resemble tree trunks, which are also known as "boles." You might need that knowledge for a trivia contest someday.

For me, the bollard idea presented design possibilities for both woodworking and lighting, which are combined in these plans for decorative path lights.

MEET THE BUILDER

GLENN HANSEN, DEPUTY EDITOR, DOESN'T LIKE TRIPPING ON DARK PATHWAYS.

UMBRELLA LIGHT

I worked on a few different versions of this umbrella light (long curved legs, stout 2x4 uprights, etc.), but I ended up making relatively short 1x2 cedar arms and capping them with a simple cedar square with a light in the middle. These uniquely stylish lights are quick to build, and the low-lumen solar lamp casts a subtle, pleasing light on your path.

HIDDEN-LED SANDWICH

This one is so easy and so striking that you could make it with kids so they can see the simplicity and power of DIY. It's just a wooden sandwich made to glow with LED light strips. If you're making several of these, go with low-voltage power. We used adhesive LED light strips that had individual solar arrays.

VALANCE POST

It's not all about cedar for outdoor projects. For this bollard light, you can choose a wood with interesting grain, like teak. I had a few eucalyptus boards in my home shop, and I like the unique tone and the way this wood cuts and sands. With this style of lighting, you can make the posts tall for path use or short for mounting to a porch wall.

CHUNKY LANTERN

I used a cedar 6x6 for the most bollard-like of my path lights. A 6x6 post seemed just the right size between a too-lean 4x4 and a too-large 8x8. The key is to find a solar lantern with its solar grids angled and off to the side. Many solar lanterns have one square solar grid flat in the center, and the top of this post would block it.

UMBRELLA
LIGHT

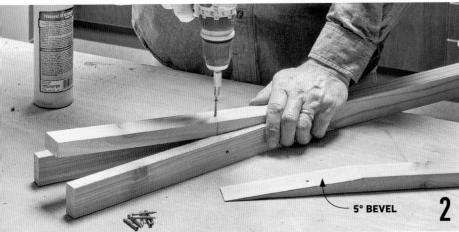

5° BEVEL

3" HOLE SAW

1 CUT THE BEVEL BOTTOM FROM 1x2 CEDAR

I kept my umbrella lights short and narrow so they would look like a row of footlights along the path. Starting 7 in. from the bottom of each 16-in. cedar arm, using a band saw, I cut a 5-degree bevel. You could also cut them with a circular saw: Just clamp the 1x2 to the edge of a 1x6 to give the saw something stable to ride on.

2 GLUE AND SCREW THE ARMS TO A POST

I connected the four umbrella arms to a treated 2x2. I took a treated 2x4 and ripped it to size on my table saw, then I crosscut it to 24 in. This gave a few inches of surface for gluing and screwing the umbrella arms, and the rest would be buried to hold the bollard upright. My short lights didn't need much below-ground support, and I can easily relocate them.

3 CUT A CIRCLE INTO THE TOP PIECE FOR THE SOLAR LIGHT

Small solar light discs that can drop into a 3-in. cutout are readily available. Before sizing my cedar to fit on top, I drilled that 3-in. hole so I had material to clamp to my bench. Then I cut the square on the miter saw and rounded the edges with an orbital sander. I gave the tops of the umbrella arms a slight bevel so the square sat flush. Then I added a clear exterior finish and set the post in the ground.

HIDDEN-LED
SANDWICH

1 MAKE THE SANDWICH

I started with three 1x6 cedar boards, each 30 in. long. I then ripped one of those to 3-1/2 in. wide and cut 6 in. off the length. I glued that narrow piece in the center of the wider boards, then added a few exterior trim screws.

2 WRAP THE LIGHTS

When you shop for outdoor-rated LED lights, look for ones that are IP65 rated. IP stands for "ingress protection," and the "65" is a code indicating they'll keep out dust particles and water spray. Buy strips you can cut to length, not silicone-coated tube-like strips. My strip lights had 3M adhesive backing—super easy.

3 ATTACH THE POST

To hold these light sandwiches upright, I took a length of gal-vanized steel pipe, connected a 90-degree street elbow (one male threaded end and one female threaded end) and then attached that to a pipe flange screwed to the bottom side of the wood. The pipe, flange and bottom couple of inches of the post get buried.

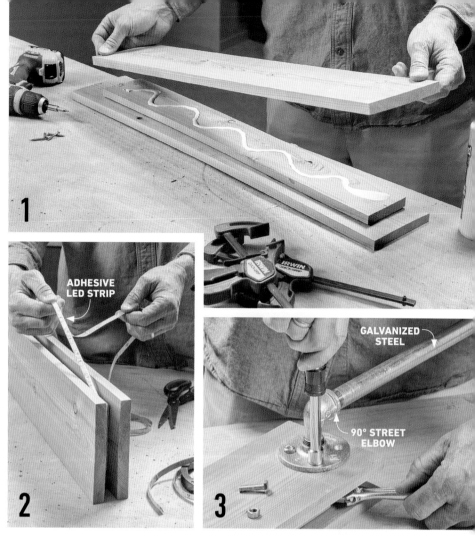

1

ADHESIVE LED STRIP

2

GALVANIZED STEEL

90° STREET ELBOW

3

LOW-VOLTAGE POWER GUIDE

The solar lights I used for these bollard lights are great for their low cost and simplicity. But they're not perfect. I'm not sure of their durabil-ity, and they are inconsistent during long stretches of cloudy days. A low-voltage lighting setup provides more reliable lighting, but at a cost of time and money. The components you need depend on the number of lights you'll connect and their combined wattage.

START WITH THIS:

Buy a larger transformer than you'll initially need so you can add lights later as your landscape (and imagination) expands. If you'll be installing 400 watts of lights, buy a 600-watt transformer.

When lighting a path, decide whether you want to light only the path or both the path and the features around it. As a rule, the broader the field you want to light, the higher the light pole you'll need. Path lights with a 20-watt halogen bulb at a 24-in. height should be spaced every 10 ft.

Consider seasonal factors when planning your landscape low-voltage lighting installation. Install lights where they won't be easily damaged by plows or shovels.

For safety's sake, before you dig for your low-voltage lighting, call 811 to have your utility companies mark the locations of underground wires and pipes. The service is usually free—and you'll avoid dangerous and costly surprises.

Connect the wires with weatherproof wire connectors. These wire connectors have a shield on the bottom and sealant inside to make them weatherproof. If your lights have press-on connections, cut them off, strip off 1/2 in. of insulation and install weatherproof connectors.

1/4" DEEP RECESS

1

2

3

VALANCE
POST

1 CUT THE RECESS AND HOLE

This simple L-shaped post has a small solar light on top that shines down the face of a long board. Before cutting my eucalyptus board to length, I clamped it to my workbench to cut a rectangle opening and an adjoining recess for the solar light pack. I placed the light upside down on the board, then traced an outline for the rectangular hole and the recessed part. I used a plunge router to clear the recess and a jigsaw to open the hole.

2 CUT THE MITER

The top that holds the solar light measures 4 x 5 in. Each end has a miter, and they're cut in opposite directions. Once you cut that small top, cut the long upright to length; mine is 32 in. tall. I added a short piece of wood to drop down the front, mostly just to hide the plastic solar light.

3 JOIN THE PIECES

I glued these miter cuts together and added nails. To secure this bollard in the ground, I used the same galvanized pipe method that I used for the Hidden-LED Sandwich bollard.

CHUNKY LANTERN

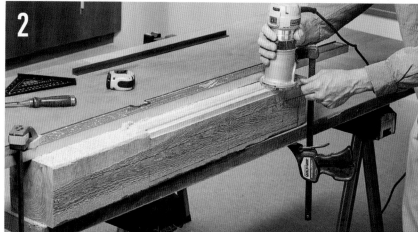

1 BEVEL THE TOP

To make my lantern post mimic the solar lantern light, I beveled the top of the 6x6 on my miter saw. I found the center of the post on each side and drew matching angles from that center point. Mine was a 30-degree angle, cut four times. I sanded off imperfections with an orbital sander.

2 ROUT THE CORNERS

I bought 3/4-in. angle iron to secure the post top to the base. I routed a rabbet to attach that angle iron flush with the post, but you could surface-mount it.

My post was 45 in. tall, including the 12-in. gap for the lantern. I determined my angle iron should be 30 in. long, with 12 in. connected to the base and 6 in. to the top. That determined the full length of my rabbet cut. Do this router work before you cut your top and base sections to length.

3 DRILL HOLES IN THE ANGLE IRON

With a bit designed to bore metal, you can easily drill the six or eight holes you need to secure the angle iron to the post. It's even easier if you have a drill press, but I just used my drill/driver on low speed. Cut your post top and base to the length you want, and then clamp the angle iron to the post before drilling.

4 ASSEMBLE THE BOLLARD

I attached the angle iron with washer-head construction screws. You can use almost any exterior-rated screws here. I like the look of washer-head screws and the strength of GRK structural screws; they're an easy replacement for meaty lag screws. After assembly, I decided I wanted the post a bit darker, so I disassembled it and brushed on a darker semitransparent waterproofing stain.

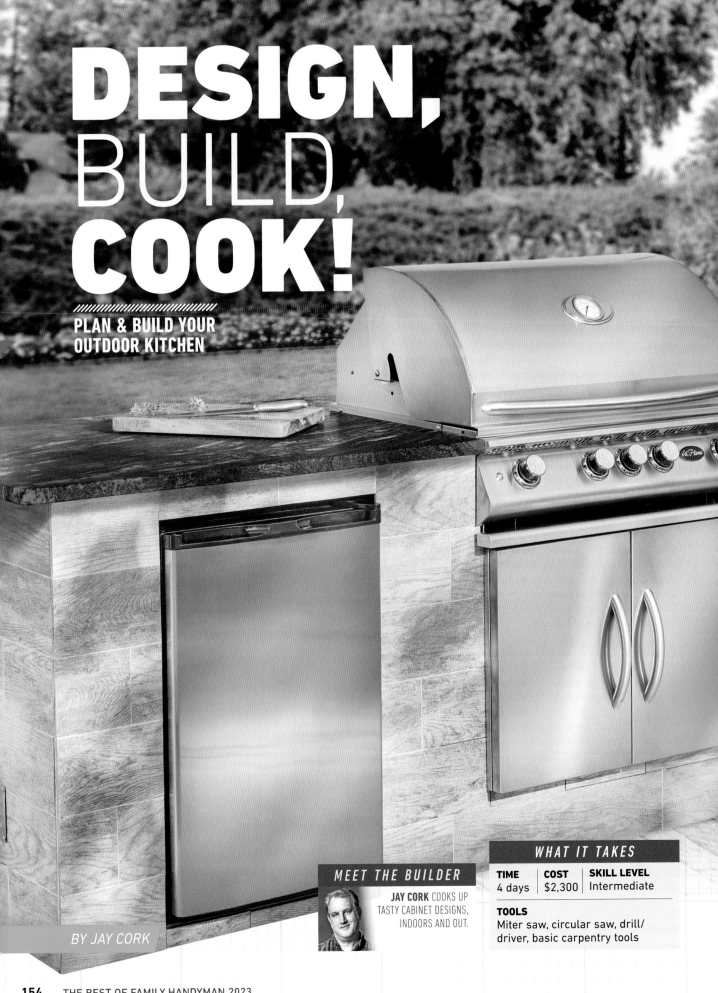

DESIGN, BUILD, COOK!

PLAN & BUILD YOUR OUTDOOR KITCHEN

MEET THE BUILDER

JAY CORK COOKS UP TASTY CABINET DESIGNS, INDOORS AND OUT.

WHAT IT TAKES

TIME	COST	SKILL LEVEL
4 days	$2,300	Intermediate

TOOLS
Miter saw, circular saw, drill/driver, basic carpentry tools

BY JAY CORK

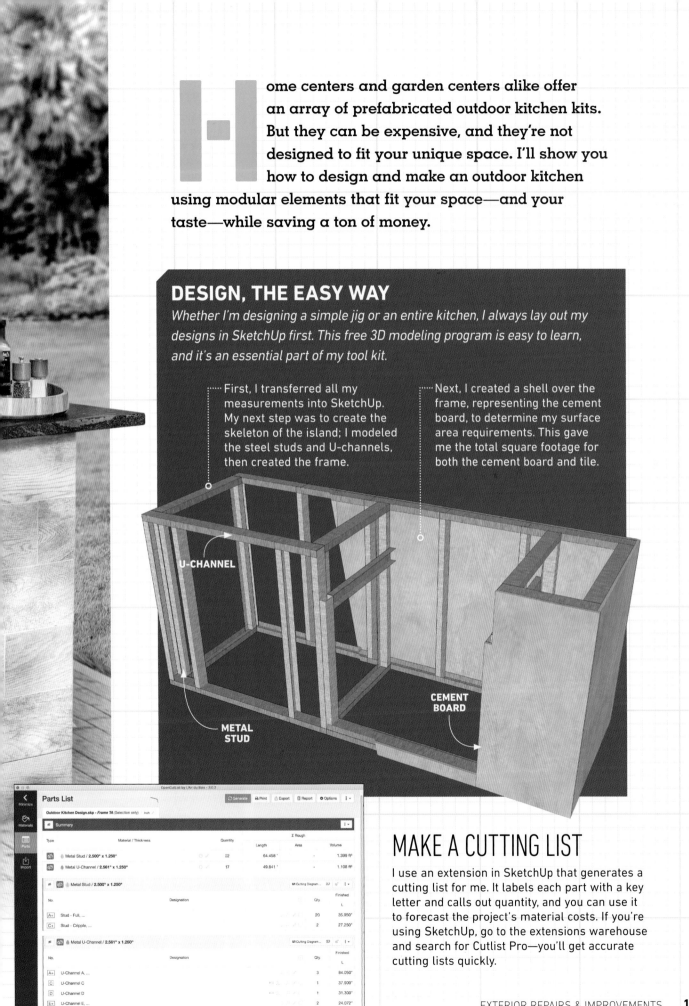

ome centers and garden centers alike offer an array of prefabricated outdoor kitchen kits. But they can be expensive, and they're not designed to fit your unique space. I'll show you how to design and make an outdoor kitchen using modular elements that fit your space—and your taste—while saving a ton of money.

DESIGN, THE EASY WAY

Whether I'm designing a simple jig or an entire kitchen, I always lay out my designs in SketchUp first. This free 3D modeling program is easy to learn, and it's an essential part of my tool kit.

First, I transferred all my measurements into SketchUp. My next step was to create the skeleton of the island; I modeled the steel studs and U-channels, then created the frame.

Next, I created a shell over the frame, representing the cement board, to determine my surface area requirements. This gave me the total square footage for both the cement board and tile.

U-CHANNEL

METAL STUD

CEMENT BOARD

MAKE A CUTTING LIST

I use an extension in SketchUp that generates a cutting list for me. It labels each part with a key letter and calls out quantity, and you can use it to forecast the project's material costs. If you're using SketchUp, go to the extensions warehouse and search for Cutlist Pro—you'll get accurate cutting lists quickly.

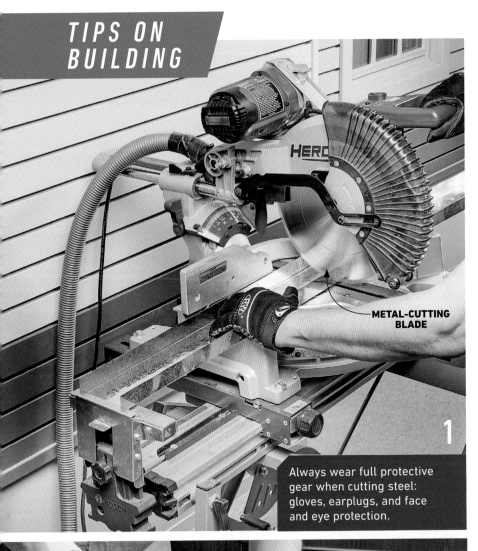

METAL-CUTTING BLADE

Always wear full protective gear when cutting steel: gloves, earplugs, and face and eye protection.

1

1 CUTTING METAL STUDS

Metal studs and U-channels are readily available, easy to work with and inexpensive. This is a perfect combination for building an outdoor kitchen from scratch. Unlike wood frames, metal studs create a light frame that's easy to move around, and it's also fireproof. When you cut metal studs, use a metal-cutting blade and appropriate PPE. I used self-tapping metal screws with low-profile heads to assemble the frame.

2 FRAME WITH METAL STUDS

Assembling metal studs and U-channels is easy with the right screws. I used 1/2-in. self-tapping stainless steel screws. A jig helped me keep the parts square to each other, and I used locking pliers with a flat jaw face to keep the two layers of steel together as the screws were driven through.

3 INSTALL ELECTRICAL CONDUIT

Once the frame is built, it's time to run the utilities. Both the refrigerator and grill need electricity, so I hid that receptacle inside the island. If you want to install outlets on the exterior, use outdoor-rated outlet boxes.

LOCKING PLIERS

1/2" SELF-TAPPING SCREWS

2

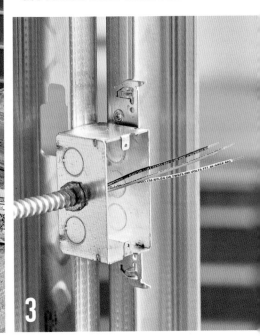

3

4 USE FIBER CEMENT BACKER BOARD

Using 1-in. self-tapping screws, attach the backer board to the steel frame. I used water-proof cement Hardie Backer Board (about $25 for a 3 x 5-ft. sheet). You can cut this material easily on your circular saw with a fiber cement blade, but you'll make a ton of unhealthy dust—wear a respirator! For a dust-free method, score it on both sides with a utility knife and snap it. This eats up blades but saves your lungs.

5 CHOOSE DURABLE CLADDING

Woods such as cedar are well suited for outdoor use but still require maintenance. To keep this island fireproof, I chose tile that emulates weathered wood grain. Installation was a bit more work, but the tile is maintenance free and will last a lifetime.

6 INSTALL VENTS

When you enclose gas—whether an LP tank or a natural gas line—in any structure, you need proper venting to avoid a dangerous buildup of gas fumes. I cut two vent holes on each end of the island and installed vent louvers with stainless steel screws.

Learn from my mistake: I forgot to cut the vent holes before tiling the exterior. Instead of getting nice, clean cuts with a tile saw, I had to use an angle grinder to cut through the tile, mortar and cement board all at once—talk about making more dusty work for myself!

CEMENT BOARD SCREWS

CONSTRUCTION ADHESIVE

LARGER-FORMAT TILE MORTAR

STAINLESS STEEL VENT AND SCREWS

DESIGNING YOUR OUTDOOR SPACE

TAKE MEASUREMENTS

Decide where your outdoor kitchen needs to be, and then grab a measuring tape, a notepad and a helper. When determining the size of your kitchen, give yourself enough room for entertaining, too, not just cooking!

ELIMINATE MISTAKES

Whether or not you have SketchUp, making a cutting list and a materials list is an important exercise; it helps estimate costs and minimize mistakes.

TALK TO THE MANUFACTURER

When installing gas grills, mistakes can be costly. If you have any questions or concerns, call the manufacturer before you start your project.

CONSIDER YOUR PLUMBING AND ELECTRICAL NEEDS

If you think you may install a sink and dishwasher, or other appliances that require electricity or plumbing, talk to a pro to make sure everything is considered before you start building.

PROPANE OR NATURAL GAS?

If you're running natural gas, now is the time to get that line installed and ready to go. Check your local building codes to see if you need a licensed professional to run the gas line.

ELEMENTS TO CONSIDER

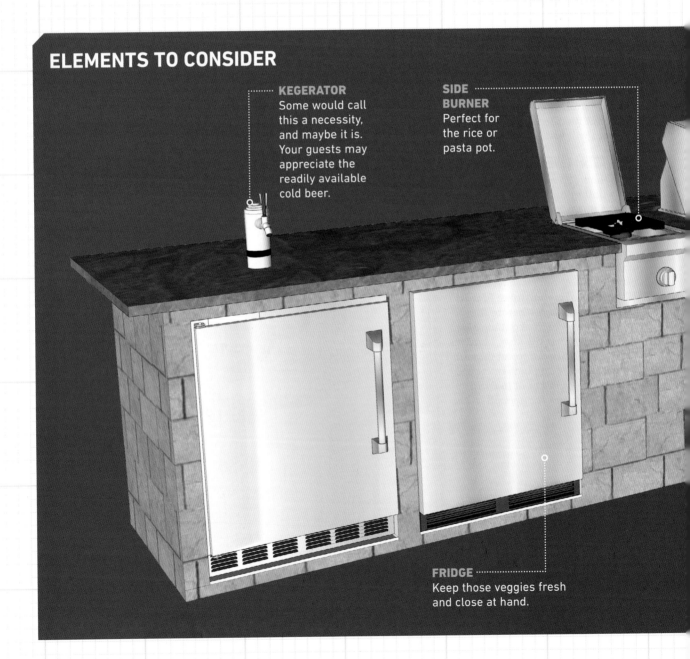

KEGERATOR
Some would call this a necessity, and maybe it is. Your guests may appreciate the readily available cold beer.

SIDE BURNER
Perfect for the rice or pasta pot.

FRIDGE
Keep those veggies fresh and close at hand.

COUNTERTOP OPTIONS

■ **WOOD.** While beautiful, wood is probably the worst choice for outdoor countertops. It will require yearly upkeep—best to just avoid this one.

■ **CEMENT.** Making your own cement countertop is a ton of fun, but it's a heavyweight project. If done right, cement can produce a long-lasting, beautiful countertop. If done poorly, it can crack, crumble and deteriorate within a single season.

■ **NATURAL STONE.** Natural stone is by far the most durable and longest-lasting outdoor counter-top choice, and this is what we chose. I thought I could find a stone countertop remnant and cut it myself, but the process isn't as DIY-friendly as I first thought. It's risky and messy, and it creates hazardous dust. Instead, I gave my SketchUp file to the artisans at *StoneSourceUSA.com*, picked out a beautiful piece of granite and had them cut it for me.

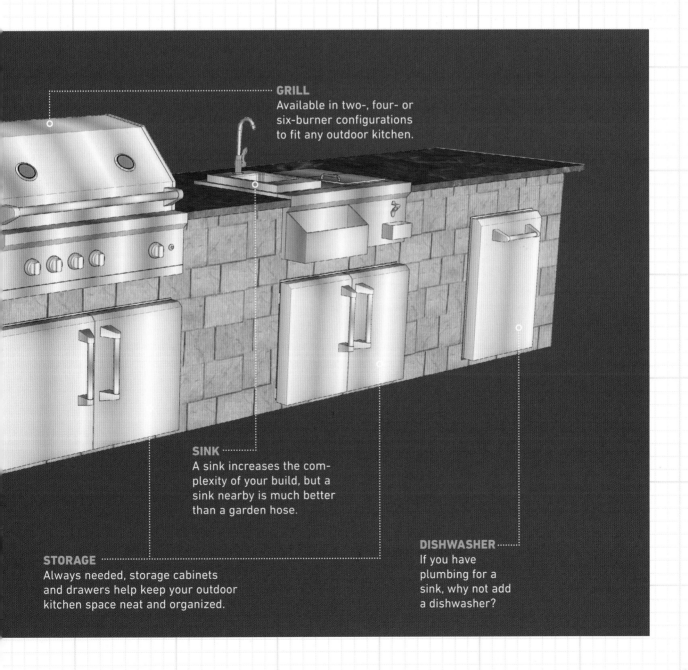

GRILL
Available in two-, four- or six-burner configurations to fit any outdoor kitchen.

SINK
A sink increases the complexity of your build, but a sink nearby is much better than a garden hose.

STORAGE
Always needed, storage cabinets and drawers help keep your outdoor kitchen space neat and organized.

DISHWASHER
If you have plumbing for a sink, why not add a dishwasher?

BY MIKE BERNER

FRONT ENTRY BUILD-OUT

TAKE A BASIC FACADE TO THE NEXT LEVEL—ADD A ROOF OVER THE ENTRYWAY

Many of the houses in my neighborhood feature a plain entryway stoop with two or three steps. Kinda boring—not to mention impractical! I'll drive by and see homeowners carrying bags of groceries, getting soaked in the rain as they struggle to open the front door with nowhere to set the bags. A covered entryway would keep these folks dry and add a shady place to sit on summer afternoons. When designed and built right, this covered, comfy entry will lift a home's curb appeal through the roof!

AFTER

BEFORE

MEET THE DESIGNER

MIKE BERNER, AN EDITOR AT *FAMILY HANDYMAN*, LOATHES UNCOVERED CONCRETE STOOPS.

THE FOUNDATION

Begin construction by installing the support system for the roof. This includes footings, posts and beams to carry the entire structure.

4

3

BRACE POSTS

1

1 POUR THE FOOTINGS

Determine the depth and width of the entryway roof and mark the corners. We designed this one to be 16 ft. wide and 10 ft. deep. The front is cantilevered past the posts by 2 ft., so the footings are placed 8 ft. away and parallel with the front of the house. The region where you live will determine the depth and diameter of these footings.

2 RAISE AND BRACE THE POSTS

Once the concrete footings have cured, fasten 6x6 post bases with correctly sized wedge anchors. (The diameter of the anchor is determined by the manufacturer of the post base, and the length is determined by local building code.) Then position the posts in the bases and brace them in opposite directions with 2x4s. Drive stakes into the ground and adjust the posts so they're plumb, then fasten the braces to the stakes.

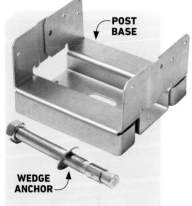

POST BASE

WEDGE ANCHOR

Post bases secure a post to a poured concrete footing, and they keep the post off the ground to help prevent rot.

3 CUT AWAY THE SIDING

On each side, place another post inside the exterior wall. You can do this from inside or outside the house. The advantage of doing it from inside is you can easily and inexpensively patch drywall. From the outside, it's more difficult to patch siding, but it's easier to position each post and beam. In either case, when you cut into the wall cavity, find the stud bay and cut down the middle of the studs. This will leave you with enough space on the stud to fasten the sheathing or drywall patch. If you're able to remove the siding instead of cutting through it, you won't have to worry about patching it or buying replacement siding.

4 ADD BEAM SUPPORT

Each beam support consists of 2-by lumber to match the framing of the existing wall (2x4 or 2x6). Each beam support will also be the same number of plies as the beam you're installing. This design called for three-ply beams, so we needed three-ply supports. To determine the length of the supports, subtract the height of a beam from the height of the studs in the wall. Align each support inside the wall so that the line between the post and the support is perpendicular to the house.

5 PLACE THE BEAM

Install each beam in one of two ways: Either build it on a pair of sawhorses and lift it into place, or build it in place on the posts. Glue and nail the plies of each beam together, making sure the tops and bottoms are flush, and then use post-beam connectors to secure it to the posts. Before installing rafters, add a fascia board to the outside of each beam.

Secure the beam to the post using specific post-beam connectors.

ROOF STRUCTURE

For the second phase of the project, build the roof support structure, including the rafter ledger against the house, the gable rafters and the ridge beam. Match the pitch of the existing roofline—the cuts in the rafters are specific to that pitch.

RIDGE BEAM

9

7

BRACE THE
GABLE TO THE
LEDGER
(TEMPORARY)

GABLE
BRACES
(TEMPORARY)

8

6

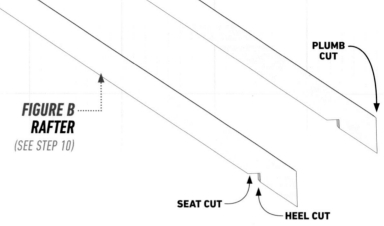

PLUMB CUT

RIDGE BEAM NOTCH

FIGURE A GABLE/LEDGER

PLUMB CUT

FIGURE B RAFTER
(SEE STEP 10)

SEAT CUT

HEEL CUT

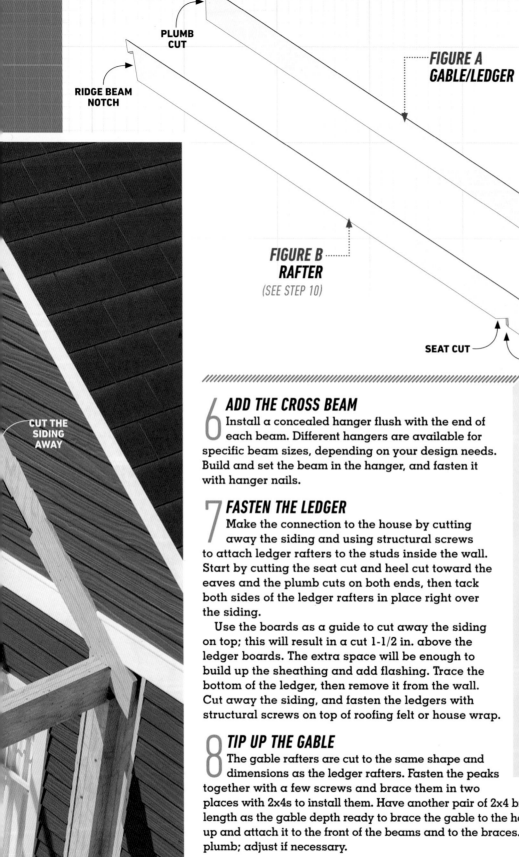

CUT THE SIDING AWAY

6 ADD THE CROSS BEAM

Install a concealed hanger flush with the end of each beam. Different hangers are available for specific beam sizes, depending on your design needs. Build and set the beam in the hanger, and fasten it with hanger nails.

7 FASTEN THE LEDGER

Make the connection to the house by cutting away the siding and using structural screws to attach ledger rafters to the studs inside the wall. Start by cutting the seat cut and heel cut toward the eaves and the plumb cuts on both ends, then tack both sides of the ledger rafters in place right over the siding.

Use the boards as a guide to cut away the siding on top; this will result in a cut 1-1/2 in. above the ledger boards. The extra space will be enough to build up the sheathing and add flashing. Trace the bottom of the ledger, then remove it from the wall. Cut away the siding, and fasten the ledgers with structural screws on top of roofing felt or house wrap.

8 TIP UP THE GABLE

The gable rafters are cut to the same shape and dimensions as the ledger rafters. Fasten the peaks together with a few screws and brace them in two places with 2x4s to install them. Have another pair of 2x4 braces cut to the same length as the gable depth ready to brace the gable to the house. Then tip the gable up and attach it to the front of the beams and to the braces. Check the gable for plumb; adjust if necessary.

9 DROP IN THE RIDGE BEAM

Build the ridge beam, then add a hanger to the peak of the ledger rafters and gable rafters. Then drop the beam into place and nail it through the hangers using the nails called for by the hanger manufacturer.

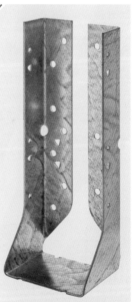

Concealed hangers keep the cross beam flush to the ends of the beams—there's no need to deal with flanges.

ADD THE RAFTERS

To finish the roof structure, make rafters by cutting two standard 2x6 or 2x8 boards. You could purchase prebuilt trusses for your project, but making your own is less expensive, and you won't have to wait for a months-long manufacturing process.

HURRICANE CLIP

There are several ways to secure rafters to their bearing points, but the easiest is to nail a hurricane clip to the ledger that the rafter is resting on and to the rafter.

10 CUT AND INSTALL THE RAFTERS

To mark the bird's-mouths and the plumb cuts at the peak and eave consistently, use one of the cut rafters as a template. Note that the bird's-mouth cannot be cut more than a fourth the width of the rafter. When the rafters are cut, space them 16 in. on-center from the house at the peak and at the eave, and then fasten them into place.

11 ADD RAFTER SUPPORTS

To support the fronts of the ridge beam and rafters, add vertical support from the cross beam to the ridge beam and gable rafters. To support the gable rafters, add a double layer of 2x6s in the center, cutting them to fit. They will help hold up the front of the structure and are decorative as well.

Install the roof sheathing to complete the structure of the entryway. Then protect it from the weather with water-resistant layers that shed water off the roof.

STEP FLASHING

TUCK WRB BEHIND SIDING

KICKOUT FLASHING

SHINGLES

ROOFING FELT

ICE-AND-WATER

SHEATHING

12

13

12 STAGGER THE SHEATHING

Lay the plywood or OSB on the rafters starting at the bottom, arranging the sheets so any seams meet with factory edges in the center of a rafter. Lay the first sheet in each course past the gable; you'll trim this later and then cut the next sheet to fit. Fasten the sheathing with ring shank framing nails and make sure the seams are staggered on different rafters. Continue attaching the sheathing through the top course, which will be cut to width.

13 WATER-RESISTANT BARRIER

The water-resistant barrier (WRB) starts with an ice-and-water shield—a self-adhered membrane applied along the eaves. Then comes a layer of roofing felt starting at the eaves and overlapping all the way to the peak. Next are the flashing and shingles. Start with kickout flashing at the eave, then add a few layers of step flashing, followed by the starter course of shingles. Overlap the shingles, alternating between shingles and step flashing where the roof meets the house. Make sure the shingle and flashing layers shed rainwater to the next layer on its way off the roof. Cover the peak with ridge cap shingles.

The final phase is to polish the look of the porch with trim and tongue-and-groove boards to hide the construction lumber.

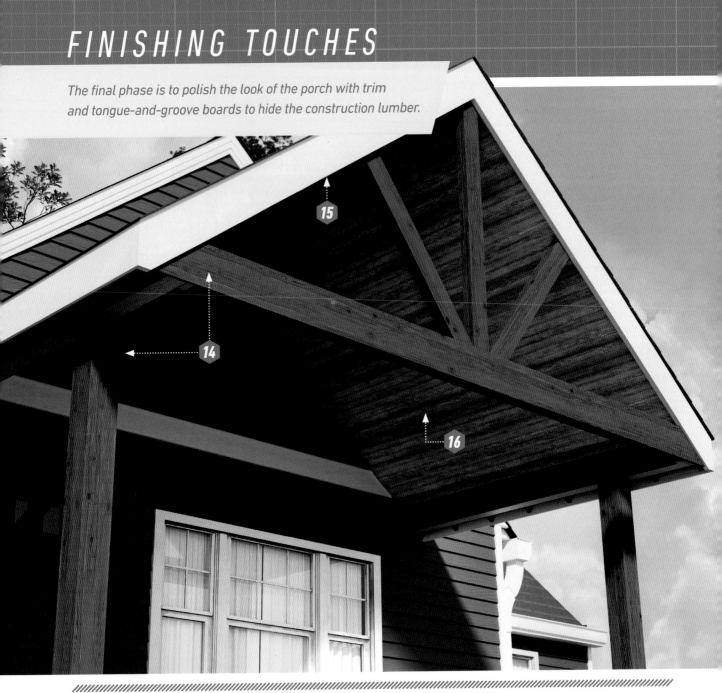

14 WRAP THE POSTS AND BEAMS

To complete the look, trim the beams and posts. Choose cedar or sealed wood for rot resistance, or use maintenance-free composite material. To cover the beams, cut boards to fit their width and fasten the boards to the bottoms, then cover the sides the same way. For each post, cut two boards to fit the width and then two more to cover the rest.

15 ADD FASCIA BOARD

Hide the rafter tails with fascia board that's 1 in. wider than their height. Cover the gable rafters on the front the same way you wrapped the beams. The miter at the peak matches the plumb in the rafters; fit the miter together and tack up the boards temporarily to mark where to cut the ends. Cut the ends and install the rest of the fascia.

16 INSTALL TONGUE-AND-GROOVE CEILING BOARDS

The final step is to install the tongue-and-groove boards for the ceiling. Tuck the first course into the beams on each side and work your way to the ridge. You can bring both sides into the peak, but it's easier to fasten a flat board to the ridge and cut the final pieces of the sides to fit.

GREAT GOOFS®

fh LAUGHS AND LESSONS FROM OUR READERS

SOUTHERN SNOW REMOVAL

As a southern girl, I didn't have much experience with snow removal. So when I moved north and got married, I decided it was high time I learned. One snowy morning, I told my husband I wanted to learn how to snow blow. We went outside, and he showed me how to move the blower side to side and make turns. He made one pass to get me started and then went back to shoveling. I eagerly got behind the blower and started down the driveway. It was a lot harder than I expected, and it took everything in me to get down to the end of the driveway. On the way back, I was nearing exhaustion and sweating up a storm. I kept wondering why it looked easy when my husband did it. When I FINALLY reached the top, my husband was waiting for me. "What the heck am I doing wrong?" I asked him. "Old people can do this!" My husband just smiled and put it in gear; then the thing took off on its own. I didn't know I had to engage the self-propel lever.

CARRIE WILKINSON

WOOD VIBRATIONS

I love my portable planer. I feed rough, ugly boards in, and beautiful boards come out. But until recently, I had never clamped it to my worktable. I'd just reposition it as it vibrated around the table. My technique changed last week when I fed in a 6-ft. board and turned around to grab the next board.

While my back was turned, the exiting board caught the planer's power cord. As the board exited the planer, the cord stayed taut and the planer pushed itself to the edge of the table. I turned around just in time to watch the planer tip over the edge, fall to the floor and keep right on planing while upside down. I still love my planer, but now it gets clamped!

KEN SCHARPENBERG

5 OUTDOOR STRUCTURES, LANDSCAPING & GARDENING

FLOOR COATINGS: WHAT'S RIGHT FOR YOUR GARAGE?

BY GLENN HANSEN

Many homeowners use garage space as an extension of indoor living space; the garage is a workshop, laundry room or recreation area. An uncoated concrete floor is an unattractive option if you spend significant time in your garage. Coat the floor and you increase its durability, make it easier to clean and improve the look as well as a home's resale value.

Epoxy is an increasingly popular floor-coating method for garages nationwide. It's a DIY option, though a plethora of coating professionals are available for affordable installation. We've been asked about polyaspartic floor coating, and whether it's a better option than the ubiquitous epoxy coating. The short answer? Yes.

WHAT IS POLYASPARTIC?

Polyaspartic coatings have been available for about 20 years but are only recently gaining ground in garages. The product is typically used on bridges and piers, or to coat parts of ships or railcars. It's similar to polyurethane, though a polyaspartic cures faster than both urethanes and epoxies and it can be applied in a wide range of temperatures.

When shopping for a polyaspartic coating, consumers could easily confuse polyureas and polyaspartics; they're related but different. Chemical differences make polyaspartics more versatile, more durable and easier to apply on your garage floor. Although polyurea coatings are also durable, they have a short cure time, which makes them quite difficult to install, especially for DIYers.

Polyaspartic coatings cure more quickly than epoxy, but slowly enough that you can work with them. By manipulating the mixture of esters, polyaspartics manufacturers have made products with a cure time that's slow enough for easy application and fast enough to quickly allow floor traffic. A polyaspartic-coated floor can cure and be ready for foot traffic in two hours and vehicle traffic in 24. In comparison, an epoxy-finish floor needs 12 or more hours of cure time before foot traffic and 72 hours before vehicle traffic.

That's all good, so is there a catch? Polyaspartic finishes do cost about 20% more than epoxies. Some companies sell polyaspartics by the gallon; Sherwin-Williams' Elladur Floor Coating is part of its Industrial product line.

More resistant to UV exposure, polyaspartic coatings hold color better than epoxy coatings and will not yellow. They also resist marking from hot car tires, making them well suited to garage use.

With a viscosity closer to water than paint, polyaspartic coatings can be a topcoat over epoxy. Versatile Building Products markets two-part kits through *GarageCoatings.com* that can be poured over a flaked epoxy floor.

EPOXY	POLYASPARTIC
12 to 72 hours cure time	2 to 24 hours cure time
$4 to $10 per sq. ft.	$8 and up per sq. ft.
$50 to $100 per gallon	$70 to $125 per gallon
55° F install temperature (low limit)	-20° F install temperature (low limit)

This lockable Husky steel garage gear cabinet is available at Home Depot.

STORING PESTICIDES SAFELY

If you use home and garden pesticides for weed and pest control, here's what you need to know to store them safely. It may seem like a lot of rules, but these products pose significant risks.

Included in this category are products for repelling and eliminating pests, weed killers, nitrogen stabilizers and other plant regulators. If you're unsure about a product, check the label for signal words like *danger, poison, warning* and *caution*, and for the presence of an EPA registration number.

Proper storage prolongs the chemical shelf life of a product and—more importantly—it protects the health of people, animals and the environment. Here are some general storage requirements, but refer to your pesticide labels for specific information about the products you've purchased.

■ The EPA recommends keeping pesticides in a locked cabinet in a well-ventilated utility area or garden shed. They should not be stored with or near food, animal feed or medical supplies.

■ Store in original containers with the labels so you'll have the directions, ingredients and first aid steps in case of poisoning. Keep the tops tightly closed. Never store pesticides in the application equipment, where they are more likely to spill and to be accessed by children.

■ Keep out of reach of children and pets. These products should be 5 ft. above the ground in that locked (preferably metal) cabinet.

■ Locate your cabinet where there is no chance of flooding and where pesticides will not leak or spill into a floor drain. From there, they would enter the sewer and cause toxic pollution.

■ The temperature in the storage area should not get below 40 degrees or over 100 degrees F. Very high or low temps can cause a pesticide to deteriorate and become ineffective. High humidity and direct sunlight will also cause pesticides to break down. Cool and dry is the goal.

■ Flammable liquids should be stored outside your living area and far away from an ignition source such as a furnace, car, grill or lawn mower.

■ Keep emergency numbers near your storage area and/or on your phone. The National Poison Center number is 800-222-1222.

■ When you need to throw away chemicals, follow the instructions on the labels. Empty pesticide containers should not simply be thrown into the trash or recycling bin. Thoroughly rinse them before disposal, and the diluted rinse water should be disposed of by applying it to the same areas you sprayed. If you have unwanted leftover pesticide, drop it off with a local program; search online for "household hazardous waste disposal near me."

■ Don't buy more pesticide than you will need soon—think in terms of what you'll need for one year or less to avoid the need to store it. To help prevent stocking up, keep your storage cabinet as small as possible.

■ Finally, and best of all, choose nontoxic alternatives whenever you can.

DONNA BIERBACH *SENIOR EDITOR*

BOOKS TO SHARE

**JOIN US BY BUILDING
A LITTLE FREE LIBRARY
IN YOUR FRONT YARD**

Little Free Library®
Pequeña Biblioteca Gratuita
Take a Book • Share a Book
Toma un Libro • Deja un Libro

BY JAY CORK

WHAT IT TAKES

TIME	COST	SKILL LEVEL
2 days	$600*	Intermediate

TOOLS
Table saw, router, cordless drill, basic carpentry tools

*Save $400 by using cedar shingles instead of copper, and painted pine instead of mahogany.

've wanted to make a Little Free Library for a long time. It's a fun project that will help a neighborhood strengthen its sense of community by bringing people together through sharing books. The whole family can enjoy this weekend project, and the whole neighborhood will appreciate it. This is our first Community Project. We hope you'll build one, too, and share the results with us.

GET STARTED

1 FINISH THE POST
I cut the 4x4 cedar post to 60 in., which leaves enough to cut the angled braces after I finish the post. Sand the post to 180 grit to prevent splinters. Apply a coat of epoxy finish to the entire post and set it aside to dry. This will seal the wood against the weather above ground and against rot below ground.

2 FIT THE BASE FOR THE POST
I attached the angled braces to the post using 3-in. coated screws. Center the post on the base (B) and mark its position. Use that as a guide to predrill and countersink holes for the mounting screws.

3 CUT THE PARTS
After gluing up the panels, cut them to size on a table saw. I used a track saw to accurately cut the angles for the roof parts. You can achieve a similar result using a circular saw with an edge guide.

PRO TIP
Keep your countersinks shallow. This keeps the screws from digging too deep.

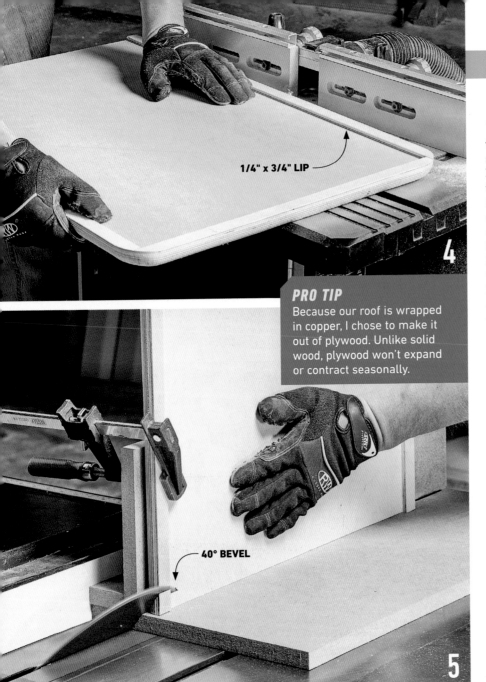

1/4" x 3/4" LIP

PRO TIP
Because our roof is wrapped in copper, I chose to make it out of plywood. Unlike solid wood, plywood won't expand or contract seasonally.

40° BEVEL

5

1/8" NAP GLUE ROLLER

6A

SEALED WITH OIL-BASED PAINT

6B

MAKE THE ROOF

4 PROFILE THE EDGES

I chose to give the roof a round-over profile. To do this, glue 1/4-in. stock around the bottom edges of the roof panels (F). Once they're dry, profile the edges with a 3/4-in. round-over bit. You can do this with a hand-held router, but a router table would be better.

3/4" ROUND-OVER BIT

5 CUT THE PEAK JOINT

After you rout the edge profiles, bevel the peak edges of both pieces at 40 degrees using a table saw. I made a simple jig to help hold the part safely.

6 APPLY THE COPPER

Roughen the copper and plywood with 80-grit sandpaper, and apply contact cement with a glue roller. I chose Weldwood original formula ($15 per qt.). After both surfaces tack up, lay half of the roof down on the copper sheet. Lay the other half down starting at the peak. Wrap the soffit, and trim the excess copper.

PRO TIP
Seal the underside of the roof. I used black oil-based paint, but you can use the same spar varnish used on the rest of the project.

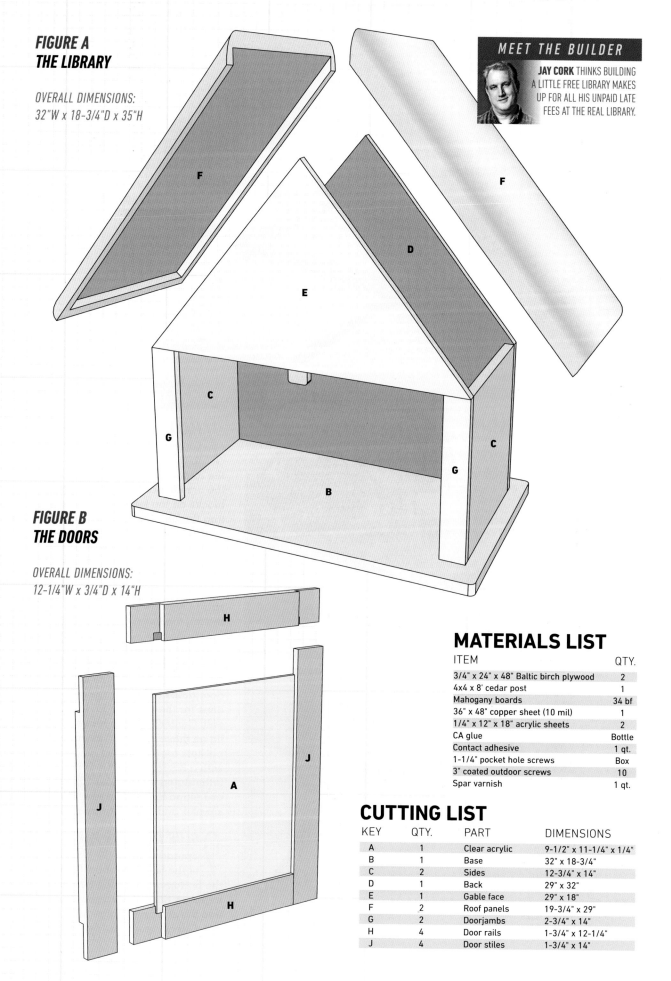

FIGURE A
THE LIBRARY

OVERALL DIMENSIONS:
32"W x 18-3/4"D x 35"H

F

F

D

E

C

G

C

G

B

FIGURE B
THE DOORS

OVERALL DIMENSIONS:
12-1/4"W x 3/4"D x 14"H

H

J

J

J

A

H

MATERIALS LIST

ITEM	QTY.
3/4" x 24" x 48" Baltic birch plywood	2
4x4 x 8' cedar post	1
Mahogany boards	34 bf
36" x 48" copper sheet (10 mil)	1
1/4" x 12" x 18" acrylic sheets	2
CA glue	Bottle
Contact adhesive	1 qt.
1-1/4" pocket hole screws	Box
3" coated outdoor screws	10
Spar varnish	1 qt.

CUTTING LIST

KEY	QTY.	PART	DIMENSIONS
A	1	Clear acrylic	9-1/2" x 11-1/4" x 1/4"
B	1	Base	32" x 18-3/4"
C	2	Sides	12-3/4" x 14"
D	1	Back	29" x 32"
E	1	Gable face	29" x 18"
F	2	Roof panels	19-3/4" x 29"
G	2	Doorjambs	2-3/4" x 14"
H	4	Door rails	1-3/4" x 12-1/4"
J	4	Door stiles	1-3/4" x 14"

7

MAKE THE DOORS

7 MAKE THE DOOR PARTS

Cut the rails (H) and stiles (J) to size. I used a 1/4-in. bit on the router table to cut the slot for the acrylic pane (A). Place stop blocks on the fence to avoid cutting through the ends. A half-lap joint is strong and easy to make on the table saw. I used a basic table saw sled to make these cuts, but a miter slider will work too. Cut the acrylic panes on the table saw in shallow passes. Don't cut the full thickness all at once.

SELF-CENTERING BIT

8

8 ROUT THE HINGE MORTISE

On the edges of the stiles and doorjambs (G), mark the center lines for the hinges 3 in. from each end. Center the Soss hinge router jig on these lines and mortise the pockets for the hidden hinges with a 3/8-in. router bit. If you're intimidated by the Soss hinges, use piano hinges instead. They're simpler and don't require routing.

1/4" SLOT

CHEEK

SPRING CLAMPS

9

9 GLUE THE DOOR PARTS

Spread glue on the cheeks of the half lap joints. Clamp the bottom rail and the two stiles together. Slide the acrylic pane into the slot and clamp on the top rail. Check for square before the glue sets.

10 PUT UP THE WALLS

I assembled the library using pocket hole joinery and stainless steel screws. Start with the back (D) and then attach the sides (C). After attaching the doorjambs on the front of each side, I attached the triangular gable face (E). I used CA glue to hold it in place, then secured it with screws from the inside.

11 ATTACH THE ROOF

With a helper, carefully lay one side of the roof down on the library. Gently lower the other side, taking care to not damage the copper on the roof peak. Attach the roof with pocket hole screws from the inside while making sure the soffit reveal remains even all the way around.

12 INSTALL THE DOORS

I made the doors a little wider than they needed to be, knowing once everything was assembled, I could trim them for a perfect fit. With the doors attached to the jambs, find the center on the gable and mark it on a bit of tape. Transfer this mark to the doors and trim them on the table saw. Reattach them and check the fit. I used a small magnetic catch to help keep the doors shut.

10

1-1/2" SETBACK

1-1/4" POCKET SCREWS

GABLE FACE

11

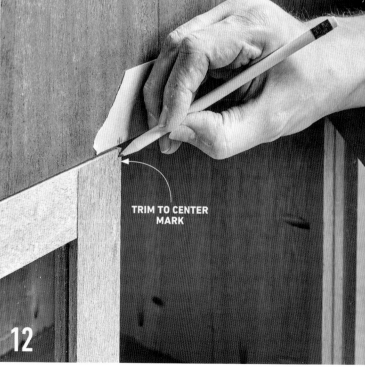

TRIM TO CENTER MARK

12

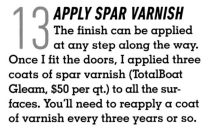

TAPE OFF THE ACRYLIC

13

13 APPLY SPAR VARNISH

The finish can be applied at any step along the way. Once I fit the doors, I applied three coats of spar varnish (TotalBoat Gleam, $50 per qt.) to all the surfaces. You'll need to reapply a coat of varnish every three years or so.

14 HAMMER THE COPPER ROOF

I chose to give this copper roof a hammered look. This is optional but well worth the hours and the sore hands—it looks amazing! You could buy hammered sheets, but they're even more expensive. Save money and DIY!

15 ATTACH TO THE POST

Once the post is secure in the ground, place the Little Free Library on top. I used 3-in. coated screws in the holes I had predrilled earlier. Now it's time for the big reveal: Register your library, fill it with books and call your neighbors!

14

MAGNETIC CATCHES

3" EXTERIOR SCREWS

15

PLANTING THE POST

You have a few options for planting the post for your Little Free Library. You can get a posthole digger and plant the post with cement or foam, but you don't have to dig a hole if you don't want to—post anchors go into the ground with no digging. I like the screw type—if I need to move this library, I can just unscrew it! Always call 811 before digging, even if you're just using a post anchor.

BUY THE PLAQUE
WHEN YOU REGISTER

Little Free Library
Pequeña Biblioteca Gratuita
Take a Book • Share a Book
Toma un Libro • Deja un Libro

Download
the app to see
the map of all the
Little Free Libraries
in your area.

ABOUT THE LITTLE FREE LIBRARY ASSOCIATION

Back in 2009, Todd Bol made a small model of a one-room schoolhouse. He placed it on top of a post in his front yard in Hudson, Wisconsin, and filled it with books. He encouraged neighbors to "take a book or leave a book," and they did. Word quickly spread of the Little Free Library, and in about three years, Bol and his nonprofit partner, Rick Brooks, knew of more than 2,500 such libraries.

Today, the nonprofit organization recognizes more than 100,000 registered libraries in more than 100 countries around the world. The group's mission is to build strong communities by expanding book access in public places around the world.

As a reader, I love finding one of these little book shelters and peeking inside to find my next literary escape. As a woodworker, I jumped at the chance to design and build one.

The editors of *Family Handyman* invite you to build a Little Free Library. You can use our design or create your own. It's a fun project, and we'd love to see photos of your completed library. Send them to **editors @thefamily handyman.com**.

You can also order a kit from *littlefreelibrary.org*. There are many models to choose from, and prices start at $160. The kits include automatic registration; if you create your own, don't forget to register it. When you do, your library will be included on the Little Free Library map and discoverable in the mobile app.

Whether you build a library or not, consider donating to the nonprofit. Ten bucks can go a long way to help place libraries where they're needed most!

BUILD A
GREENHOUSE

EXTEND YOUR GROWING SEASON BY MONTHS!

Here in the Upper Midwest, the gardening season is short, typically May through September. By building a greenhouse, we can harness the sun's rays to let plants thrive as early as March and extend harvest into late fall. A greenhouse is also a great place to store less hardy plants during harsh winters. Even if you live in a more temperate region, a greenhouse will create a perfect climate for plants, protecting them from temperature swings, storms and pests.

We built our greenhouse from cedar, which weathers beautifully, and polycarbonate sheets, which diffuse the sunlight and give even exposure to all the plants.

BY MIKE BERNER

KEITH AND RENEE JOHNSON
live on a picturesque plot of land amid rolling hills in rural Wisconsin. They have run a small hobby farm for about 30 years and have always wanted a greenhouse. *Family Handyman* teamed up with them to build this greenhouse so they could start seedlings for their garden just a few steps away.

WHAT IT TAKES

TIME	COST	SKILL LEVEL
About a week	$8,000 to $10,000	Intermediate

TOOLS
Circular saw, miter saw, table saw, reciprocating saw, impact driver, drill/driver, hammer drill, framing nailer, compressor, level, sawhorses, basic hand tools

MEET THE BUILDER

MIKE BERNER ENJOYS WRAPPING HIS HEAD AROUND PROJECTS OF ALL SIZES AND HELPING PEOPLE BUILD COOL STUFF.

SECURE THE SEAMS

LANDSCAPE TIMBER RETAINING WALL

1

1 BUILD THE FOUNDATION

We removed 8 in. of topsoil to make room for our base layer of rock. We leveled and compacted the dirt, rolled out heavy-duty landscape fabric, then added at least a 2-in. layer of 3/4-in. limestone. Next we created a mini retaining wall using landscaping timbers. We placed, leveled and squared three sides of the retaining wall, leaving the fourth side off until most of the rock was dumped.

We secured the timbers at the corners with 8-in. timber screws and fastened a pressure-treated board to keep the timbers together at the seams. When most of the rock was dumped and evenly spread, we built the fourth side. Then we leveled off and compacted the rock with a tamper.

BRACE EACH CORNER PLUMB

16" ON-CENTER

DOUBLE BOTTOM PLATE

2

2 BUILD THE SIDE AND BACK WALLS

To build the walls, we used pressure-treated 2x4s for bottom plates and cedar 2x4s for top plates. We cut them to the length of each wall and marked the stud layout on them. Because the studs will be visible inside and outside, we wanted the walls to be symmetrical, so we found the center of the wall and marked the studs every 16 in. on-center from there. We nailed the cedar 2x4 studs through the plates and then fastened a second bottom plate. After tipping up each wall, we kept it plumb with braces at each corner and nailed the corners together, making sure the top plates were flush on top.

LEAVE OUT CENTER STUDS

3

3 FRAME THE FRONT WALL

Since the walls are only 6 ft. tall and the door is taller than that, we didn't frame its rough opening during this step. We wanted all the walls tied together while the rest of the structure gets built, so we built the wall all the way across, leaving out the center studs where the door will eventually be framed. We tipped this wall up, braced it plumb and nailed it to the side walls.

FIGURE A GREENHOUSE

OVERALL DIMENSIONS:
10' W x 14' D x 12' H

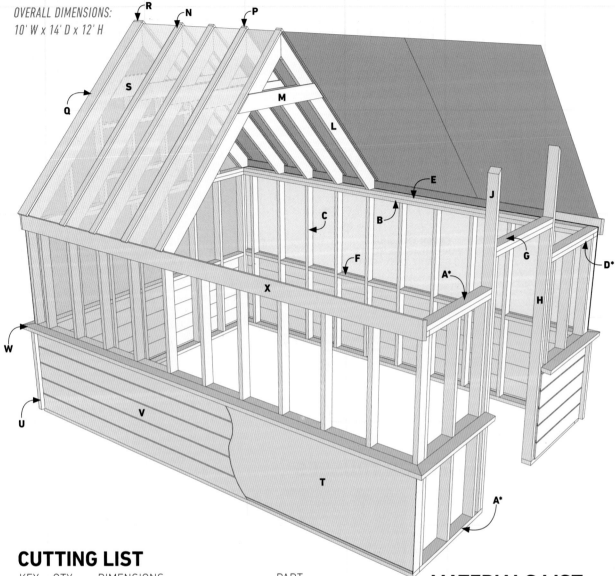

CUTTING LIST

KEY	QTY.	DIMENSIONS	PART
A	4	1-1/2" x 3-1/2" x 9' 5"*	Front/back wall top/bottom plates
B	4	1-1/2" x 3-1/2" x 14'	Side wall top/bottom plates
C	40	1-1/2" x 3-1/2" x 5' 9"	Wall studs
D	2	1-1/2" x 3-1/2" x 10'*	Front/back wall, second top plate
E	2	1-1/2" x 3-1/2" x 13' 5"	Side wall, second top plate
F	35	1-1/2" x 3-1/2" x cut to fit	Wall/sill blocking
G	2	1-1/2" x 3-1/2" x 3' 3-1/4"	Door header for 36" door
H	2	1-1/2" x 3-1/2" x 6' 8-3/4"	Door trimmer stud
J	2	1-1/2" x 3-1/2" x cut to fit	Door king stud
K	12	1-1/2" x 3-1/2" x cut to fit	Gable cripples (Figure C)
L	28	1-1/2" x 5-1/2" x 6' 7-1/2" (short edge)	Rafter
M	10	3/4" x 5-1/2" x 3' 11-1/2" (point to point)	Collar tie
N	10	3/4" x 3-1/2" x 7' 3"	Batten, short side
P	10	3/4" x 3-1/2" x 7' 3-3/4"	Batten, overlap
Q	2	3/4" x 5-1/2" x 7' 3"	Gable batten, short side
R	2	3/4" x 5-1/2" x 7' 3-3/4"	Gable batten, overlap
S	4	1-1/2" x 5-1/2" x 2' 7" (point to point)	Gable collar tie
T	7	7/16" x 32" x cut to fit studs	Sheathing
U	8	1-1/2" x 1-1/2" x 32"	2x4 corner trim
V	30	9/16" x 7-1/4" x cut to fit	Cedar lap siding
W	4	1-1/2" x 3-1/2" x cut to fit	2x4 cedar sill
X	2	3/4" x 5-1/2" x cut to fit	Cedar fascia
Y	4	3/4" x 5-1/2" x cut to fit	Cedar frieze board (Figure C)
Z	8	3/4" x 3-1/2" x cut to fit	Cedar corner trim (Photo 18)

*(The front wall plates will be cut to frame the door opening)

MATERIALS LIST

ITEM	QTY.
5"x5" x 8' ground-contact timbers	8
Cedar 2x4 x 14'	6
Cedar 2x4 x 10'	6
Cedar 2x4 x 8'	55
Pressure-treated 2x4 x 14'	2
Pressure-treated 2x4 x 110'	2
2x4 x 12' framing lumber (bracing)	8
Cedar 2x6 x 8'	26
Cedar 1x4 x 8'	20
Cedar 1x6 x 8'	8
Cedar 1x6 x 16'	2
11/16" x 8' x 14' cedar bevel siding	12
11/16" x 8' x 12' cedar bevel siding	12
7/16" x 4' x 8' weather barrier sheathing	7
8mm x 4' x 8' polycarbonate sheets	14
10' polycarbonate ridge cap	2
No. 9 3" construction screws	
2" stainless steel rubber gasket roofing screws	
3" framing nails	
No. 9 2-1/2" construction screws	
2" stainless steel ring-shank siding nails	
Butyl sealant tape	
Wooden screen door	

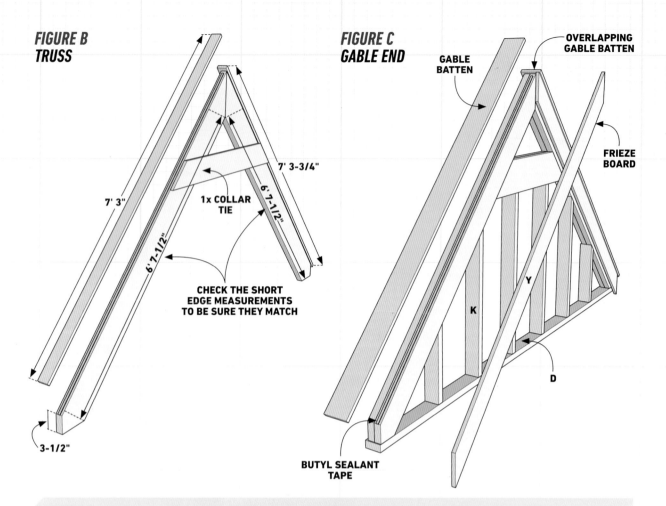

**FIGURE B
TRUSS**

7' 3"

7' 3-3/4"

6' 7-1/2"

6' 7-1/2"

1x COLLAR TIE

**CHECK THE SHORT
EDGE MEASUREMENTS
TO BE SURE THEY MATCH**

3-1/2"

**FIGURE C
GABLE END**

GABLE BATTEN

**OVERLAPPING
GABLE BATTEN**

**FRIEZE
BOARD**

Y

K

D

**BUTYL SEALANT
TAPE**

MAKE A TEMPLATE FOR TRUSSES

**MARK RAFTERS
ALONG TEMPLATE**

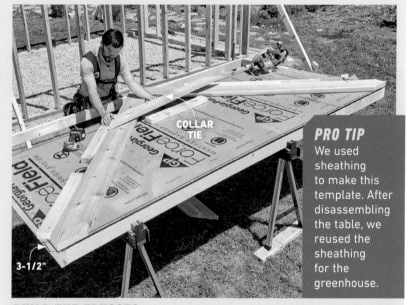

**COLLAR
TIE**

3-1/2"

REPEAT PARTS WITH A TEMPLATE

Make a template to accurately cut the rafters and assemble the trusses to ensure they're all identical. We built a simple 2x4 frame on a pair of sawhorses and fastened a piece of sheathing to the top. Be sure to build the frame to the exact span of the walls, then draw a line up from the center point to locate the ridge miter. We fastened a block 3-1/2 in. up from the corner on each side of the template at a 45-degree angle. With this setup, we could accurately mark and make all the necessary cuts before assembly.

PRO TIP
We used sheathing to make this template. After disassembling the table, we reused the sheathing for the greenhouse.

BUILD THE TRUSSES

After making the cuts, place the parts of the truss back on the template, line them up and fasten the peak together with a screw. Then cut and fasten 1x6 cedar collar ties. After determining the location of the collar tie, fasten another block to the template so you can repeat the location on the rest of the trusses.

DRIVING ROD

3" BULLET ANCHOR

QUICKVISE WASHER

CRIPPLE

TRUSS TEMPLATE

COLLAR TIE

4

SCRAP BLOCKS

FASTEN BRACE HERE

6

4 ANCHOR THE WALLS

To anchor the structure to the ground, we used bullet anchors by American Earth Anchor. After drilling holes in the bottom plates to fit the anchors through, we drove the anchors into the ground with a hammer drill outfitted with a driving rod. Then we pulled the cable through the Quickvise washer to set the anchor in the ground and hold the structure firmly in place.

5 ASSEMBLE GABLE WALLS

The gable walls on the front and the back of the greenhouse follow the same process as the trusses, with a few exceptions. First, the gable ends are doubled up. Second, the collar ties are cut from 2-by material and fit between the two rafters. Third, we added cripples to match the layout of the wall they will be sitting on. We used the same template to position the parts, then fastened the second top plate to the bottom of the trusses, and cut the collar tie and cripples to fit.

6 POSITION AND BRACE THE GABLE END

We lifted the gable end onto the walls. Before tipping it upright, we fastened a few scrap 2x4s to the back of the wall to prevent the gable from slipping off. We fastened a long board to the center cripple toward the top of the gable to use as a brace, pushed the gable upright and then braced it plumb. With it in place, we added a second top plate to the side walls where we'll rest the trusses.

USE BLOCKS FOR EVEN SPACING

KING STUD

TRIMMER STUD

DOOR HEADER

7 POSITION THE TRUSSES

When the gable end is plumb, braced and fastened to the wall below, it is time to set the rest of the trusses. First, precut cedar 2x4 blocks to match the spacing of each stud bay. Fasten the blocks to the gable 36 in. from the peak, tip up the next truss, fasten it to the blocks and then add the next blocks. Repeat this for each truss until all are attached. As we tipped up trusses, we checked that their tails lined up with the studs in the walls and toe-screwed them to the top plates.

8 CUT OUT THE DOOR OPENING

When the trusses are fixed to the walls, cut away the top plates and a bottom plate to frame the door. We marked out a 42-1/2-in. opening in the center of the front wall and cut it out to fit the 36-in. door and its framing. This left room for the framing and space for the door to swing open.

9 FRAME THE DOOR

Cut king studs to fit from the bottom plate to the gable truss, plumb and fasten them in place. To finish the framing, add trimmer studs cut to fit the height of the door and a header across the top. Because there is no doorjamb, these components must be perfectly plumb and level. Keep about 3/16-in. space at the sides and top, and about 3/8 in. at the bottom when the door is in place. Install the door temporarily to make sure it fits.

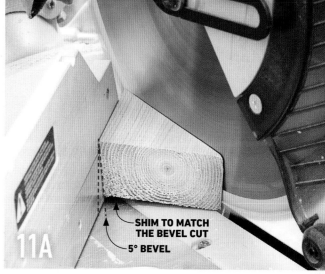

SHIM TO MATCH THE BEVEL CUT

5° BEVEL

10 SHEATHE THE BOTTOM

To install siding on the bottom half of the greenhouse, we added sheathing to the studs. The sheathing also adds rigidity to the entire structure. We ripped the sheets and nailed them to the studs with ring-shank framing nails, making sure all the seams landed on a stud. We kept the factory edge of the sheets up for easier leveling.

11 ADD THE SIDING SILL

Before adding the siding, we needed to cut and install a siding sill to keep water from getting behind it. We started by cutting a 5-degree angle on the edge of a 2x4 with the table saw, then we cut a miter at both ends to turn the sill around the corner. To get these miters to snug up at the corner, we matched the bevel cut with the miter saw. We marked the miters and set the back of the board on a shim to keep the beveled edge flat against the fence (11A). This trick makes it easy to make more precise compound cuts.

Once the miters were cut, we cut a 1/4-in.-deep kerf in the bottom of the sill about 1/2 in. from the outer face of the sill (11B). This kerf will keep water from wicking backward and getting behind the siding.

We fastened 2x4 blocks between the studs to attach the sill (11C). We set the sill on top of the plywood sheathing, flushing up the top of the blocks with the top of the sill. Then we fastened the blocks through the studs and the sill through the blocks.

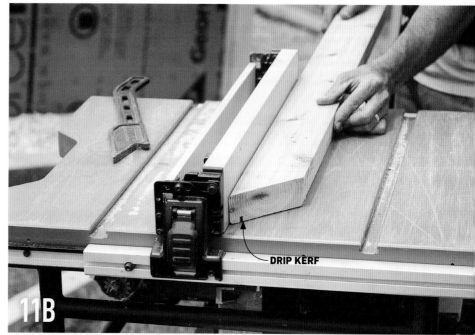

DRIP KERF

BLOCKS TO FASTEN THE SILL

CORNER TRIM

13

12

14

12 INSTALL CORNER TRIM

There are several ways to handle the corner detail of the siding. We chose an inverted corner trim that the siding butts into. We used leftover 2x4s ripped in half and nailed them to the corners. This makes cutting the siding right up to the trim a breeze and adds a unique look. We also didn't have to order thicker trim boards, spend time cutting angles into each piece of siding or install individual corner hardware for each course.

13 INSTALL SIDING

The corner trim makes the siding installation fast and easy. We recommend buying lap siding that's long enough to span an entire side, if available. Cut the siding to length and nail it to the studs using ring-shank nails compatible with cedar (some galvanized siding nails will leave a blue streak on the cedar when water passes over it). Each course of siding overlaps the next, leaving 6 in. of each course exposed.

14 FINISH SHEATHING THE WALLS

With the sill and siding finished, we started sheathing the rest of the greenhouse walls with polycarbonate sheets. We cut the sheets to length, made sure each seam landed on a stud and then used 2-in. stainless steel roofing screws to fasten the sheets.

CLAMP FOR EASY NAILING

15

BUTYL TAPE

16A

FASTEN BATTEN THROUGH THE POLYCARBONATE INTO THE RAFTER

16B

15 FASTEN THE FASCIA

Cut a piece of 1x6 cedar to fit beneath the edge of the roof. Fasten the fascia so that a straight-edge placed on the rafter contacts the top outer edge of the fascia. Drive nails into each truss and top plate.

16 MAKE A POLYCARBONATE SANDWICH

Apply a strip of butyl tape down the center of each truss (16A). This tape is very sticky, especially in hot weather! Cut the pieces of poly-carbonate to overhang the fascia by about 1-1/2 in. Double-check the truss layout to verify that the edge of each sheet will land on a truss, then set the sheets in place. The butyl tape sticks to the polycarbon-ate instantly, so be precise when laying each sheet down.

As you position the sheets, fasten a piece of cedar 1x4 over each truss with a 3-in. exterior construction screw (16B). Drive the screw through the butyl tape to seal the penetra-tions and secure the polycarbonate sheets. To be on the safe side, we added a second strip of butyl tape where two sheets met on one truss to make sure all the screw holes would be sealed.

17 TRIM THE ROOF

We trimmed the gable edges of the roof with 1x6 cedar. This batten needed to overhang the frieze board, so we positioned it 1 in. proud of the sheathing on the gable end. Then we installed cedar frieze boards to trim the peak. We cut two scraps of 1x6 at a 45-degree angle to check the fit at the peak and fastened one of them temporarily. We positioned the frieze board on one side, then removed the scrap to install the other side.

TEMPORARY SCRAP

FRIEZE BOARD

GABLE BATTEN

17

1x4 CORNER TRIM (Z)

18

POLYCARBONATE RIDGE CAP

19

20

18 ADD CORNER TRIM
Cut 1x4 cedar boards to fit between the sill and the fascia, and fasten them to fit around the corners using siding nails.

19 FASTEN THE RIDGE CAP
To finish the outside of the greenhouse, we covered the peak with a polycarbonate ridge cap. We lined up the ridge of the cap with the peak of the roof all the way down and fastened it through each batten into the trusses with 2-in. stainless steel roofing screws.

20 INSTALL THE SCREEN DOOR
We purchased a screen door from a home center to fit our door opening. We removed the screen and replaced it with a clear version of the polycarbonate we used on the rest of the greenhouse. Then we hung the door using 3-in. galvanized utility hinges. Finally, we installed a screen door closer and fence gate latch to keep it from blowing open in the wind.

BUILT-IN POTTING BENCH

1 START WITH A LEDGER

Fasten cedar 2x4s to the studs inside the greenhouse so the top of one 2x4 is 34 in. from the ground. Level it across and then fasten two more 2x4s to create the ends of the bench. Fasten the 2x4 front of the bench to the end pieces. Next fasten 2x4 stretchers between the front and the back 2x4s to complete the frame of the bench.

2 ADD BRACES

Add a 2x4 on the bottom of the bench where braces will be fastened. Cut a 45-degree angle at each end of a 2x4 to make a brace about 40 in. long from point to point (trim the brace to fit). Then fasten the brace from the underside of the bench to one of the studs. We spaced three braces evenly along the bench.

3 TOP WITH CEDAR DECKING

Top the bench with cedar decking, fastening it to the frame with trim screws. The incense version we used is mostly used for saunas and closet lining, but it's much cheaper than typical cedar decking. It was perfect for the greenhouse and made it smell amazing inside.

FIGURE A BUILT-IN POTTING BENCHES

OVERALL DIMENSIONS: 10'5" W x 27-1/2" D x 35" H

MATERIALS LIST
(for 2 sets of benches)

ITEM	QTY.
Cedar 2x4 x 14'	6
Cedar 2x4 x 8'	12
Cedar 5/4x6 x 8' deck boards	20
2" deck or trim screws	
No. 9 3" construction screws	

CUTTING LIST (for 2 sets of benches)

KEY	QTY.	DIMENSIONS	PART
A	6	1-1/2" x 3-1/2" x cut to fit	Ledger board/front/bottom
B	20	1-1/2" x 3-1/2" x 24-1/2"	Stretcher
C	6	1-1/2" x 3-1/2" x cut to fit	Brace
D	28	1" x 5-1/2" x 27-1/2"	Cedar top deck boards

GREENHOUSE UPGRADES

To make this a perfect place for plants to thrive, we outfitted the inside of the greenhouse with some useful features—both high tech and practical.

CIRCULATING FANS

We installed two wall-mounted fans on the back wall. These fans circulate air and simulate wind inside the greenhouse. It's important for young plants to be exposed to wind so their stems will mature strong enough to support their growth.

GROW LIGHTS

We attached several eye hooks to the rafters above the benches so we could install cafe lights with full-spectrum grow lightbulbs. These bulbs will give the plants the light they need early on in the growing season.

VENTILATION FAN

We added an automatic ventilation fan in the gable end of the roof to help control temperature and humidity. This is a complete kit that allows you to program when the fan will turn on based on the temperature and humidity found by built-in sensors.

It comes with a controller that's easy to program from inside the greenhouse, but the kit also includes access to an app that monitors the temperature throughout the day and gives you the ability to change the settings remotely.

BUILT-IN POTTING BENCH

This simple floating bench is sized perfectly to pot plants and to store trays of starter plants. We built it right inside the greenhouse.

SIMPLE GARDENING BENCH

YOU CAN BUILD IT IN HALF A DAY

BY JOE CRUZ

When you get into serious gardening, you need a sturdy bench where you can perform all your potting chores. I designed this one using cedar 2x4s and deck boards. All you need to do is cut the parts to length and assemble. Your bench can be ready for use in just a few hours. If you want to save a little money, use pressure-treated lumber instead of cedar.

SPACER BLOCK

1

1 BUILD THE FRAMES

After cutting your parts to length, assemble the top and shelf frames by attaching the short frame members (A) to the front and back frame members (B) using 3-in. screws. Use a block for even spacing.

2 MAKE THE LEGS

Each L-shaped leg has two parts: a front and a side (C). Fasten the fronts to the sides as shown in Photo 2 using 3-in. screws. Keep the outer edges of the fronts flush with the faces of the sides.

If you're adding the upper shelf, cut two leg/shelf supports (D) at 60 in., and be sure to assemble them as a right and left leg.

3 ASSEMBLE THE BENCH

Lay the left and right back leg assemblies on a flat work surface. Place the frame assemblies between the two legs, the top frame flush with the top of the legs and the lower shelf frame 5 in. from the bottom of the legs. Secure the legs to the frames with 3-in. screws (3A). Then fasten the front leg assemblies to the frames using 3-in. screws (3B). Stand the bench on the floor and finish screwing the back legs to the frames.

2

3A

3B

FIGURE A GARDENING BENCH

OVERALL DIMENSIONS:
58" W x 30" D x 60" H

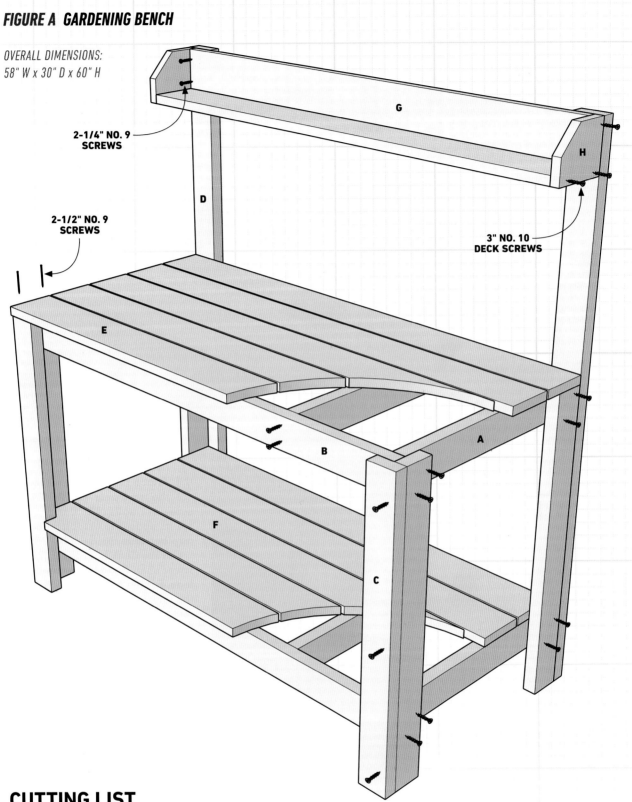

2-1/4" NO. 9
SCREWS

2-1/2" NO. 9
SCREWS

3" NO. 10
DECK SCREWS

CUTTING LIST

KEY	QTY.	DIMENSIONS	PART
A	10	1-1/2" x 3-1/2" x 23-3/4"	Short frame members
B	4	1-1/2" x 3-1/2" x 55"	Front and back frame members
C	6	1-1/2" x 3-1/2" x 34"	Leg fronts and sides
D	2	1-1/2" x 3-1/2" x 60"	Back leg/shelf supports
E	5	1" x 5-1/2" x 58"	Top deck
F	5	1" x 5-1/2" x 55"	Lower shelf deck
G	2	1" x 5-1/2" x 56"	Upper shelf
H	2	1" x 5-1/2" x 6-1/2"	Upper shelf ends

MATERIALS LIST

ITEM	QTY.
2x4 x 8' cedar	9
5/4 x 6 x 8' cedar	12
3" No. 10 deck screws	2-lb. box
2-1/2" No. 9 screws	1-lb. box
2-1/4" No. 9 screws	4

SPACER

4A

LEG CUTOUT

4B

4 INSTALL THE DECKING

Attach the decking (E) to the top frame with 2-1/2-in. screws or nails (4A). Use a 1/4-in. spacer to establish the gap between the deck boards.

Cut the deck boards for the lower shelf (F) to fit between the legs. For the front deck board of the lower shelf, cut a 1-1/2 x 2-in. rectangle out of each end of the board using a handsaw or jigsaw (4B), then attach it.

5 ADD THE UPPER SHELF

Next, cut your upper shelf parts (G), and assemble them as shown in Figure A. Attach the shelf ends (H) using screws or nails. Then use a quick clamp to hold the upper shelf assembly while you fasten it to the back legs/shelf support with 2-1/4-in. screws.

5

MEET THE BUILDER

JOE CRUZ, AN ARTISAN AND HANDYMAN FOR 50+ YEARS, BRINGS SIMPLE, ELEGANT DESIGN TO EVERYDAY DIY.

MODERN
FENCES

**BOOST YOUR HOME'S
CURB APPEAL WITH
THE RIGHT FENCE**

BY DAN STOUT

Fences lay out the borders of our property and keep children and pets safely away from the street. But a well-designed fence can be more than just functional—a beautiful front-yard fence can make a good first impression.

This is a perfect DIY project, letting you stretch your skills without worrying about load-bearing walls, plumbing or electricity. One important note: Always check your local requirements before buying materials or starting work.

CONTRASTING MIXED MATERIALS

By combining two or more distinct materials, you can build an attractive fence. Shown here are two styles of mixed-material fences: blended and layered.

BLENDED FENCES, such as this wood and brick example, mix different materials into a single fence. Remove either material and you no longer have a fence. Each part is essential.

LAYERED FENCES are stand-alone fence structures with additional elements. Think of a metal grid fence with horizontal cedar planking. If you removed the wood planking, the metal grid would stand as a fully functional fence. Layered fences can make striking design features; modular construction allows for more creative use of secondary elements to build a unique fence.

POSTHOLE HOW-TO

Designing a mixed-material fence is the fun part. Digging postholes is where the real labor comes in. Here's what you need to know before you dig.

MANUAL VS. MACHINE. For loose soil or a small fence, you can dig the holes by hand. For larger projects or in areas with heavy clay and roots, it's worth renting a power auger. Either way, start by calling 811 to locate underground utility lines. Digging holes is dangerous, even when you think you know your own front yard.

If you dig manually, start with a spade, then switch to a posthole digger (sometimes called a clamshell digger) to reach the required depth. Use a spud bar to knock rocks out of the way, and a reciprocating saw to cut through roots. If you use a power auger, start slowly; let the weight of the auger do the work. You can speed up once the auger is a few inches into the ground.

A SOLID BASE. Loose soil at the bottom of the hole should be removed with a shop vacuum or tamped down into a firm base. (Loose soil will eventually shift, knocking the post out of level and straining the fence.) A layer of gravel can add stability and improve drainage.

Some municipalities require hole inspections before you set the posts. Don't forget this step! You don't want to tear down a new fence because you skipped the hole inspection.

GUIDELINES FOR POST FOOTERS

The exact depth and diameter of the posthole is determined by local ordinances, but in most areas it should be at least one-third of the above-ground post height, and the diameter should be three times the post's width. (As an example, a 6-ft. 4x4 post should sit at least 2 ft. deep in a 12-in.-diameter hole.)

Caution: Always call 811 before you start to dig!

SECURING THE POST

Many DIYers opt to secure fence posts with quick-setting concrete that mixes with water right in the posthole. But your local ordinances may allow for other options.

GRAVEL BACKFILLING works well in areas with heavy clay soil, which the gravel can bite into. Fill the hole with 1 to 3 in. of material at a time, tamping it down before adding more. **CRUSHED ROCK** is another option. It has finer particles that pack together more tightly than gravel but still allow water to filter through. Fill the hole as you would with gravel, working in shallow layers.

EXPANSION FOAM is a two-part product, sold in gallon jugs or in single-use bags. When combined, it rapidly expands, curing into a secure material, fixing the post in place. Foam is more expensive than concrete but easier to use. It's a good choice if you don't want to haul heavy bags of concrete or for projects in areas where you won't have access to water. Two options are Sika PostFix and Postloc.

CONCRETE MIX is the best-known method for setting fence posts. You can find fast-setting concrete mix options at hardware stores. The manufacturers' how-to steps might differ, and some suggest a gravel base first. For most, you place a post in the hole, then mix the dry material with water right in the hole. Keep the post plumb, and the mix will set in about 30 minutes.

MAINTENANCE

Most fences require some maintenance, including management of bushes and saplings that grow near the slats. A thin sapling will quickly grow into a strong tree, damaging the fence and undoing all your hard work.

Other maintenance depends on the materials. Wood fencing can be stained, sealed or allowed to weather naturally. Metal fencing may need rust protection, while organic elements will require watering and pruning. The good news is that a well-built, well-maintained fence can last for decades.

SCREWS OR NAILS?

Although nails are less expensive and faster to install, choose screws for your wood fencing project. Deck screws work best for most fences, even those built with pressure-treated wood, which corrodes some hardware. And you can find color-matched deck screws at home centers.

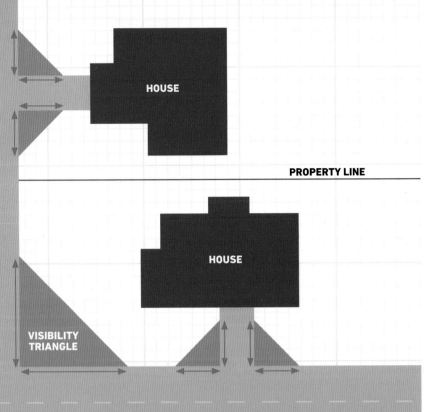

PROPERTY LINE

HOUSE

HOUSE

VISIBILITY TRIANGLE

CODES AND PERMITTING

Most DIYers are surprised to learn fences often require a permit. Some communities restrict fence size and materials, or specify construction that can withstand local conditions such as high winds or frost heave. Homeowner associations (HOAs) often have even more restrictive fencing regulations, with emphasis on materials and design.

BUDGET

Your cost will depend on the materials you choose and the total length of your fence. Expect to pay $15 to $40 per linear foot for fence supplies.

Chain-link fence is on the low end of that price range, and also the low end of the curb appeal scale. Wrought iron fencing is on the high end. A fence kit option can be easy on the pocketbook and a good option for beginning DIYers. With the materials cut and sized, you just need to put up panels.

LOT LINES AND CORNER LOT CONSIDERATIONS

Local regulations will determine whether you need a survey to begin work, as well as whether you can place the fence directly on the lot line or need a setback.

Front-yard fences and corner lots often have their own set of requirements, including lower heights and setbacks from the street. Even if these aren't requirements where you live, it's a good idea to give drivers a line of sight for oncoming traffic.

EXTRAS

A fence isn't just a boundary; it's a blank slate just waiting for you to add a little character.

PLANTERS AND BIRD FEEDERS bring a touch of nature to your fence, but can increase maintenance time.

ACCENT LIGHTING can highlight plants and add a level of security to your property. Low-voltage LED kits are easy to install and look great.

HOUSE NUMBERS make your address easy to read. A distinctive style can echo the architecture of your home (such as a Frank Lloyd Wright–inspired typeface on a Craftsman home).

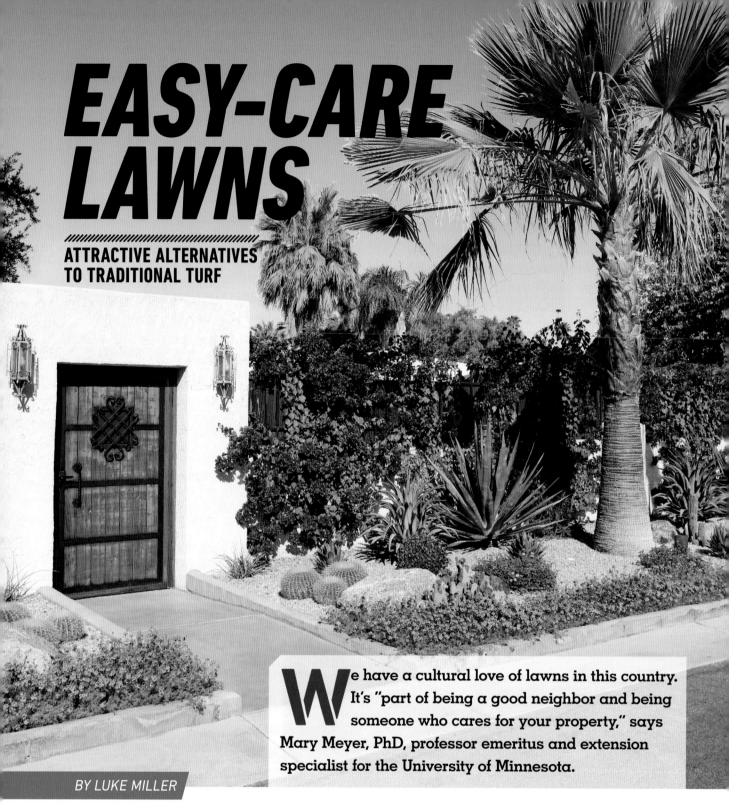

EASY-CARE LAWNS

ATTRACTIVE ALTERNATIVES TO TRADITIONAL TURF

We have a cultural love of lawns in this country. It's "part of being a good neighbor and being someone who cares for your property," says Mary Meyer, PhD, professor emeritus and extension specialist for the University of Minnesota.

BY LUKE MILLER

A lawn makes a great play area for children and dogs while keeping mud from being tracked into the house. It's invaluable for both sports and lawn games. And it's a nice way to visually frame a house and garden. But some homeowners are rethinking grass.

"Especially in the last 10 years, we see a lot more interest in the function of the lawn rather than just aesthetic appearance," Meyer notes. "If we're not playing soccer on it or using it for recreational purposes, why are we putting so much time and effort into a lawn?"

The lion's share of that time and effort goes to mowing—perhaps a couple of times a week during peak seasons, but other things factor into lawn care. "If you want a pristine lawn, it takes a lot of maintenance and a lot of input. It's the mower, fertilizer, irrigation, and maybe pest and weed control," says Meyer. "Those are a lot of environmental inputs; most of them are really negative."

Homeowners looking for more eco-friendly alternatives have plenty of options. These require less work and water and fewer chemicals than traditional sod.

GRASSES

LOW-MAINTENANCE grass is an option for those who wish to keep a more traditional-looking lawn. Often labeled **NO-MOW**, "most mixes are a combo of four to seven fine fescues," says Meyer. "No-mow is great. At the arboretum, we cut it maybe twice a year. It's a good choice for areas you don't want to cut very often."

Prairie Nursery (*prairienursery. com*) is one national retailer of no-mow and native plant and seed mixes, including mixtures for erosion-prone areas.

DROUGHT TOLERANT GRASSES are another option. **BLUE GRAMA GRASS** (*Bouteloua gracilis*) is a prairie bunch-grass often used as an ornamental but capable of handling lawn duties as well. Grown from seed or plugs, it needs minimal mowing, watering and fertilizing. **BUFFALOGRASS** (*Buchloe dactyloides*) is one of the few native grasses that can be grown as turf-grass and has less moisture and nutrient requirements than most other grasses. **ZOYSIAGRASS** (*Zoysia japonica*) is a dense, weed-snuffing turf that's drought tolerant. It's a good candidate for warm regions of the country.

POLLINATOR-FRIENDLY GRASS mixes have developed a following, due in part to concern about the health of our pollinators. **FLEUR DE LAWN**, developed with the help of Oregon State University, includes ryegrass, fescue, clover, white yarrow, English daisy, sweet alyssum and baby blue eyes (*Nemophila*). This grass can be kept at 3 in. for a more manicured look or 5 in. for a mini-meadow effect.

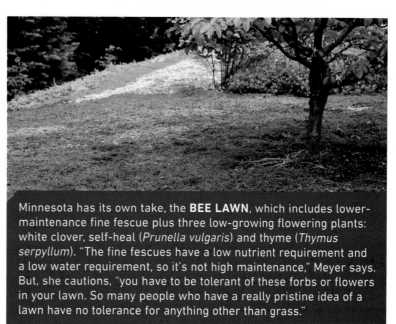

Minnesota has its own take, the **BEE LAWN**, which includes lower-maintenance fine fescue plus three low-growing flowering plants: white clover, self-heal (*Prunella vulgaris*) and thyme (*Thymus serpyllum*). "The fine fescues have a low nutrient requirement and a low water requirement, so it's not high maintenance," Meyer says. But, she cautions, "you have to be tolerant of these forbs or flowers in your lawn. So many people who have a really pristine idea of a lawn have no tolerance for anything other than grass."

WILDFLOWERS

WILDFLOWER MEADOWS are a beautiful sight when in bloom. And they're cost-efficient to install, too. "It can be done exclusively from seed, which from a cost standpoint makes it bearable," says Larry Weaner, of Larry Weaner Associates, an ecology-based landscape design firm in Pennsylvania featuring native species. Also, "it is a landscape you can see around if you want to preserve open space but don't want to mow your lawn every week."

An established wildflower garden doesn't need a lot of attention, with a weeding session once per season—spring, summer and fall—and an annual mowing at the end of winter, Weaner says. "That schedule is very realistic if you pick the right plants; it is very unrealistic if you pick the wrong plants."

With a mix of short-lived annuals, you may eventually end up with a big patch of weeds. Instead, choose a mix that fits the conditions (sun vs. shade, moist vs. dry) and look for perennials, which will outcompete weeds once they are established in two to three years. "It's not about picking out the flowers that look pretty or picking out the cheapest mix, which is likely short-lived plants," Weaner says. "This is really about understanding the environmental conditions you have and determining what are the native species to your area that grow in those environmental conditions."

A big bonus is the meadow's ecological impact. "Native species that occur in meadows are the most rapidly declining species of all types of native plants," Weaner says. "Consequently, the insects and birds that depend on those particular native species are also rapidly declining. From a wildlife habitat standpoint, when you plant a meadow, you are planting a combination that is in part reversing the decline of two very important elements of nature: native plants and native fauna."

MORE ALTERNATIVES

ARTIFICIAL TURF is the Jekyll and Hyde alternative: While fossil fuel is used to manufacture artificial turf, none is needed to maintain it. And while it offers no wildlife value, it does withstand heavy foot traffic and stay green during drought. Its best use may be in small pockets that would be difficult to mow.

GROUND COVERS are low-growing plants that spread by underground rhizomes to quickly cover a lot of territory. They make a fine lawn substitute as long as you're not walking on them regularly. Most are sold in flats, so you can plant in clumps and see them fill the gaps within one or two growing seasons. Popular ground covers include vinca vine, ajuga, lamium, dichondra, sedum and Boston ivy. There are ground covers for sun and shade, so you can grow them alone or incorporate them into a mixed shrub bed.

XERISCAPING isn't so much a landscape style as it is a landscape *lifestyle*. While the goal is to minimize irrigation, it goes beyond simply choosing drought-tolerant plants. In fact, some xeriscapes have plants that are not drought tolerant but instead grouped together to make watering more efficient. They're also located strategically where soil moisture is more abundant—near a drainpipe or at the bottom of a swale. Amending the soil with compost and topping it with mulch are other water-conserving strategies of a xeriscape.

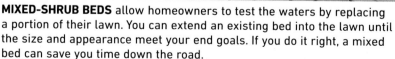

MIXED-SHRUB BEDS allow homeowners to test the waters by replacing a portion of their lawn. You can extend an existing bed into the lawn until the size and appearance meet your end goals. If you do it right, a mixed bed can save you time down the road.

The trick is to choose low-maintenance shrubs that won't outgrow their space or need constant pruning or watering. Fill the gaps with similarly well-behaved perennials for more color. Finally, lay down landscape fabric and 2 to 4 in. of mulch to thwart weeds. Spreading a pre-emergent weed preventer, such as Preen, also keeps weeds from sprouting.

HARDSCAPING includes paths, pavement and seating areas that require no watering, fertilizing or mowing. Options include laying down wood chips, pea gravel or decomposed granite, or installing permeable pavers that allow water to percolate back into the soil rather than running off. You can even leave planting pockets to fill with low-growing ground covers.

GETTING STARTED

First, consider how a lawn alternative would fit your neighborhood. Bear in mind that homeowners' associations and local codes may prohibit certain types of front-yard landscaping. Also consider neighbors. "In your backyard, whatever pleases you and the wildlife, go after it," says Weaner. "I would take a different approach in the front yard, where all the neighbors see it. In the front yard, it may be shorter, it may have mowed areas that define it as a planting as opposed to something that grew up because you stopped mowing your lawn."

Second, prepare the area.

- To turn an existing lawn into an eco-friendly one, scalp the grass, then dethatch and aerate before seeding.
- To replace a lawn with meadow, rent a sod remover, loosen the soil to a depth of 3 to 4 in. with a tiller, then rake the soil level and spread seed.
- To plant a mixed bed, mow turf short, plant in pockets, then smother surrounding area with wet cardboard topped with 4 in. of organic mulch, such as wood chips.

REGIONAL PLANTS FOR A WILDFLOWER GARDEN

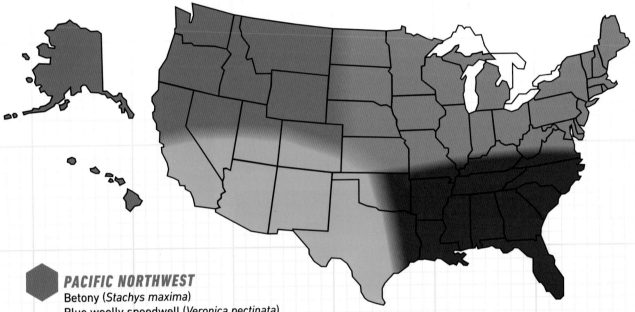

PACIFIC NORTHWEST
Betony (*Stachys maxima*)
Blue woolly speedwell (*Veronica pectinata*)
Candytuft (*Iberis sempervirens*)
Cooper's hardy ice plant (*Delosperma cooperi*)
Creeping gold buttons (*Cotula tiffindell*)
Creeping thyme (*Thymus serpyllum*)
Juniper leaf thyme (*Thymus neiceffii*)
Mossy sandwort (*Arenaria 'Wallowa Mountains'*)
Partridge feather (*Tanacetum densum*)
Poppy mallow (*Callirhoe involucrata*)
Self-heal (*Prunella grandiflora*)
Snow-in-summer (*Cerastium tomentosum*)
Soapwort (*Saponaria lempergii*)
Thyme-leaf speedwell (*Veronica oltensis*)
Woolly thyme (*Thymus lanuginosus*)

NORTH & MIDWEST
Candytuft (*Iberis sempervirens*)
Cooper's hardy ice plant (*Delosperma cooperi*)
Creeping gold buttons (*Cotula tiffindell*)
Creeping thyme (*Thymus serpyllum*)
Lamb's ears (*Stachys byzantina*)
Poppy mallow (*Callirhoe involucrata*)
Self-heal (*Prunella grandiflora*)
Snow-in-summer (*Cerastium tomentosum*)
Soapwort (*Saponaria lempergii*)
Thyme-leaf speedwell (*Veronica oltensis*)
Woolly thyme (*Thymus lanuginosus*)

DESERT SOUTHWEST
Candytuft (*Iberis sempervirens*)
Cooper's hardy ice plant (*Delosperma cooperi*)
Creeping germander (*Teucrium*)
Creeping shrubby ice plant (*Ruschia pulvinaris*)
Evening primrose (*Oenothera speciosa*)
Lamb's ears (*Stachys byzantina*)
Self-heal (*Prunella grandiflora*)
Wild zinnia (*Zinnia grandiflora*)

SOUTHEAST
Betony (*Stachys maxima*)
Bugleweed (*Ajuga reptans*)
Candytuft (*Iberis sempervirens*)
Cooper's hardy ice plant (*Delosperma cooperi*)
Evening primrose (*Oenothera speciosa*)
Self-heal (*Prunella grandiflora*)
Spotted dead nettle (*Lamium maculatum*)

MULCH OR ROCK?

//

BY GLENN HANSEN

"I hate putting down mulch every year. No mulch for me," says Larry, my neighbor to the west. "Mulch is way easier for landscaping and our annual flowers, and that's why Amy likes it," says Amy's husband, Tom, my neighbor to the east, "but I prefer rock, and we use both."

For me? Mulch. "Rock can look nice, yeah, but once you have to dig through or move rocks, they turn from beauty to beast," I told them both.

That's the type of chatter you hear in my neighborhood. Want more substance? Here are the facts of the Mulch vs. Rock battle. (To be clear, we're talking about organic mulch here, not inorganic mulch like recycled rubber.)

MULCH   ROCK

ADVANTAGES

LESS WATERING: Mulch helps soil retain moisture, and it reduces evaporation on the soil surface; you can water less often.

MORE NUTRIENTS: Mulch is a natural product, and its breakdown adds nutrients to feed plants and soil.

FEWER WEEDS: With small pieces and a fine texture, mulch covers soil more completely to help prevent weed growth.

JUST THE RIGHT TEMPERATURE: Mulch is a natural insulator, keeping plants warm in the winter and cool in the summer.

EASY INSTALL: If you buy bags of mulch, it's simple to tote them around your yard to places where you'll spread the goods.

DISADVANTAGES

ANNUAL REPLACEMENT: While mulch decay is good for plants, it's bad for your purse. Mulch needs to be replaced, and it can move in heavy rains and wind.

TOO MUCH MULCH: A layer of mulch more than 3 in. deep can stress plants.

TIMING MATTERS: Spread mulch too early and your soil won't warm naturally, meaning late blooms. If it's spread too late, weeds will develop.

SEEDS & WEEDS: Spreading organic mulch might introduce new weeds to your landscape.

ADVANTAGES

LOW MAINTENANCE: Rock doesn't decay, and it will stay where you place it for years.

FIREPROOF: If you live in an area with wildfires, rock can make a good fire break.

VARIETY: Rock gives you countless options of size, shape and color.

LOW LONG-TERM COST: Rock costs more than mulch initially, but there is little to no replacement cost.

FEWER BUGS: Unlike mulch, rock will not attract bugs or pests, which are drawn to decaying matter.

EROSION PROOF: Rock can prevent soil erosion, and it will stay in place on hillsides.

DISADVANTAGES

TOO HOT: Dark rock holds heat and raises ground temps, and light-colored rock will reflect heat onto plants. Both increase evaporation; you'll need to water more.

NO BENEFIT TO PLANTS: Rock doesn't aid plant growth or soil health.

MESSY pH: In different parts of the United States, different types of rock will increase the acidity or alkalinity of your soil.

WEED BED: The spaces between rocks invite leaves, seeds and weeds.

REMOVE BY HAND: Moving rock, whether for replanting or new landscaping, is simply dreadful work.

TOO HEAVY: Gravel is heavy, hard to transport and not DIY friendly.

STUCCO-LOOK WALL
Just frame it, sheathe it and add paint-ready panels.
P. 217

VERTICAL PANELS
We added composite decking panels to accent the boardwalk.
P. 227

GABION WALL
Stone-filled steel baskets—easy to build!
P. 214

BUILT-IN BENCHES
This attractive, durable seating can handle any weather.
P. 219

BACKYARD
LIVING

We knew we wanted to create a backyard living room, a spot where you could put up your feet and enjoy the company of family and friends around a fire. Because we were stuck in the Midwest in late winter, we decided to take the project on the road—all the way to Santa Fe.

Your backyard may not look like this one, but you can adapt these stylish, low-maintenance options to suit any yard. Build one or all, and then sit back and relax, knowing there's little to no upkeep ahead.

BEFORE
We started with a walled, but undeveloped, backyard.

FIRE ON THE ROCKS
Relax in the glow of your backyard fire pit.
P. 228

COMPOSITE DECKING BOARDWALK
A path that's no-maintenance? We're on it!
P. 224

GABION & STUCCO WALLS

BY BRAD HOLDEN

GABION

EASY STYLES YOU CAN BUILD YOURSELF

You can add beautiful stone and stucco-look walls to your patio without being a skilled mason. Gabion baskets provide the structural support for stacking any type of stone. These steel baskets can be used as retaining walls, landscaping structure or decorative elements. James Hardie Architectural Panels over simple framing make quick work of adding the look of stucco.

WHAT IT TAKES

TIME	COST	SKILL LEVEL
4–5 days	$250 per gabion*	Beginner

TOOLS
Pickax, shovel, level, rake, tamper, drill/driver, straightedge, tin snips, putty knife, ZIP tape roller, angle grinder with metal-cutting blade(s), circular saw with blade (for Hardie panels)

*about $55 per Hardie panel and per sheet of ZIP System sheathing

GABION BASKETS

1 PLOT GABION LOCATIONS
This step is important if you are setting several baskets in a line. You'll set stakes and masonry string to keep everything straight. We used single baskets in this installation, so alignment wasn't an issue.

2 ESTABLISH YOUR FOOTING
Level the area where your baskets will sit to keep the baskets from leaning. If you're placing the baskets on soft soil or clay, you'll need to dig down about 1 ft. and add a gravel base, or footing, to prevent the baskets from sinking. Our site in New Mexico was firm, so it needed only leveling and tamping.

TAMPER

3 ASSEMBLE THE BASKETS

Your gabion baskets may come partially assembled, with the sides already connected to the basket bottoms. You fold up the sides and secure them with special wire or easy-to-use spiral binders. Close the top to ensure the basket is level, but don't secure the top in place yet.

SPIRAL BINDER

4 FILL THE BASKETS

With your basket level and in place, add the center stretcher to keep the sides from bulging. There's more to filling a basket than just dumping in rocks. You'll want to "face" the basket, using the best-looking stones on the visible faces and filling in the center with smaller and/or less attractive stones. As you build up the faces, use the interior fill stones to support the face stones.

5 CAP THE BASKETS

When you've filled the basket level with stones, set the top in place and fasten it using wire or the spiral binders. Crimp these tight at the corners and file or grind off sharp edges.

CENTER STRETCHER

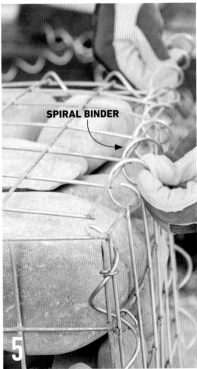

SPIRAL BINDER

STUCCO-LOOK WALLS

1 BUILD THE FRAMING
Assemble the wall framing to your specifications, using standard stud-wall construction to form rigid boxes. These are exterior installations; use either treated dimensional lumber or steel studs for the framing.

2 WRAP SHEATHING EDGES
You'll need sheathing that will hold up to the elements; we used ZIP System sheathing panels. The bottom edges of this sheathing will contact the ground, and the panels could wick moisture and swell. To prevent that, wrap the bottom edges of each panel with ZIP tape or another adhesive-backed moisture barrier after you cut the parts to size.

ZIP SYSTEM TAPE

MATERIALS LIST

ITEM	QTY.
Gabions	4
Rocks	2 cu. yds.
2x4s	50
4' x 8' ZIP sheathing	8 sheets
ZIP tape	
4' x 8' Hardie Panels	10 sheets
Screws	

3 ATTACH THE SHEATHING

Fasten the sheathing using construction screws. Then tape all the seams—including corners—with ZIP tape. Be careful not to sink fasteners more than halfway through the thickness of the sheathing.

4 ATTACH THE HARDIE PANELS

With your box frames built and sheathed, cut your Hardie panels to fit. Attach the panel parts using approved fasteners, such as ring-shank nails. Fill any nail holes with an exterior putty. The manufacturer stipulates that the edges of Hardie panels need to be 6 in. above grade or 1 in. above hardscape. Because this isn't a dwelling, we were comfortable voiding the product warranty to get the look we wanted.

5 PAINT THE BOXES

These Hardie panels come primed and ready for paint. The only prep you'll need to do is to fill any nail holes and seams and give any sharp edges a slight round-over with a sanding block. Apply an exterior paint using a brush or 1/2-in. nap roller.

ZIP SYSTEM SHEATHING

ZIP SYSTEM TAPE ROLLER

BUILT-IN BENCHES

MAINTENANCE-FREE SEATING FROM COMPOSITE DECKING

BY MIKE BERNER

We all want to sit back and enjoy the best weather in our backyards. That's why we chose to build this custom-fit bench with composite decking. No need to spend precious summer hours keeping up with its appearance —there will be no sanding, restaining, or replacing warped or splintered wood.

We built our bench to fit against an angled wall and between two gabion walls, but you can modify the plans to fit your own space. We designed the bench to have waterfall sides to hide the cut ends, but you could change this detail to simplify it further.

The bench can be built in just a couple of days, and the composite decking has the beautiful look of hardwood—without the hassles.

WHAT IT TAKES

TIME	COST	SKILL LEVEL
2 days	$1,000	Beginner

TOOLS
Circular saw or miter saw, drill/driver, hidden fastener installation tool (recommended)

TO SEE HOW TO BUILD THESE WALLS, SEE P. 217

2" GAP

1 LAY OUT YOUR BENCH WITH 2x4s

To determine where to place your bench and its approximate size, lay out 2x4s to outline the base. This will give you a good visual for the bench's placement and length. We left a 2-in. space between the framing and the abutting walls to allow room for decking and to make installation easier.

2 MARK THE PLATES

The top and bottom of the bench are identical, and each is built just like a very short wall. We started by marking the stretcher locations on the plates. With the plates cut to length (and miter angles cut), flush the end and mark stretcher locations 12 in. on-center with a Speed square. Repeat this for all four pairs.

12" ON-CENTER

PLATES FLUSH AT THE END

HOW TO DETERMINE AN ODD MITER ANGLE

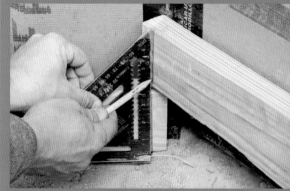

PIVOT THE FENCE ON THE CORNER OF THE STUD

ANGLE MEASUREMENT

FIND THE INTERSECTION

Stack the 2x4s so their corners fit into the angled wall. With the boards pressed against the walls, hook the fence of a Speed square under the bottom board and slide it toward the corner until it contacts the adjacent board. Then trace a line on both faces.

CONNECT THE DOTS

Remove one of the 2x4s from the corner and align the square's fence with the corner that was against the wall. Pivot the fence until the opposite edge of the square lines up with the mark, and then trace a line. The square works like a protractor to give you the angle measurement.

3 BUILD THE BASE AND TOP

Space the two plates apart and nail or screw the stretchers through the plates. With our angled bench design, we built two matching pairs and then placed them against the corner to make sure they fit. If the miter is tight when the two sides are against the wall, cutting the deck boards to fit will be much easier.

STRETCHERS

FIGURE A ANGLED OUTDOOR BENCH

OVERALL DIMENSIONS: 18"H x 186"W x 24"D

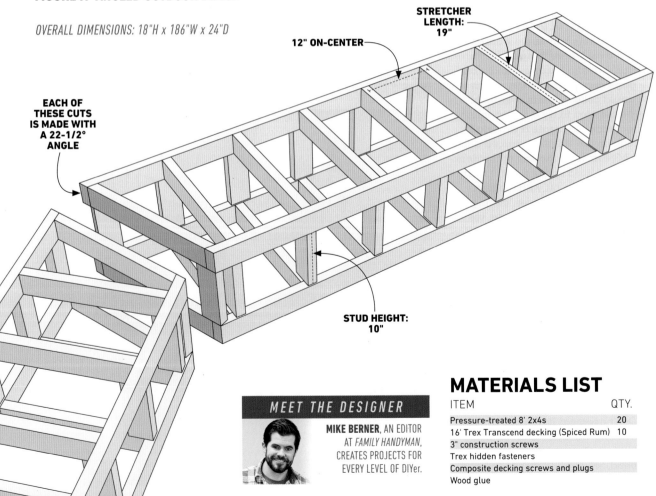

STRETCHER LENGTH: 19"

12" ON-CENTER

EACH OF THESE CUTS IS MADE WITH A 22-1/2° ANGLE

STUD HEIGHT: 10"

MEET THE DESIGNER

MIKE BERNER, AN EDITOR AT *FAMILY HANDYMAN*, CREATES PROJECTS FOR EVERY LEVEL OF DIYer.

MATERIALS LIST

ITEM	QTY.
Pressure-treated 8' 2x4s	20
16' Trex Transcend decking (Spiced Rum)	10
3" construction screws	
Trex hidden fasteners	
Composite decking screws and plugs	
Wood glue	

ORIENT ALL SCREWS TO FACE UP

4 ATTACH THE STUDS

Place one of the top sections on a work surface, and then align the studs with the stretchers and flush with the edge. Toe-screw each stud into the top/bottom with 3-in. construction screws. Once the studs are attached to the top, align the bottom with the studs and toe-screw the bottom to the studs. When the section is flipped upright, all the screws will face upward, preventing water from entering and rotting the wood.

5 MITER-FOLD THE END

For this bench, we wanted to avoid three things: a picture frame design; ugly cut ends; and gaps at a mitered edge, which would collect debris over time. We decided to try a folded-miter technique to create a waterfall look on the sides. We traced a line 17-3/4 in. from the end of the decking and lined up the point of a large 2-in. V-groove bit with the line.

With several passes, cutting with a Speed square guide, we made a deep groove on the underside of the board, leaving just under 1/8 in. of thickness at the deepest part of the groove. You can also achieve this with a circular saw with two precise, opposing 45-degree bevel cuts.

6 HEAT UP AND FOLD THE CORNER

Hold the board over the edge of the bench, and slowly heat the surface until it folds by itself. Don't overheat it; the cap of the decking will melt or break while folding. Once we got the board to bend, we applied wood glue and then installed the deck boards.

17-3/4" FROM THE END

TREX STARTER CLIPS

TREX UNIVERSAL FASTENERS

TREX UNIVERSAL FASTENER INSTALLATION TOOL

7

This Trex Universal Fastener Installation Tool made installing all the decking in the project a breeze. It allowed us to push or pull the boards tight, hold the fastener and guide our bit to the screw head all at once. It was well worth its $23 price tag.

7 PROPER FASTENERS ARE THE KEY

To clad the bench with decking, start with the top and fasten a solid-edge (no groove) board, having it overhang the front framing by 2 in. Solid-edge deck boards are fastened with composite screws and matching plugs through the faces of the boards. The next board is grooved and slides into a J-shaped clip fastened to the framing to maintain a 3/16-in. gap. The boards "in the field" are held down with T-shaped hidden fasteners.

8 TRIM THE ANGLE

We left the boards on the bench top long until the entire top was fastened. Then we set up a straight-edge and cut the boards flush with the framing using a circular saw.

9 FINISH THE FRONT

Once both sides of our bench were built, we dropped them into place, joined them with a few construction screws, then attached deck boards on the front. We placed starter clips 1/4 in. from the bottom of the framing to fit the bottom course of decking and worked our way up the front.

GROOVED-EDGE DECK BOARD

SOLID-EDGE DECK BOARD

8

WATERFALL SIDE

9

WORRY-FREE CLADDING

To clad the bench, we chose the Transcend line of decking by Trex. It's a wood/plastic composite that doesn't have a scalloped bottom. The solid bottom makes it easy to secure composite fasteners through the face. It also allows us to achieve a small overhang along the edge of the decking.

BOARDWALK & WALL PANELS

HOW TO CREATE A WALKWAY AND ACCENT WALLS, STEP BY STEP

WHAT IT TAKES

TIME	COST	SKILL LEVEL
3 days	$3,500	Beginner

TOOLS
Circular saw/miter saw, drill/driver, hidden fastener installation tool (recommended), landscaping tools

BY MIKE BERNER

An inviting boardwalk and unique wall accent panels are the finishing touches to this backyard. The boardwalk provides an elegant path, and the accent walls tie it all together. Best of all, they're built with composite decking, which is easy to clean and will look good for years to come.

The boardwalk is a quick and easy build. The flexible composite decking will follow slight contours in your yard and can span roots and rocks that would otherwise require excavation. You may have to do a little digging to make the boardwalk flush with the ground and create a seamless walkway through your yard.

The walls surrounding this backyard were bland, so to liven them up and match the rest of the new space, we used extra deck boards to outline the new seating area. These two projects take just a few days to build, but they can have a big impact.

Lead friends and family into your backyard with a simple, beautiful, maintenance-free boardwalk.

1 PREP THE GROUND

To build the boardwalk at ground level, dig a trench along the path. We needed to fill our trench with drainage rock to keep the pressure-treated lumber dry, so we dug out 6 in. of soil to fit a 2-in. layer of rock topped with our 2x4 frames. Tamping the area before and after laying the rock gave us a solid foundation.

MATERIALS LIST

ITEM	QTY.
16' pressure-treated 2x4s	16
16' composite decking boards	30
3" No. 10 construction screws	
Hidden fasteners	
Deck joist tape	
Drainage rock	

MEET THE DESIGNER

MIKE BERNER, AN EDITOR AT *FAMILY HANDYMAN*, LOVES A GOOD DESIGN CHALLENGE.

STRETCHERS

12" ON-CENTER

2 BUILD THE BOARDWALK FRAMES

The frames of the boardwalk are simple boxes made from pressure-treated 2x4s. Place two long 2x4s along the edge of the boardwalk to determine their length. Then fasten the stretchers between them 12 in. on-center with construction screws.

3 ADD BLOCKING AT THE MITERS

To turn the boardwalk with a miter, as shown in our design, both ends of the mitered boards need to be supported and fastened. We added two 2x4 stretchers at a 45-degree angle from the corners and cut stretchers to fit.

4 PROTECT THE WOOD FRAME

To further protect the framing members, I used Trex Protect, a butyl tape that comes in convenient widths (1-5/8 in. and 3-1/8 in.) to fit on the edges of 2-by lumber. The tape can be applied to vertical and horizontal surfaces, making it perfect for these projects.

5 LET THE DECK BOARDS RUN LONG

Running the deck boards past the miter allows us to make one clean cut using a circular saw and a straightedge. Cut the same angle in the adjacent boards and repeat the process.

DIAGONAL BLOCKING

STRETCHERS CUT TO FIT

COVER TOP EDGES WITH DECK JOIST TAPE

STRAIGHTEDGE

VERTICAL WALL PANELS

To tie the space together and to hide some of the plain block wall, we installed two wall panels.

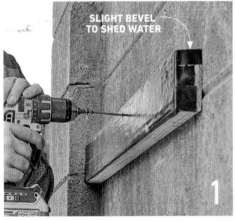

SLIGHT BEVEL TO SHED WATER

1

DECK JOIST TAPE PROTECTS AND HIDES THE LEDGERS BEHIND THE PANELS

2

1 FASTEN LEDGER BOARDS

The wall panels are attached to the block wall on 2x4 ledger boards. The 2x4s are cut about 2 in. short of the total width of the wall and installed with concrete anchors. Put the ledger in position and drill through it and into the block with a hammer drill outfitted with the correct-size bit. The hole should be deep enough to seat the anchor completely.

2 FASTEN DECK BOARDS

Fasten a solid-edge deck board vertically with composite screws and matching plugs, making sure it's plumb. Then attach the grooved deck boards with starter clips and hidden fasteners, and finish with a final solid-edge board on the end.

FIRE ON THE ROCKS

A PROPANE FIRE PIT
YOU CAN BUILD IN
A WEEKEND

BY GLENN HANSEN

I use propane often at my house to cook on my gas grill. I'm careful with propane tanks, especially when transporting them, and I trust that the manufacturer of my grill considered my safety when designing this enclosure of gas and flames.

If you've replaced burner elements in a gas grill, you know it's a fairly simple appliance. A 20-lb. propane tank feeds burner tubes made of steel, brass or even ceramic or porcelain through a thermoplastic hose with a pressure regulator. Those burner tubes are perforated with small holes or slits where gas exits to be burned. Fuel, delivery, ignition. A backyard fire pit is even simpler than your gas grill—there's no device to hold food over the flames—but you still need to consider safety with such a unit.

LOCATING YOUR FIRE PIT

To decide on the location of any fire pit, start with three main considerations: clearance, ventilation and drainage. As part of our larger backyard project, I fit the fire pit burner into a gabion basket, which is a steel mesh rectangle filled with rocks. You can order any size basket you want, then fill it with boulders to serve as a functionally ornamental border or barrier. For complete details on gabion basket construction, see p. 214.

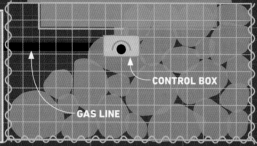

96" DISTANCE MINIMUM CLEARANCE

FIRE PAN, FIRE GLASS & BURNER

PROPANE TANK

36" DISTANCE MINIMUM CLEARANCE (EACH SIDE)

AIR VENTS

CONTROL BOX

GAS LINE

NONCOMBUSTIBLE BOX

WHAT IT TAKES

TIME	COST	SKILL LEVEL
1 weekend	$1,000	Intermediate

TOOLS
Table saw, hole saw, caulk gun, drill/driver, hand tools, tin snips

MATERIALS
Metal studs, boulders, gabion baskets, treated lumber 2x4s, fiber cement panels, 1/2-in. cement board, fire pit components, vent covers

IS THIS DIY-ABLE?

I look at most projects and ask, "Can I do this myself?" (I like to answer, "Of course," and my wife then says, "Really?") So I looked at fire pit kits, then asked and answered, "Of course." But just because you *can* DIY something doesn't mean you *should*.

My original plan involved making my own fire burner pipes from either black steel or stainless steel pipe. I thought I'd then buy all the necessary connections, drill holes, assemble it and light the fire. I wanted the freedom to create a shape and size for my pit. And I hoped to test the different pipe types to see which would look better. But the more I discussed this with coworkers, the worse the idea sounded. We're talking about gas and fire here. While many "experts" have shared similar projects online, we want to be more careful. Follow along as I build a propane-fueled fire pit and show you how to do it safely.

INNER GABION BASKET

1 FILL THE BASKETS

Inside a larger rectangular gabion basket, I placed a 30 x 10-in. basket that would support my fire pit pan-and-burner combo. I filled the larger outer basket with rocks, and then I filled the inner basket about halfway, adding just enough rocks to help hold its shape. The boulders in this fire pit are large enough to allow air spaces around all sides. And it's all noncombustible.

2 SECURE THE CONTROLS

The fire pit control box fit neatly after a simple modification to the gabion basket. I cut away a couple of metal pieces to fit the wide box, then I added metal struts below and above the control box to hold it securely in place and to support one layer of rocks above it. This box includes gas flow control, a pilot switch, on/off control and a battery-operated igniter button.

I purchased this UL-listed device separate from my fire pit burner, but the control box included the igniter element that mounts alongside the burner in the fire pit pan. It's the most expensive part of this whole fire pit, and it's worth it. Find one online or from a local fireplace store, then follow the instructions to connect the propane line and the gas out to the fire pit. I used PTFE gas-ready thread tape on all connections and tested them all with a leak detector spray before use.

CONTROL BOX

3 DROP IN THE PAN

Fire pit burners and pans come in all shapes and sizes. So do gabion baskets. I started with a 30 x 10-in. fire pit pan and ordered a gabion basket of the same size—a perfect fit. Make sure your burner pan has weep holes to let water escape.

> **NOTE:** You can use natural gas for this fire pit. If you go that route, you'll need to hire a licensed pro to run the gas line.

BURNER

FIRE PAN

PILOT ASSEMBLY

PRESSURE-TREATED 2x4

HARDIE PANEL

DUROCK CEMENT BOARD

4

5

4 FRAME THE BOX

To enclose the propane tank and its gas hose, I built a noncombustible box to sit adjacent to the gabion box. I wrapped treated 2x4s inside metal studs and nailed the structure together.

5 FINISH THE BOX

To cover the box, I chose fiber cement siding, aka "Hardie Panel," using the same material Brad used for his project on p. 214. These sturdy panels are normally used as siding for houses. Because I wanted the top of this box to be even stronger, I first layered 1/2-in. Durock cement board there. Then I covered that and the rest of the box with the 1/3-in.-thick Hardie panels. I nailed the panels on, setting each nail just below the surface, then caulked all the holes and joints before painting.

6 ADD AIR VENTS

I added two 5-in.-diameter air vents to the enclosure, even though I left the back of the box open on the fire pit side. It's vital to keep good airflow around that propane tank. Drilling the vent holes is slow going—you can count on burning through a hole saw—and you need a proper respirator mask when you cut or drill the fiber cement board.

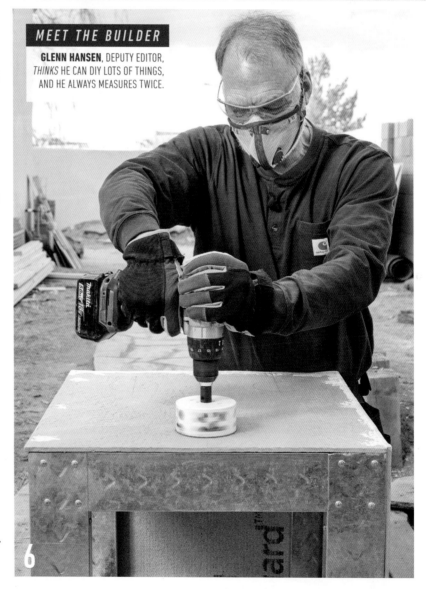

MEET THE BUILDER

GLENN HANSEN, DEPUTY EDITOR, *THINKS* HE CAN DIY LOTS OF THINGS, AND HE ALWAYS MEASURES TWICE.

6

7 INSTALL A DOOR

You could skip the vents and forgo the door on your box, but I like having the door in place. I built a simple doorframe using square aluminum tubing, sized to nest inside the door opening. Add a couple of hinges, a door latch or a heavy magnetic closure, and a handle.

8 POUR IN THE GLASS

I purchased fire glass to surround my fire burner pipes; lava rocks work too. Whatever you choose, just make sure it's tempered to withstand the fire. Regular glass would smoke, melt or even explode. I chose reflective fire glass (instead of nonreflective) because it acts like many tiny mirrors to enhance the look of the fire. Fill the pan with enough glass or rocks just to cover the burner holes. Especially when you use propane, too much fire glass can trap the gas and be dangerous upon ignition.

SAFETY & MAINTENANCE

- Follow the manufacturer's operating instructions for any fire pit components you purchase.
- Establish a kid-free zone and maintain adult supervision while children are near the fire.
- Insects and rodents could nest in your fire pit or near the propane tank enclosure. Check before using.
- Clean the fire glass periodically with a vinegar-and-water mix.

GREAT GOOFS®

HOLY INTRUDER!

I built a permanent roof over my patio a couple of years ago. Recently I noticed water stains on the inside wall directly below the step flashing that seals the new roof to the house siding. I climbed up there to track down the leak. I looked for holes, checked for flashing that had slipped out of place and even flooded the area with a hose. No dice.

Then I climbed a ladder and held my head close to the wall behind a rafter to see if any light was shining through to reveal a hole. Inches away and staring right back at me was a bat. And directly below him were his urine stains.

ED LEJCHAR

THE BATHROOM IS OCCUPIED

To save a few bucks, I decided to cut down one of our trees myself. I easily removed all the lower branches with my pole saw, and then I had the brilliant idea of taking the saw upstairs and hanging out the second-story bathroom window to remove the upper branches.

All went well until the last (pretty large) remaining limb. I planned the cut so the branch would fall into the "safe and open space" in the yard. Unfortunately, the nearly 12-ft. limb had other ideas. I narrowly avoided being skewered as it crashed through the window opening and came to rest a few inches from the door. People do a variety of things in their bathrooms—but how many have cut firewood while standing in the bathtub?

GREG RUVOLO

6 USING DIY TOOLS & MATERIALS

WORKSHOP
WORKHORSE

MASTER YOUR CIRCULAR SAW WITH THESE TIPS

BY MIKE BERNER

One of the most reached-for tools in my garage, the circular saw is an essential tool for DIYers of all skill levels. The "circ" saw is uber-versatile; if you need a straight cut of any kind, a circular saw can do it. Follow along to learn circular saw skills and to find out what type of saw you should reach for in your shop.

SAFETY FIRST

Always wear hearing and eye protection when you use any power saw, and keep loose-fitting sleeves, long hair and hoodie drawstrings tucked away. When making a cut, keep hands in front of and away from the saw, never behind it.

ADJUST BLADE DEPTH

When a lot of the saw blade extends beneath your material, you increase the possibility of cutting something you don't intend to cut. As a rule of thumb, set your blade depth so that just a bit more than the teeth protrudes through the material.

PINCH POINT

DON'T BIND THE BLADE

When a circular saw blade gets pinched or twisted while making a cut, the blade can kick back toward you with force. This is almost completely avoidable. Don't rush, keep your saw cuts straight and position the cutoff side of your workpiece to fall away from the blade. Never cut between supported ends, such as in the middle of two sawhorses, where the cut will fall into the saw blade.

CUTS OF ALL KINDS

Whether you're cutting 2x4s to length, breaking down plywood sheets into a manageable size, creating joinery, or making angled and beveled cuts, reach for a do-it-all circ saw.

ANGLE: Changing the angle of the saw relative to the material you are cutting

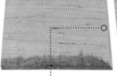
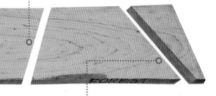

RIP CUT: Sawing with the grain of solid lumber

CROSSCUT: Sawing across the grain of solid lumber

BEVEL: Changing the angle of the blade relative to the saw's shoe

COMPOUND: Sawing at an angle with the blade set at a bevel

Your circular saw can cut far more than just 2x4s and plywood, and specialty blades are available to help you cut other materials.

MASONRY: Repair a driveway crack or cut landscape blocks and pavers with a diamond blade in your circular saw. These blades are common for tile saws or angle grinders but also come in sizes to fit your circular saw.

METAL: Install a steel-cutting blade to cut cleanly through tough metal. Check that your circular saw does not exceed the blade's rpm rating. The Cermet blade by Diablo is a heat-tolerant blade that cuts up to 3/8-in.-thick steel, without heating up the material or leaving sharp burrs.

PLASTIC: I learned to cut material such as vinyl siding by flipping the blade to spin backward. This is a bad idea. Instead, use a blade for cutting composite material. They are configured to cut—not melt—plastic and other composite materials, as well as aluminum.

TYPES OF SAWS

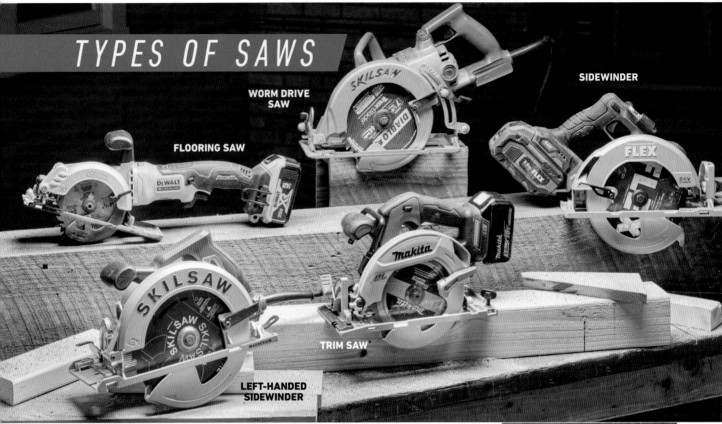

WORM DRIVE SAW

SIDEWINDER

FLOORING SAW

TRIM SAW

LEFT-HANDED SIDEWINDER

A specific circular saw exists for the work you do most often. If you only cut 2x4s, you don't need a bigger saw. If you need to cut flooring easily, there is a saw that does that better. Getting the right saw for the job makes your work easier. Here are the types of saws and what they're best at cutting.

TRADITIONAL/ SIDEWINDER

This is the circular saw that everybody knows. The motor is mounted on the left and spins a 7-1/4-in. blade on the right. Tried and true, this saw can handle most of the jobs a DIYer has on his or her weekend projects list. It is also available in a left-handed version with the motor on the right and the blade on the left.

COMPACT/ FLOORING SAW

Equipped with a much smaller 4-1/2-in. blade, this saw still has the ability to cut 2-by material, but it excels at cutting flooring and sheet goods. The barrel handle design on these saws gives them a unique operating feel, and they demand different use habits for safety.

WORM DRIVE

Most circular saws are direct drive, meaning the saw blade is connected directly to the motor's spindle. A worm-drive saw has the blade in front of the motor. Gears perpendicular to the motor spin the blade. Some framing carpenters favor gear-driven saws. They're narrower and heavier than traditional circular saws but are more powerful and track straight when you're making long cuts. Two versions of this saw, worm drive and hypoid drive, use slightly different style gears; both need gear oil for maintenance.

TRIM SAW

A smaller version of a traditional circular saw, a trim saw has a 6-1/2-in. blade and typically comes in a blade-left orientation, although some use a blade-right setup. This saw's smaller blade results in less cutting-depth capacity, but its light weight and easy handling make the trim saw shine for out-of-shop tasks.

BEAM CUTTER

When you need to cut large timbers for landscaping or a thick slab for a project, check out a beam cutter, such as this one by Prazi (praziusa.com). This attachment fits a variety of 7-1/4-in. sidewinder saws. Bolt one on and you'll be able to cut lumber up to 12 in. thick.

SO SIMPLE— A SPINNING BLADE, RIGHT?

Circular saws might all look similar, but they vary in significant ways. Cutting capacity, for example, is mostly a factor of blade size, but can differ slightly among saws. When choosing the best saw, look for these features, which improve safety, make the saw more versatile or stand up better to the rigors of the job site:

■ **ELECTRIC BRAKE:**
An electric brake stops the blade as soon as you release the saw's trigger.

■ **MAGNESIUM SHOE:**
Magnesium is lighter and stronger than steel.

■ **NO-CATCH BLADE GUARD:**
Some blade guards catch on the edge of your material, which is annoying and also unsafe. A blade guard shaped to avoid snagging the edge of a board means you don't have to lift it to make your cut. Keeping safety features in place is always a good thing.

■ **POSITIVE BEVEL STOPS:**
This feature makes it easy to change the bevel angle from 90 degrees to 45, or other common angles, with speed and consistency.

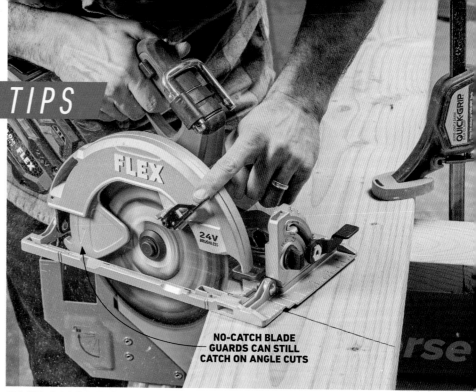

TIPS

NO-CATCH BLADE GUARDS CAN STILL CATCH ON ANGLE CUTS

CUT ANGLES EASIER

Cutting angles can be tricky because the blade guard often catches on the material as the saw begins to cut, even with a no-catch blade guard. Before starting the cut, lift the blade guard lever with your opposite hand until the blade guard can rest on the material.

PREVENT SCRATCHES AND CHIP-OUT

Apply tape to the material you're cutting. This accomplishes three things: It prevents the saw's shoe from scuffing your wood, allows you to make an accurate and visible (dark) mark you won't have to sand away, and helps prevent chip-out.

CUT PLYWOOD ON A FOAM BACKER

Cut full-size sheets of plywood on top of a sheet of 1-in. rigid foam. The foam won't dull the blade, and the cut-off parts won't crash to the floor.

RIGID FOAM BACKER

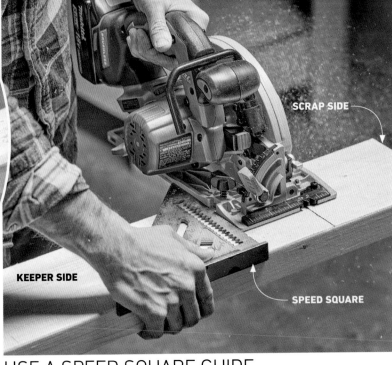

SCRAP SIDE

KEEPER SIDE

SPEED SQUARE

MAKE A NOTCH

Mark the width and depth of your notch, then set the saw's depth and make several cuts between your marks. Knock away what's left with a screwdriver or chisel.

If the notch is less than 1-1/2 in. wide, use your circular saw to smooth out the bottom by slowly dragging the saw blade over the notch sideways. If the saw's shoe can't be supported on both sides of the blade, smooth out the bottom with a chisel.

USE A SPEED SQUARE GUIDE

To quickly make square cuts, use a Speed square as a saw guide. You'll get a perfect cut, fast. Be sure to place your square and the bulk of the saw on the keeper side of the board and line up the blade so it cuts on the scrap side of the board. If necessary, adjust the saw's blade depth to prevent the motor from hitting the square.

SKILSAW

MAGNESIUM

BRAKE SAW

SUPPORT BOTH SIDES OF THE SHOE

PRO TIP

If you're notching a narrow piece of lumber, clamp scrap lumber on both sides of the piece to give the saw's shoe more solid footing.

SECURE MATERIAL

Whether you're ripping or cross-cutting, if your material shifts, you risk a potentially dangerous kickback. Secure the material to a workbench or sawhorse with nails, screws or clamps.

BORA
Speedhorse

SCORE FOR A CLEAN CUT

A saw blade tends to lift the surface wood fibers as it cuts, giving you a fuzzy or splintered edge. Score your cutting line with a razor blade to cut the fibers on top and give you a clean edge.

CUT ON THE HIGH SIDE

PROP

PROP THE BOARD

When making cuts on a pile of lumber or on a flat work surface, prop up the piece you're cutting with a small scrap about 2 in. long. It prevents you from cutting into the work surface and will allow the cutoff piece to fall away from the blade. Make your cut on the high side of the prop.

TROUBLE CUTTING STRAIGHT? CHECK THE SHOE

If you're having trouble with your saw not cutting straight along a guide, and leaving burn marks, check that the edge of the shoe is parallel to the blade. The shoe can bend and become crooked if your saw has been dropped or jostled too much. It might be time for a new saw or to find a replacement shoe online.

POINT THUMB THROUGH THE CUT

MAKE STRAIGHT CUTS

A veteran carpenter once suggested I unwrap my thumb from the saw's handle and align my wrist and thumb with the direction I'm pushing the saw. When I changed my grip, I was able to make much straighter cuts without the aid of a saw guide.

PRO TIP
For straighter cuts, watch the blade cut along your line instead of focusing on the saw's guide.

SUPPORT BLOCK

MAKE STEEP BEVEL CUTS

Most circular saws will make bevel cuts up to 55 degrees. What if you need a steeper bevel? Subtract the bevel you're after from 90 and set your saw at that bevel. Next, clamp or screw a block even with the end of the board to support the saw base while you cut. If the blade doesn't complete the cut, finish it with a handsaw or reciprocating saw. This trick works for compound cuts as well. Cut the angle first with the saw's bevel at 90 degrees, and then use the off-cut to support the saw while you cut the steep bevel.

4x4 POST

KERF FROM FIRST CUT

CUT AND ROLL THROUGH POSTS

Even though the cutting capacity for traditional 7-1/4-in. circular saws is only about 2-1/2 in., you can easily cut through thicker posts. Mark the cut and make the first full-depth cut on one side, then roll the material backward and use the saw kerf to line up the next cut. A third roll and cut will saw through a 4x4 post. If you're working with larger lumber such as 6x6 posts, you'll have to cut on all four sides and finish it off with a handsaw or reciprocating saw.

ADJUSTMENT SETSCREW

CHECK FOR 90 DEGREES

If the blade on your circular saw isn't 90 degrees against its shoe, any bevel you adjust to will be inaccurate. Check the blade with a machinist's square. If it's not square, flip the saw upside down and adjust the setscrew on the bottom until it is square. Once the saw is dialed in at 90 degrees, adjust it to 45 degrees and check the angle with a Speed or combination square. Unplug the saw or remove its battery when making such adjustments.

THE FIRST CUT SETS THE WIDTH TO MATCH YOUR SAW

WEAR A DUST MASK WHEN YOU CUT MDF

LEAVE SPACE FOR A CLAMP

LINE UP THE TRACK, MAKE THE CUT

UPGRADE WITH A DIY TRACK GUIDE

A simple and inexpensive track guide will let you cut straight, accurate lines with any circular saw. The track consists of a straight board fastened with glue and nails to a piece of 1/4-in. hardboard. Use the board as a fence and run the saw along the track, cutting the hardboard to match your saw blade exactly. Then to make a cut, just line up the edge of the guide with your marks. Making one long and one short version of this guide will give you a rip guide and a crosscut guide.

MEET THE EXPERT

ASSOCIATE EDITOR **JAY CORK** HAS YET TO FIND ANY TAKERS FOR SAW BLADE FRISBEE AROUND THE OFFICE.

THE BEST CUTS

SAW BLADE SAVVY TO GIVE YOU AN EDGE

BY JAY CORK

Saw blades seldom get the attention they deserve. We might purchase based on price, or just grab what's on the shelf in the correct size. And we think it'll be OK. It probably will be—just OK. The right saw blade—a better saw blade—will produce cleaner and more accurate cuts, and will do so safely. That means better DIY results the first time. Here's what you need to know about blades for table saws, miter saws and circular saws.

ALL BLADES ARE THE SAME, RIGHT?

A saw blade is more than its teeth. I prefer laser-cut blades with vibration-dampening slots cut into the blade body. Here's why: Blades with these slots cut cleaner and quieter. Blades without vibration-dampening slots are loud. This vibration makes your saw ring like a bell.

SHOPPING FOR SAW BLADES

Home centers stock many mid-level construction blades. If you're looking for a high-end woodworking blade, find your way to a specialty woodworking store like Rockler or Woodcraft. The experts at these stores will help you find what you're looking for.

COMBINATION
IDEAL FOR RIPPING & CROSS-CUTTING SOLID WOOD, PLYWOOD & PARTICLE BOARD

10"
254mm

50 TEETH

MAX RPM 6,000

RECOMMENDED APPLICATIONS

HARDWOODS	★★★★
SOFTWOODS	★★★★★
PARTICLE BOARD	★★★★★
PLYWOOD	★★★★
LAMINATE	★★★
FERROUS	NOT RECOMMENDED
NON-FERROUS	NOT RECOMMENDED

Not for use on masonry

WARNING: Do not operate tool without proper saw blade guard in place. Read and understand your machine owner's manual before using this blade.

**ATB-R
(SEE ACRONYM
GUIDE, P. 247)**

THIS IS THE BLADE YOU NEED

A combination blade for the table saw is perfect for the casual user. It produces clean crosscuts in solid wood or plywood, and rips plywood with acceptable results. Most combo blades expose their weakness when ripping thick lumber; the gullets are too small to effectively eject chips and keep the blade cool.

1/8"   3/32"

THIN KERF VS. STANDARD KERF

Which type should you buy? The correct answer is determined by the power of your saw. My rule of thumb is to use a thin-kerf blade for any table saw under 3 hp, which includes all portable job-site saws. A thin-kerf blade is 25% thinner than standard kerf, therefore it has 25% less cutting resistance. With a thin-kerf blade installed, your job-site saw will feel like a powerhouse.

THESE ARE THE BLADES YOU WANT

1. PLYWOOD/MELAMINE BLADE
With a less aggressive rake angle and a steeper top bevel, these blades are designed to minimize chip-out in manufactured sheet material.

2. RIPPING BLADE
A proper ripping blade can do more than produce glue-ready straight cuts along the grain. A ripping blade with flat teeth will produce a true flat-bottom kerf, which makes the blade perfect for joinery cuts such as dadoes, rabbets and tenons.

3. CROSSCUT BLADE
With teeth designed to cleanly sever wood fibers, this blade will give you glass-smooth cuts across the grain.

3 ATB

1 HATB   **2** FTG

freud INDUSTRIAL MADE IN ITALY ITEM NO. LU88R010

CROSSCUT

Wood River

freud INDUSTRIAL MADE IN ITALY ITEM NO. LU79R010

THIN KERF ULTIMATE PLYWOOD & MELAMINE

10"   80T

10"-24T

USE FULL-KERF BLADES

Miter saws, especially sliding miter saws, may subject the blade to higher torsional stress. That's why I always use a full-kerf blade on my sliding miter saw. With a stiffer body and larger teeth, this blade will resist flexing and give you a clean, accurate cut.

THESE CUTS
REDUCE VIBRATION

freud ®

INDUSTRIAL

MADE IN ITALY

ITEM No. LU85R010

ATE CUTOFF

80T
10" HOOK

ATB

Non-Stick
perma-
SHIELD™
Coating

Before using, read all warnings in machine manual & blade package.

CES GLASS SMOOTH CUTS

Rip Wood			
rosscut Wood			
Chipboard			
Plywood	1" Max. Thickness		
Laminate			
Non-Ferrous	Not Recommended		

Copyright of
Freud Inc.
1990

Fair   Good   Excellent

ANTI-VIBRATION

NEGATIVE HOOK ANGLE

In miter saws, especially sliders, use a blade with a negative hook angle. The tips of the teeth lean backward in relation to the material. This design greatly reduces the risk of kickback and produces less chip-out as the blade exits the wood. In contrast, a positive hook angle can grab and lift the workpiece, and give you fuzzy cuts— not safe, not good!

TOOTH COUNT MATTERS

A 10-inch finish saw blade has 60 to 80 teeth. That tooth count helps produce beautiful cuts, but my rule of thumb has always been to use a high-tooth-count blade in stock that's 1/4 in. or thinner, and use a lower-tooth-count blade for thicker stock.

THESE AREN'T YOUR DAD'S BLADES

When I first used my father's circular saw, the cheap stamped steel blade smoked and burned, and also disappointed. Blades like this are still made—for some reason. You can spot them easily, but there is no reason to ever use them. A high-quality carbide-tipped circular saw blade costs only about $15; it will cut cleaner and won't burn your wood.

SMALL SAW, BIG CHOICES

You can improve your circular saw game by owning a range of job-specific saw blades. For less than $100, you can expand the usefulness of this saw with dedicated blades for demolition, solid lumber, plywood, even cement composites. You'll make better cuts and your saw will last longer.

GENERAL-PURPOSE CONSTRUCTION

FIBER CEMENT COMPOSITE

DEMOLITION—WOOD AND NAILS

RIPPING SOLID WOOD

FINISH CUTS IN PLYWOOD

BLADES FOR CUTTING METAL

Don't cut metal with that nice crosscut blade! Sure, it might cut, but metal will damage the teeth. Blades for cutting nonferrous metals are designed for that work. With a negative hook angle, the teeth don't flare out to the sides. Before cutting metal, invest in a blade made for that purpose and save your wood blade for wood.

freud®

THIN KERF ALUMINUM BLADE
FOR ALUMINUM, BRASS, COPPER, PLASTICS, & OTHER NON-FERROUS METALS

ITEM: LU89M012

MADE IN ITALY

12" po/pulg. 72T Dents / Dientes

TCG **FULL KERF** 7/64" 0.11" → 2.8mm -5° Hook

NEGATIVE HOOK ANGLE, TCG

USE PLASTIC BRISTLE BRUSHES

POSITIVE RAKE ANGLE FOR TABLE SAWS

Positive rake angle on the table saw not only produces a better cut, but is safer, too.

YOUR BLADE ISN'T DULL

It's dirty. And if you keep cutting with a dirty blade, it's going to get dull—fast! Cleaning the teeth regularly will keep the blade sharper longer. Make a habit of cleaning your blades immediately after use. You can easily remove any pitch buildup, and the next time you reach for that blade, it will be ready to go.

POSITIVE OR NEUTRAL FOR MITER SAWS

Stationary miter saws can safely accept any hook angle; the blade is not moving in relationship to the work, so the material being cut can dictate the rake angle.

AFTMCTG (ACRONYMS FOR THE MOST COMMON TOOTH GRINDS)

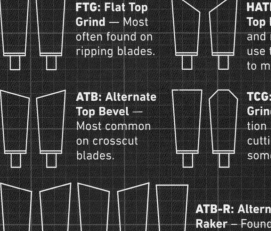

FTG: Flat Top Grind — Most often found on ripping blades.

HATB: High Alternate Top Bevel — Plywood and melamine blades use this tooth geometry to minimize fuzzy edges.

ATB: Alternate Top Bevel — Most common on crosscut blades.

TCG: Triple Chip Grind — This configuration is found on metal-cutting blades and some ripping blades.

ATB-R: Alternate Top Bevel with Raker — Found on combination blades for the table saw.

NEGATIVE HOOK ANGLE FOR SLIDING SAWS

Taking the crosscut blade off your table saw and putting it on the sliding miter saw could have dangerous consequences. Have you ever had a piece of wood jump out of your hands on a sliding miter saw? It might be because you're using the wrong blade. Sliding miter saws and radial arm saws require a blade with negative hook angle. As the blade spins, the teeth will push the part down and into the fence rather than catching it and pulling it up.

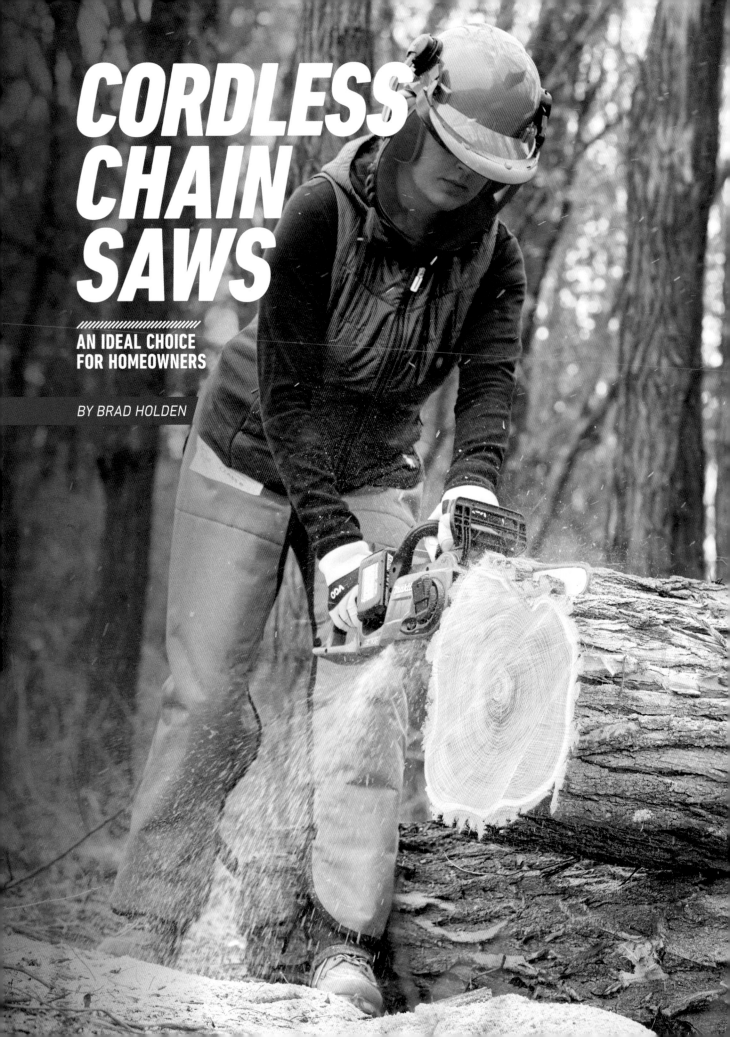

CORDLESS CHAIN SAWS

AN IDEAL CHOICE FOR HOMEOWNERS

BY BRAD HOLDEN

Thinking about buying a chain saw? Consider a battery-powered one. While these saws can't go toe-to-toe with gas-powered chain saws when it comes to run-time and power, they'll do the job for most homeowners. And for many people, their advantages—no hard-to-start two-cycle engine, no mixing gas and oil, and no fouled spark plugs—make up for any shortcomings. We put a few models through their paces to find out what you can expect from a battery-powered chain saw. Here's what we found out.

WHAT WE LOOKED FOR

RUN-TIME
We tested run-time two ways. First, by cutting through a 16-in.-diameter log. That's a tough slog; so many teeth carving at the same time draws a lot of battery power. Second, by cutting through 8-in. logs—work that's more typical for the average homeowner.

CHARGING TIME
As you'll see, most battery chargers won't keep up with a saw's run-time. For any battery-powered saw, you'll want an extra battery (or two) if your work requires more than just trimming a few branches. Extra batteries are essential for chain saw work that's away from home and your plugged-in charger.

SPECS & FEATURES
Criteria included bar length; weight; whether they feature a hand-guard/chain brake, bucking spikes and tool-free chain adjustment; and the ease of locating replacement chains.

CHAIN SAW SAFETY GEAR

You must take chain saw safety seriously. In a split second, a slip or errant cut can cause severe injury. Here are a few safety measures you should take.

- Protect your hands with gloves containing fibers that stop chains.
- Protect your feet with steel- or composite-toe boots.
- Battery-powered chain saws are quieter than their gas-powered counterparts, but they're still noisy. Wear hearing protection.
- Protect your eyes and face from flying wood chips with a minimum of safety glasses. A full face shield is better.
- Protect your legs with chaps woven with fibers that will stop a chain.
- If you're cutting branches or limbs overhead, wear a hard hat. Hard hat/face shield/earmuff combos are readily available.

(DISCONTINUED. NEW 56V MODEL NOT AVAILABLE FOR OUR TEST.)

ECHO 58V

$240 TOOL ONLY
+ $216 FOR ONE BATTERY

- **BATTERY VOLTAGE** – 58V 4Ah. Extra battery: $216
- **ELAPSED TIME** for a single cut through a 16-in.-dia. log – 1:25
- **RUN-TIME** cutting a 16-in.-dia. log – 6:47
- **RUN-TIME** cutting 8-in.-dia. logs – 9:05
- **CHARGING TIME** – 52 minutes
- **BAR LENGTH** – 16 in.
- **CHAIN BRAKE** – Yes
- **BUCKING SPIKES** – Yes, plastic
- **HIGHER Ah BATTERY** – No
- **TOOL-FREE CHAIN ADJUSTMENT** – No
- **WEIGHT** – 15 lbs.
- **REPLACEMENT CHAIN** – Commonly at home centers

GREENWORKS ULTRAPOWER 60V

$350 INCLUDING BATTERY

- **BATTERY VOLTAGE** – 60V 4Ah. Extra battery: $250
- **ELAPSED TIME** for a single cut through a 16-in.-dia. log – 1:37
- **RUN-TIME** cutting a 16-in.-dia. log – 5:37
- **RUN-TIME** cutting 8-in.-dia. logs – 8:30
- **CHARGING TIME** – 23 minutes
- **BAR LENGTH** – 18 in.
- **CHAIN BRAKE** – Yes
- **BUCKING SPIKES** – Yes
- **HIGHER Ah BATTERY** – 8Ah battery available for $350
- **TOOL-FREE CHAIN ADJUSTMENT** – No
- **WEIGHT** – 15 lbs.
- **REPLACEMENT CHAIN** – Commonly at home centers

RYOBI 40V

$280 INCLUDING ONE
4Ah BATTERY

- **BATTERY VOLTAGE** – 40V 4Ah. Extra battery: $160
- **ELAPSED TIME** for a single cut through a 16-in.-dia. log – 3:22
- **RUN-TIME** cutting a 16-in.-dia. log – 4:38
- **RUN-TIME** cutting 8-in.-dia. logs – 3:40
- **CHARGING TIME** – 36 minutes
- **BAR LENGTH** – 16 in.
- **CHAIN BRAKE** – Yes
- **BUCKING SPIKES** – No
- **HIGHER Ah BATTERY** – 6Ah available for $200
- **TOOL-FREE CHAIN ADJUSTMENT** – No
- **WEIGHT** – 14 lbs.
- **REPLACEMENT CHAIN** – Usually need to order

EGO 56V

$370 INCLUDING BATTERY

- **BATTERY VOLTAGE** – 56V 5Ah. Extra battery: $250
- **ELAPSED TIME** for a single cut through a 16-in.-dia. log – 50 seconds
- **RUN-TIME** cutting a 16-in.-dia. log – 7:21
- **RUN-TIME** cutting 8-in.-dia. logs – 8:57
- **CHARGING TIME** – 64 minutes
- **BAR LENGTH** – 18 in.
- **CHAIN BRAKE** – Yes
- **BUCKING SPIKES** – Yes
- **HIGHER Ah BATTERY** – 7.5 and 10Ah batteries are available starting at $150
- **TOOL-FREE CHAIN ADJUSTMENT** – Yes
- **WEIGHT** – 14.5 lbs.
- **REPLACEMENT CHAIN** – Commonly at home centers

MAKITA XCU04

$329 INCLUDING TWO BATTERIES (TWO REQUIRED TO RUN)

- **BATTERY VOLTAGE** – 36V 5Ah. Extra battery set: $170
- **ELAPSED TIME** for a single cut through a 16-in.-dia. log – 1:14
- **RUN-TIME** cutting a 16-in.-dia. log – 7:53
- **RUN-TIME** cutting 8-in.-dia. logs – 8:08
- **CHARGING TIME** – 50 minutes
- **BAR LENGTH** – 16 in.
- **CHAIN BRAKE** – Yes
- **BUCKING SPIKES** – Yes
- **HIGHER Ah BATTERY** – No
- **TOOL-FREE CHAIN ADJUSTMENT** – Yes
- **WEIGHT** – 11.5 lbs.
- **REPLACEMENT CHAIN** – Commonly at home centers

WORX-NITRO

$300 INCLUDING TWO BATTERIES (TWO REQUIRED TO RUN)

- **BATTERY VOLTAGE** – 40V 4Ah. Extra battery set: $120
- **ELAPSED TIME** for a single cut through a 16-in.-dia. log – 1:21
- **RUN-TIME** cutting a 16-in.-dia. log – 6:25
- **RUN-TIME** cutting 8-in.-dia. logs – 8:15
- **CHARGING TIME** – 60 minutes
- **BAR LENGTH** – 16 in.
- **CHAIN BRAKE** – Yes
- **BUCKING SPIKES** – Yes, plastic
- **HIGHER Ah BATTERY** – 4, 5 and 6Ah batteries are available for $100 to $130
- **TOOL-FREE CHAIN ADJUSTMENT** – Yes
- **WEIGHT** – 11 lbs.
- **REPLACEMENT CHAIN** – Commonly at home centers

BRAD'S BEST PICK

The battery run-time for these saws surprised me—I had expected it to be longer. But for our test, we cut continuously, with the trigger held down the whole time. A more typical scenario for a homeowner might be limbing a downed tree, for example. In that case, nine (or even four) minutes of actual cutting time takes off a lot of limbs in brief cuts. An extra battery doubles your cutting time. For some avid users, the run-time might be a deal breaker.

Also, when we cut the 16-in. logs, the air temperature was 32 degrees F, which I thought might affect battery life. So, to cut the 8-in. logs, I brought them into a heated shop to take temperature out of the equation. The differences were marginal. For the amount of chain sawing I do, I'd still opt for battery over gas.

But which saw is best? For me, the Makita stood out as having a comparatively long running time and light weight, and the saw cut quickly and aggressively. It has a balanced feel and metal bucking spikes that protrude well beyond its housing. Bucking spikes poke slightly into the bark during the cut, giving you a solid fulcrum to tip the bar into the cut. This eases the work and makes it safer as well.

Makita's tool-free chain tension adjustment—a feature three of the saws have—is really nice as well. The Worx and Greenworks were excellent performers with nice price tags. All said and done, the six saws work well, so weigh the factors that are important to you.

TOOLS WITH HORSEPOWER

CHOOSE THE RIGHT WORK VEHICLE FOR YOUR LAND

UTILITY VEHICLE

Some of my favorite tools don't fit in a toolbox or on a workbench. Take a close look at the tools on the following pages. If you have land to care for, you should consider adding a utility vehicle, tractor or zero turn radius (ZTR) mower to your tool shed. Here's what you need to know.

BY GLENN HANSEN

TRACTOR

ZERO TURN RADIUS MOWER

UTILITY VEHICLES

With the capabilities of small pickups and a much higher fun factor, utility vehicles (UTVs) are soaring in popularity with landowners nationwide. Consider them grown-up four-wheel ATVs; utility vehicles can carry up to six passengers while doing a whole lot more work. Yes, that makes them more difficult to store and tow than a small ATV, but if you have land, a UTV is worth the effort.

I've spent a lot of time testing UTVs over the years, and I recently added a Polaris Ranger 570 NorthStar ($19,299, suggested retail price) to my tool kit for our greenhouse project. Here's what I learned.

If you've driven a car or truck in the last 100 years, you can drive a UTV. On the ease-of-use scale, UTVs are the champ. They have power steering, gas and brake pedals, automatic transmission and seat belts just like a truck. It might take a while to master the

response characteristics of a UTV's belt-drive continuously variable transmission (CVT). Finding the engagement point (how far to move the foot pedal before the vehicle moves) takes time to get used to. The advantages of a CVT? It automatically finds a good gear range for the situation, and the simple belt-and-pulley design allows performance upgrades with aftermarket components. The driver can easily select high- or low-range gearing, plus reverse.

Not all UTVs use a belt-drive CVT. The Honda Pioneer 1000 UTV uses a unique six-speed automatic dual-clutch transmission that features a manual paddle-shift option. This transmission won't slip in muddy or wet conditions like a belt drive can, but it's far more complicated mechanically. Kubota UTVs, like the company's compact tractors, use a hydrostatic transmission.

ON THE JOB

The first thing I did with the Polaris Ranger 570 NorthStar during our greenhouse build was load the cargo bed with the gravel we used for our foundation. This UTV can carry up to 500 lbs., and the bed's gas-assist lift helps dump loads easily. With its short wheelbase and tight turning radius, I easily transported tools, lumber and materials to the work site. One of my favorite features is the vehicle's TurfMode rear differential. With the push of a button, I can unlock the rear differential to make this a one-wheel-drive machine that treads lightly across any area I don't want torn by aggressive tires.

This Polaris Ranger 570 is powered by a fuel-injected four-stroke gas engine, making a reported 44 hp. UTVs with more powerful engines are widely available and may be a good choice if your work includes pulling a boat and trailer out of the lake or taking a work crew into mountain terrain. Bobcat, Kubota, Kawasaki and John Deere are among the manufacturers offering diesel-powered UTVs, a good option for owners of diesel tractors or other equipment. Polaris recently introduced the industry's first electric UTV; it was not in production at the time of this test.

You find the worth of a UTV like this when driving on rough terrain. On-demand all-wheel drive is standard on this UTV (and many of its competitors). With 11 in. of ground

DRIVE SYSTEM SELECT BUTTON

clearance and four-wheel independent suspension, this Ranger confidently covers rough terrain. If you're doing fence work, accessing a tractor in the field or just need to get to a remote location, a UTV is an ideal choice. Plus, it delivers the convenience of your on-road pickup—passenger seats, power steering, a cab enclosure and more—while being purpose-built for off-road use. If you need the ultimate in off-road capabilities, consider a six-wheel Can-Am Defender with an 82-hp V-twin engine, six-wheel drive and a locking differential.

If you're interested in a work vehicle that plays, too, a UTV is

your best choice. At 60 in. wide or less, most of these vehicles will fit on public-access off-road vehicle trails, and UTVs can drive on these roads legally in many states (check the local regulations).

MAKE IT WORK FOR YOU

By adding the right accessories, you can make your UTV the perfect work or play machine. This Polaris Ranger 570 NorthStar comes equipped with a winch mounted to the frame in front, plus a full cab with windows and a windshield wiper. Those are add-ons for many UTVs on the market. Many accessories are aimed at recreational users: Hunters can add rifle cases; sport riders can choose specific tires and wheels, and engine-performance kits.

Plenty of add-ons will help you get more work done too. You can add light bars and utility light options, mount a snowplow or powered snowblower, or add a heavy-duty bumper kit and brush guards. And a wide range of cargo racks and tool holders help you carry tools to the task. A UTV also makes it easy to tow a log splitter or chipper right to your fallen trees. Or tow a pull-behind mower or leaf vac to maintain turf-covered acreage.

TRACTORS

With long-running diesel engines and chassis made for chores, tractors are workhorses for any landowner. If you measure your property in the thousands of acres, you need a full-size tractor. For those with 1 to 100 acres, consider a compact or subcompact tractor.

A tractor's hp rating is one mark of whether a tractor is compact (about 25 to 50 hp) or subcompact (typically less than 25 hp). Specification charts aside, buy the tractor capable of doing the work you need done. If you need a tractor that can lift round hay bales, choose a compact or larger model. Many subcompact models have compact-tractor features in packages that are smaller, lighter and less expensive. And for most homeowner chores, a subcompact tractor will get the job done.

ON THE JOB

I spent some time on a Kubota BX2380 ($13,615, suggested retail price) to learn the capabilities of a subcompact tractor. When I set up a test with a local dealer, the first question he asked was, "What implements do you want with it?" That's the thing about a tractor. It doesn't do much on its own, but it can do a ton of work with the right attachments. Tractor shopping begins with that "Whadda ya wanna do?" question. From there, you determine which tractor can do that work easily and within your price range.

Popular attachments include a front-end loader ($3,750), a mid-mount mower ($2,400), and a scraper blade ($500) or disc harrow ($2,100). These add-ons show how tractors work with different implements. Tractors use a hydraulic system to lift and articulate a front-end loader. The mid-mount mower is driven by a power-take-off (PTO) shaft. Many of the rear-mount implements you'll pull are simply lifted and lowered to work. You can also run powered implements, like a posthole digger or brush cutter, with a separate PTO at the rear of the tractor.

To effectively carry and pull nearly any rear-mounted accessory, tractors use a three-point hitch system. This triangular steel attachment transfers the implement's load to the tractor's drive wheels and lets you easily switch between implements.

Most subcompact tractors use a Category 1 three-point hitch, while the largest farm tractors use Category 4 hitches. The three-point hitch on my Kubota BX was equipped with an additional quick-hitch accessory, allowing me to swap implements from the driver's seat. As the popularity of subcompact tractors has increased, the availability of Category 1 three-point attachments has blossomed, making subcompacts much more than just big lawn mowers.

With its hydrostatic transmission, the Kubota BX tractor is a clutch-free automatic, and most subcompact tractors use a similar transmission. During my test drive I was reminded of the unique character of this transmission and the tractor's forward foot pedal. While trying to fill the front-loader

bucket, I needed to use a bit more of the Kubota's horsepower. I pressed down hard on the forward pedal as if I was driving that Polaris UTV and pulling a heavy trailer up a hill. With a hydrostatic transmission, that pedal-to-the-metal action essentially shifts the tractor into a higher gear range—the opposite of what I wanted. The tractor bogged down and I couldn't fill the bucket. I realized my mistake, backed off the foot pedal, put the tractor in low and 4WD, then eased the throttle and loaded the bucket. The tractor's reverse employs a separate heel-operated pedal.

Some subcompact tractors use gear-driven manual transmissions. These gear-drive transmissions are more efficient horsepower-wise, meaning there's more power for your PTO-driven implements, plus better overall fuel mileage.

Because you might sit on a tractor for hours, comfort is a factor to consider. While seated, you're using a variety of controls, from drive and gear operations to hydraulics, hitches and PTO controls. Sometimes armrests help, and sometimes they're in the way. And depending on your climate, a cab could be essential. A soft-sided cab keeps out wind, dust and bugs, and it can cost less than $2,000. A hard cab costs four times that but enables heat and AC, plus comfort features like a stereo and more. You can save money by buying an aftermarket cab, but spending a bit more for a factory-made cab system ensures a perfect fit.

THREE-POINT HITCH

ZERO TURN RADIUS MOWERS

You can pull a mower behind your utility vehicle. Or you can use your subcompact tractor for finish mowing or rougher, brush-cut mowing. But if you have acres of turf to cut weekly, you need a zero turn radius (ZTR) mower. Not just for golf-course superintendents or landscape pros, ZTR mowers are increasingly popular for any landowner with an acre or more to cut, especially if you want a precise cut around trees, gardens, or a pool and patio.

When shopping, consider cutting width, cost and construction (and, of course, the cup holder!). I'll cover feature details and what to look for, but you should start with a budget. In the $4,000 price range, you'll find many competitive mowers with 40- to 50-in. mowing decks. If you can spend about $7,000, you can buy a ZTR with a 60-in. cutting width. To flip a cliché here, money is time. If you spend more to buy a mower with a larger deck, you'll cut more grass more quickly—usually. The extra width may make it harder to mow around trees and landscaping features.

ON THE JOB

I tried an Exmark Radius E-Series mower with a 52-in. cutting width ($6,499, suggested retail price). As with most ZTR mowers, you turn the Exmark by manipulating individual lap-bar levers. The levers control the speed of the wheel on that side of the mower. When you push both levers forward simultaneously, both wheels turn at the same rate, propelling the mower in a straight line. To turn left, you push the right lever forward and pull back on the left lever. Do the opposite to turn right. The front tires swivel and are not connected to any steering input. Individual speed control on the powered rear wheels gives these mowers their unique capabilities. It also makes driving one a learned skill, especially on side hills where, lacking front-end control, a ZTR mower can be difficult to handle.

Cub Cadet makes a ZTR mower that features a traditional steering wheel for directional control. Using mechanical gearing and linkages to both front wheels and rear-end transmissions, Cub Cadet claims its mower can accomplish zero-turn-radius precision with a steering wheel you can operate with one hand.

Be sure your mower seat is comfortable and holds you in place well. Armrests are vital for lap-bar mowers. The Exmark Radius has height-adjustable lap bars, which is nice if you have more than one operator. Some Radius models feature a seat suspension system for increased driver comfort.

Most ZTR mowers use gasoline engines, as does the Exmark Radius, which is powered by a carbureted V-twin engine making about 24 hp. I don't want to say the engine doesn't matter, but ZTR mowers aren't sold on horsepower or speed, which is usually limited to about 10 mph anyway. A higher-hp engine can help if you're cutting long or wet grass, but the engine is not the differentiating feature of a ZTR mower.

A few companies, however, beg to differ. Ryobi expanded its outdoor tool offering last year with a line of battery-powered ZTR mowers. The company offers different battery platforms and cutting deck sizes, depending on the amount of work you need to do. You can also find electric ZTR mowers made by Greenworks, EGO and Cub Cadet.

WHAT TO LOOK FOR IN A ZTR MOWER

I appreciated a few other features on the model I drove. Consider items like this if you're shopping for a ZTR mower:

- **Ease of maintenance.** With no tools, I can access typical maintenance items for oil changes or belt replacement.
- **Deck lift system.** I can lift the deck with foot controls to navigate over obstacles.
- **Receiver hitch.** I don't need to tow with this mower, but I can if I want to.
- **Easy-adjust deck height.** The cutting height is easy to adjust at 1/4-in. increments.
- **Quick-adjust ROPS.** The rollover protection system folds easily for trailering or storage.
- **Accessories.** I can add a bag system and vacuum attachments, and more.

Look closely at a ZTR mower's cutting deck. The deck on the Exmark Radius is made from 10-gauge seam-welded steel. Some residential mowers use cutting decks made of thinner steel stamped from a single sheet. If you're mowing a few acres once a week, a mower with a stamped-steel deck will most likely be durable enough. But if you mow many acres or several properties, a fabricated steel deck might be worth the extra cost and weight.

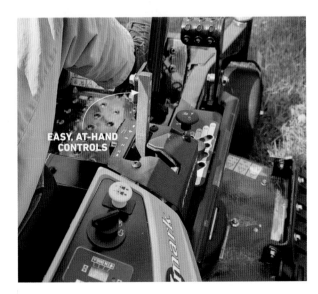

EASY, AT-HAND CONTROLS

BELT ACCESS COVER

HART 80V RIDING MOWER

If your lawn is an acre or less, you might need this Hart 80V riding mower with a 30-in. cutting deck ($3,397). I spent several hours mowing an average-size suburban lawn or two over the summer, and here's what I learned.

REDUCED CUTTING TIME

I used to mow my lawn with a 56V walk-behind mower with a 21-in. deck. I could cut my grass in an hour—a little longer when I needed to do some string trimmer work (same 56V battery, all on one charge). With a 30% larger cutting area and more speed than my feet, this Hart rider cut my mowing time to less than 30 minutes. I was able to mow both my lawn and my neighbor's on one battery charge.

SMALL, BUT NOT TOO SMALL

This mower takes up minimal garage space (about 32 x 56 in.). At 6 ft. 2 in., I sat comfortably on the suspended seat. Thanks to the seat's fore-aft adjustment, it doesn't feel cramped; the three pedals (forward, reverse, brake) are easy to use, and the short wheelbase aids maneuverability.

QUALITY CUT

With two 15-in. blades under a 12-gauge steel deck, the Hart mower cuts well. I tested it on long and damp grass, on shorter grass, on hills and around a variety of lawn obstacles. I set the deck for different heights from 1.5 to 3 in. The cut was always clean and even, though controlling the mower's speed downhill takes practice. I did bump the adjustment lever with my left arm a couple of times, and I didn't notice the cutting height change until a few passes later. The mower can mulch and side discharge, and an optional rear-mount bagging kit is available.

SHARP, BUT NOT ZERO TURN

A tight turning radius is essential in a riding mower; that's what makes ZTR mowers so popular. The Hart turns well, but I quickly learned to appreciate that this mower also cuts in reverse. I used that feature often when mowing around the trees in my yard. The Hart mower's rear wheels will get caught on bigger tree roots, but I learned to rock the vehicle so the spinning wheel can grab some turf—minor inconvenience.

NO GAS, NO OIL, LESS NOISE

I wish all my neighbors cared about quiet lawn tools as much as I do. While the spinning blades do make noise, this mower is much quieter than any other riding mower in my neighborhood. And when I'm finished mowing, I simply insert the plug from the charger into the mower's charging port. I admire that ease and convenience.

DR POWER BRUSH CUTTER

When we built our *Family Handyman* Getaway cabin, we faced the same problem many landowners do. We had brush to cut; we had unwanted flora that was too much for a lawn mower and too small for a chain saw—and we had a lot of it. So we fired up a PRO MAX34 DR Power Brush Cutter ($4,700).

Powered by a Briggs & Stratton engine with electric start, the PRO MAX34 looks like a lawn mower on steroids. It's a walk-behind unit with simple handlebar controls to engage the cutting blades and the self-propulsion drive system.

The area we needed cleared was mostly weeds and saplings. The PRO MAX34 is rated to cut weeds and brush up to 8 ft. high and saplings up to 3 in. thick. Our weeds weren't that high, but we pushed the limits on the sapling size. With its single cutting blade, the PRO MAX34 sliced through our growth with ease. The machine's two 18-in. tires roll smoothly over roots and stumps, and the mower deck glides on steel rails.

If you have weeds and growth to eliminate, a brush cutter might be right for you.

DIGITAL MEASURING DEVICES: WHAT ARE THEY & DO YOU NEED ONE?

BY GLENN HANSEN

A tape measure is a pretty reliable tool. You probably have several around your house and work area. They're inexpensive and easy to use. So, do you need a digital measuring device? I mean, if it ain't broke ... right? But we love new digital devices, and we found three unique tools all promising a better way to measure. It just depends on what you need to measure.

DIGITAL TAPE MEASURE

The KOISS model K519 digital tape measure looks like any other tape, aside from the buttons and small LCD screen. This tool uses a standard pull-out, retractable, locking tape that reaches 16 ft. When you pull the tape across a board, wall or table—whatever you're measuring—the LCD screen reads the length continuously.

With the push of a button, you can set it to measure from either end of the device. It will store two measurements, can instantly figure the halfway point if needed, and displays in feet, feet and inches, inches, or centimeters. And the tape itself has bold markings in both metric and standard, though it

doesn't highlight 16s or even feet. It's a sleek and simple package available in multiple colors for about $30.

LASER DISTANCE MEASURE

The Bosch GLM 20X (shown) is a laser distance tool that reads

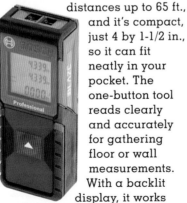

distances up to 65 ft., and it's compact, just 4 by 1-1/2 in., so it can fit neatly in your pocket. The one-button tool reads clearly and accurately for gathering floor or wall measurements. With a backlit display, it works indoors or outdoors and is rated to work in temps as low as 14 degrees F. This tool is available at home centers for about $50.

If you need more advanced features, try the Bosch GLM165-27CG, which measures up to 165 ft. with a bright green laser display and Bluetooth connectivity (we did not test this device). This tool stores 30 measurements, adds and subtracts, and calculates area and volume. It retails for $170.

DUAL TAPE & LASER DISTANCE MEASURE

The HISS laser tape is a dual-function device with a 16-ft. pull-out tape and a side-mounted laser that measures up to 60 meters (nearly 200 ft.). The tape measure is auto-locking with a grippy, rubber-coated, magnetized hook end. The nylon-coated tape is highlighted for feet and at 16s, has metric markings, and is two-sided, with the bottom side showing convenient fractional notations.

The laser measuring feature is simple to use and calculates distance from the front or the rear of the unit. Just place the device, aim its red laser light and press the "Read" button. The laser gave accurate readings across the several lengths I tested. The "Unit" button lets you toggle between standard and metric readouts.

The tool runs on two AAA batteries, has a convenient strap handle and is enveloped in a durable plastic. I dropped the device several times—as I do with tape measures— and have had no problems with its functioning. This tool is available online for $50.

POWER PLAY

BATTERY EVOLUTION PUTS POWER CORDS ON THE ROPES

"**W**e're to the point where we can launch a battery-powered tool that actually delivers better performance than corded solutions. That's just come around in the last couple of years of lithium-ion technology advancements," says Bryson Stewart, VP of product management for Ridgid.

BY GLENN HANSEN

MEET THE EXPERT

GLENN HANSEN, DEPUTY EDITOR, IS ALSO COMPLETELY RECHARGEABLE AND POSSIBLY RECYCLABLE.

Evolution favors reliable tool technology that helps us do better work. Juicing tools with electricity—whether cordless or tethered—has never been the main goal. It's about helping users get work done more easily. Today's progression is mostly about cordless tools and battery power. "We can simplify workplaces by moving to batteries and away from power cords, air hoses and gas," says Gabriel Sandoval, director of product management for Ryobi Tools.

That was the goal of NASA when it contracted with Black & Decker in the early '60s to make battery-powered tools—hammer drills and wrenches—that astronauts could use in outer space. The power wrench needed to spin bolts in zero gravity but not spin the astronaut holding the tool. The goal was simplicity and usability, not power.

THE ROAD TO LITHIUM-ION

That cordless space wrench used a nickel cadmium (NiCad) battery pack. Developed by a Swedish scientist in 1899, NiCad batteries had several advantages over lead-acid batteries—durability, long life and high energy density—and we continue to buy them as rechargeable AA, AAA and other cell sizes. However, these batteries suffer from

In 1963, a cordless tool was used to spin space bolts (above), but before that, in 1961, Black & Decker made a cordless drill for earthlings (right).

memory effect, where the cells will remember a lower energy capacity if you recharge them from a partial discharge state. In addition, cadmium is a toxin and environmental hazard.

Nickel metal hydride (NiMH), in use since the mid-1980s, delivered an even higher energy density than NiCad batteries and used no toxic cadmium or lead. The problem with NiMH was, and still is, their self-discharge rate. Leave a charged NiMH battery in a drawer or tool bag and it's likely to lose its charge; how's that for usability? Some newer NiMH battery cells are manufactured with low self discharge

(LSD) construction, but LSD NiMH batteries also have lower overall voltage output.

That is how we got to lithium-ion batteries. High energy density, no toxicity, no memory effect, a low self-discharge rate and an overall higher usability. Yes, Li-ion battery cells are more expensive than NiCad and NiMH, but the benefits outweigh the cost difference. Li-ion cells are preferred by nearly every tool manufacturer, as well as by some automakers.

BUILT FOR (SOME) ABUSE

Tools endure heat and cold, they vibrate and spin, and they're tossed around on job sites and in your shop. Is your battery pack tough enough for how you work? Some manufacturers share details of a product's construction. In the battery pack, thin and light conductive materials connect cells to an intricate circuit board and the terminals that touch the tool. The tool itself has terminals and wires that lead to a motor enabling your sanding, drilling, sawing and more. Consider all that next time you drop a tool, throw one into your pickup bed or use a drill battery as a hammer (you know you've done that).

A BATTERY IS A COLLECTION OF CELLS

The battery packs on cordless tools look alike for a reason: Most of them hold rows of similar cylindrical cells. The new DeWalt Power Stack battery uses Li-ion pouches (see below), not cylinders. But most toolmakers choose cylinder-shaped cells because they're the most cost effective.

Li-ion cylinders are manufactured in different sizes, and toolmakers generally use the 18650 size, though some are choosing the newer 21700 size. The first two numbers tell the diameter of the cylinder in millimeters. The next two numbers tell the length (or height); the final

"0" denotes the cylinder shape. Tesla, with its Gigafactory partner Panasonic, developed the 21700 cell in 2018. Its advantage? Higher energy density. But it comes at a cost in size and weight, which can make your tools heavier. Tesla recently developed a 4680 cell (much fatter, a little taller), claiming that it has greater storage capacity and costs less to build.

In the 18V battery pack on your cordless circular saw, five Li-ion cylinders, whether 18650 or 21700, lie neatly next to each other. Some 40V or 60V batteries

18650 lithium-ion cells from a Ryobi battery pack

for your lawn mower and the smaller 12V battery on your compact drill/driver have cells in groups of three or four. The 24V battery packs use groups of six cells. And the 2019 Tesla Model 3 electric car uses 4,400 Li-ion (21700) battery cells, more or less, to drive itself right past the gas station.

DESIGN

As battery packs evolve, we see slight but important design updates. When Bosch built its Core 18V packs with the 21700 cells, for example, it arranged them in a wave design of sorts, not a flat layer of five cells. This enabled a slightly shorter but thicker pack design and gave more space for cool air to flow around the cells. Bosch claims this "cools the battery 17% faster and provides 135% longer life" when compared

with Bosch batteries without "CoolPack 2.0 technology."

DeWalt can take a different design direction with its new Power Stack battery technology. The use of lithium-ion pouch cells instead of cylindrical cells "represents the next step forward for our industry," says Sean Fitzgibbons, DeWalt's group product manager. Does he think cylinder cells will go away? "I think it will happen gradually in time. Not since we changed from NiCad to lithium-ion have we seen such a change in

results/performance." He points, for one, to the large, laser-welded connective tabs on the pouch cells that improve the electrical connection and, therefore, performance.

Toolmakers know that design is about performance, and they listen to tool owners. Ridgid dropped its Octane line of batteries last year following user feedback. "Octane was big and heavy," said Ridgid's Stewart, "and we want to move away from that, based on end-user feedback. Users told us they want smaller with the same performance."

While the future of battery design will bring big changes sooner rather than later, what's most important in the design realm is to "keep the compatibility and keep it affordable," says Ryobi's Sandoval.

Several Bosch tools can use the Core 18V with the 21700 cells and cooling fins. DeWalt similarly boasts broad application for its new 20V Power Stack battery. Design must be functional first or it won't do much good in your toolbox.

DeWalt claims its new pouch cells make a battery pack lighter, smaller and more powerful.

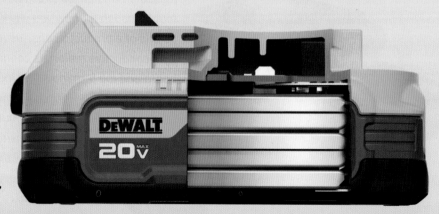

BATTERIES & TOOLS IN USE

We disassembled a Ryobi 18V 2Ah battery and found five 18650 cells. Wired in series, those 3.6V cells combine energy to reach the nominal 18V rating. Had they been wired in parallel, the battery pack would be rated at 3.6V and 10Ah, not usable in shop tools.

Actual battery pack construction uses series wiring, or a combination of series and parallel cell connections. For example, to achieve an 18V 4Ah battery pack, a toolmaker adds a second layer of five 18650 (3.6V, 2Ah) cells, with each of the two five-cell groups wired in series and then wired in parallel. Ryobi's 18V 6Ah is noticeably taller, with three layers of five-cell groups inside.

Bosch is one of a few tool manufacturers using the higher-Ah 21700 cells in its battery packs. Its Core 18V 4Ah battery uses a single layer of five 21700 cells in a pack that is noticeably smaller than competitors' 4Ah battery packs using two layers of 18650 cells (see the weight chart below). While Bosch announces "21700 cell technology" on its website, Milwaukee marketing materials don't, even though many of its M18 batteries use 21700 cells.

So how do you know which battery cells are inside each battery pack? Amp hours. Milwaukee's M18 line includes an 18V 3Ah battery pack stamped with Milwaukee's "High Output" badging; it's powered by 21700 cells. There is also an M18 pack with the same 18V 3Ah rating, but its much larger size tells the inside story of two layers of 18650 battery cells. With twice as many cells, that non-High Output battery pack weighs nearly 1 lb. more than the High Output battery. Less weight and equal power mean the advantage goes to the battery pack using 21700 cells.

But even though the cells and their numbers are important, they're not the whole story.

DEFINITIONS & A LITTLE MATH

Voltage is the maximum potential energy of a battery cell or group of cells. It's the amount of energy provided to the electric circuit that spins your drill. Each of the 18650 and the 21700 cells inside a tool's battery pack has a nominal voltage of 3.6 (some might say 3.7, but 3.6 is the norm).

When you connect five 3.6V cells (wired in series), you get an 18V battery (5 x 3.6 = 18). Tool manufacturers that stamp a tool with "20V Max" are referring to the battery's maximum *initial* voltage. A cell reaches maximum voltage when fully charged, but then it quickly settles to its *nominal* voltage for the remainder of its charged cycle. That's the difference between nominal voltage of a cell (3.6V) and maximum voltage (4V).

Most makers that go with the "maximum" voltage place an asterisk after 12V or 20V on their tools and in literature. DeWalt, for example, says, "*Maximum initial battery voltage (measured without a workload) is 20 volts. Nominal voltage is 18." A 12V battery uses three 3.6V cells for a total nominal voltage of 10.8 and max of 12. Manufacturers in European countries are required to use the nominal voltage in labeling.

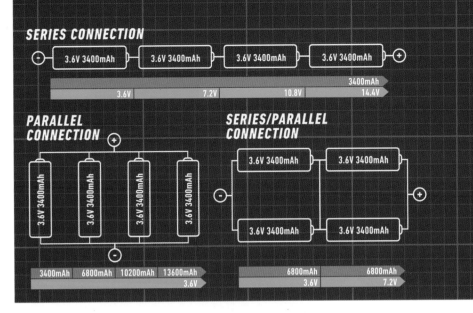

SERIES CONNECTION

3.6V 3400mAh — 3.6V 3400mAh — 3.6V 3400mAh — 3.6V 3400mAh

3400mAh
3.6V | 7.2V | 10.8V | 14.4V

PARALLEL CONNECTION

3.6V 3400mAh | 3.6V 3400mAh | 3.6V 3400mAh | 3.6V 3400mAh

3400mAh | 6800mAh | 10200mAh | 13600mAh
3.6V

SERIES/PARALLEL CONNECTION

3.6V 3400mAh — 3.6V 3400mAh

3.6V 3400mAh — 3.6V 3400mAh

6800mAh | 6800mAh
3.6V | 7.2V

Weight matters! And 12V power can be enough.

WEIGHT CHART

BRAND	V	Ah	BATTERY	TOOL & BATTERY	CELL SIZE
Bosch	18	4	18.8 oz.	(jigsaw) 48.2 oz.	21700
Bosch	18	8	34.4 oz.	(jigsaw) 63.8 oz.	21700
Ryobi	18	2	15.5 oz.	(jigsaw) 66.2 oz.	18650
DeWalt	12	2	7.8 oz.	(drill) 40.3 oz.	18650
DeWalt	12	5	14.4 oz.	(drill) 46.9 oz.	18650
DeWalt	20	1.5	12.2 oz.	(drill) 51.2 oz.	18650
DeWalt	20	5	22.1 oz.	(drill) 64 oz.	18650
Ridgid	18	4	24.4 oz.	(drill) 47.5 oz.	18650
Ridgid	18	5	27.9 oz.	(drill) 51 oz.	18650

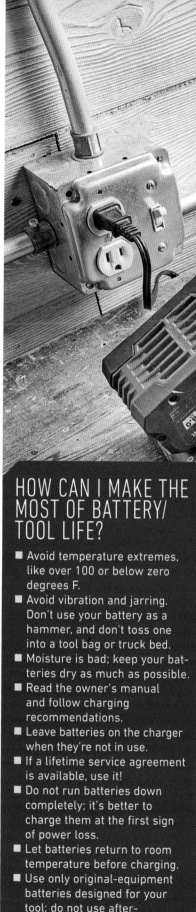

WHAT'S AN AMP-HOUR?

Amp (short for "ampere") is a measure of current flow, and amp-hour is that flow over time. A battery's amp-hour (Ah) rating tells the amount of energy charge that allows one amp of current to flow for one hour. For example, an 18V 4Ah battery will supply one amp at 18V for four hours, or two amps for two hours, or the current needed for as long as it can. Battery cells have individual Ah ratings as well as V ratings. And this is where the

21700 cells step away from the smaller 18650 cells.

While most tool manufacturers don't announce if their battery packs use 18650 or 21700 cells, the battery's Ah rating can tell the story. The 18650 cells are generally rated from 1.5Ah to 2.5Ah. The larger 21700 cells have a higher cell capacity and increased energy density, which leads to high Ah ratings, from 3.0 to nearly 5.0. And that means longer run-time for your tools.

 ## COST

Yes, it's enticing to buy the most powerful battery pack available, but that's not what most DIYers need. Start by purchasing a kit that includes a tool, like a drill/driver, with an included battery and charger. From there, buy bare tools and batteries separately, always making sure there is a lifetime service agreement available. Shop for batteries by first considering your power needs, and then the price. If your cordless work is mostly in remote locations where you can't easily access freshly charged batteries, then go for the packs with the high amp-hour ratings. But if you're working near home with the convenience of battery chargers, then choose low-Ah batteries. They're smaller, lighter and cost less.

HOW CAN I MAKE THE MOST OF BATTERY/TOOL LIFE?

- Avoid temperature extremes, like over 100 or below zero degrees F.
- Avoid vibration and jarring. Don't use your battery as a hammer, and don't toss one into a tool bag or truck bed.
- Moisture is bad; keep your batteries dry as much as possible.
- Read the owner's manual and follow charging recommendations.
- Leave batteries on the charger when they're not in use.
- If a lifetime service agreement is available, use it!
- Do not run batteries down completely; it's better to charge them at the first sign of power loss.
- Let batteries return to room temperature before charging.
- Use only original-equipment batteries designed for your tool; do not use after-market batteries.

CHOOSE A COMPANY, THEN CHOOSE YOUR TOOL

Finding the right cordless power tool for you—one that spins the bolts without spinning the astronaut—starts by considering the second and third tools you will need, not just the first.

"It is all about the platform," says Ridgid's Stewart—and he means for both the user and the manufacturer. Tool users who own a half-dozen of a single brand of tools might need just three batteries and one charger. That saves money and shop space.

Manufacturers that build a complete line of tools to all work with the same battery are more likely to build brand loyalty. Makita claims it makes more than 270 tools that work with its 18V battery (though some tools need two batteries). Ryobi's One+ tool lineup now includes more than 260 tools.

Choosing one tool brand does place your future purchases into one voltage category, but you won't be limited to one amp-hour option.

That means you can use an 8Ah battery in your circular saw if you're cutting stacks of framing lumber or ripping heavy sheet goods. Or you can use the 2Ah battery when you want a lighter-weight tool and you have access to a charger and a backup battery.

"Your tool platform choice is dependent on many factors," says Christopher Gregory, Bosch product marketing manager, "including tool usage, power needs, run-time and application."

Most of the brands know you want to keep your tools for years. The DeWalt drill/driver with 20V 2Ah battery I purchased nearly four years ago still works well, so I was thrilled to learn that a brand new 20V 5Ah battery will also work with that same old drill. And my old battery works with new tools! As battery and tool tech evolve, I hope old and new continue to work together.

GREAT GOOFS®

THE BENEFITS OF HIGHER EDUCATION

My husband and I bought some lumber at the local lumberyard and proceeded to tie it to the top of our car. We're intelligent and educated people with an abundance of common sense.

(Between us we have 11 years of higher education: an architectural degree, an undergraduate in prelaw and a master's in social work.) We placed a blanket on the car to protect the roof, lowered the windows and proceeded to secure our purchase. When we were done and trying to get into the car, we two "geniuses" discovered that we had tied the doors closed! Our mouths dropped. Then we looked around, quickly climbed in through the open windows and drove off before anyone could see us. So much for higher education.

KAREN ADELWERTH

FURNITURE FLAMBÉ

I decided to strip my old kitchen chairs using a gel paint stripper. After working on the first chair for hours and making slow progress, I decided that a little heat from my propane torch might loosen the stain in hard-to-reach places.

It definitely moved things along—until suddenly I saw that the chair was on fire! I ran with the burning chair to the backyard and smothered the flames before the fire did any serious damage. I decided to pay a furniture stripper to do the remaining three chairs. I'm still planning to stain and refinish the chairs, but now I'll be using an "ebony" wood stain to hide the burn marks.

JIM SCANLAN

INDEX

Visit **familyhandyman.com** for hundreds of home improvement articles.

p. 174

p. 48

p. 80

p. 248